Other books by Nathan Miller

War at Sea: A Naval History of World War II

Theodore Roosevelt: A Life

*Stealing from America: Corruption in American Politics
from Jamestown to Whitewater*

The U.S. Navy: A History

Spying for America: The Hidden History of U.S. Intelligence

FDR: An Intimate History

The Naval Air War: 1939–1945

The Roosevelt Chronicles

The U.S. Navy: An Illustrated History

*The Founding Finaglers: A History of Corruption
in American Politics*

Sea of Glory: A Naval History of the American Revolution

The Belarus Secret (with John Loftus)

STAR-SPANGLED MEN

AMERICA'S TEN WORST PRESIDENTS

★

NATHAN MILLER

A LISA DREW BOOK

SCRIBNER

A LISA DREW BOOK / SCRIBNER
1230 Avenue of the Americas
New York, NY 10020

SCRIBNER and design are trademarks of Simon & Schuster Inc.
A LISA DREW BOOK is a trademark of Simon & Schuster Inc.

Set in New Baskerville
Designed by Colin Joh

Manufactured in the United States of America

1   3   5   7   9   10   8   6   4   2

Library of Congress Cataloging-in-Publication Data

Miller, Nathan, 1927–
Star-spangled men : America's ten worst presidents / Nathan Miller
p. cm.
"A Lisa Drew Book."
Includes bibliographical references (p. 257) and index.
1. Presidents—United States—Biography. I. Title.
E176.1.M665 1998
973'.099—dc21
[B]
97-35655
CIP

ISBN 0-684-83610-6

To Henry L. Mencken
Would that you were living today

To please your ghost, I have forgiven a sinner
and winked at a homely girl.

ACKNOWLEDGMENTS

First of all, I would like to express my appreciation to my wife, Jeanette, for suggesting the basic idea for this book and for her encouragement and support throughout the writing of it. Once again, for the fifth time—which must be something of a record in modern publishing—Lisa Drew has been the most able and sympathetic of editors. Her assistants, Blythe Grossberg and Marysue Rucci, made every effort to make my task easier. David Black, my agent, deserves recognition for his efforts on my behalf in this and other projects. I owe a special debt of gratitude to the distinguished Civil War historian Ernest B. Furgurson, and to Dr. Kenneth J. Hagan, professor of history and museum director emeritus at the U.S. Naval Academy, for reading the manuscript and suggesting numerous changes that improved it. The staff of the Nimitz Library at the Naval Academy also deserve my thanks for their assistance.

CONTENTS

CONTENTS

The day of greatness in the Presidential chair is over. . . .
Greatness in the Presidential chair is largely an illusion.
—Harry M. Daugherty,
attorney general under Warren G. Harding

There are a lot of mediocre judges and people and lawyers.
They are entitled to a little representation, aren't they?
—Senator Roman Hruska of Nebraska

STAR-SPANGLED
MEN

PROLOGUE

Picking America's best presidents is easy. George Washington, Abraham Lincoln, and Franklin D. Roosevelt usually top any list. Theodore Roosevelt, Harry S Truman, and Woodrow Wilson belong among the near greats. But choosing the nation's *worst* chief executives requires much more thought. Warren G. Harding and Ulysses S. Grant are easy choices. But what about Richard M. Nixon? Except for Watergate and its concomitant crudities, he was not a bad president. Nevertheless, he was the only one forced out of office—and for no less than trying to make off with the Constitution. Does Herbert Hoover belong on such a list? How about Jimmy Carter? Ronald Reagan? Or William Jefferson Clinton? The possibilities are almost endless.

Ranking presidents is a popular sport among Americans. Perhaps the first such list appeared back in 1948, when Professor Arthur M. Schlesinger of Harvard asked fifty-five leading historians for their ratings of the nation's chief executives. Nearly a half century later, his son, Arthur Jr., put the same question to thirty-two experts. A startling result of all the polls in between is that those named the best and the worst presidents remained pretty much the same over the years despite the adding of new presidents. The major reshufflings have been in the near-great and average categories.

My selection of the worst presidents is purely subjective. It is not the result of a scientific sampling of historians or leading Americans. I have made my choices based upon a lifetime of reading American history, graduate study, a career in political journalism on the local, state, and national levels, and as a Capitol Hill staffer, as well as having written two presidential biographies and other books with a political slant. If the reader suspects me of partisan bias, let me state that in the last thirteen presidential elections, I voted Democratic seven times, Republican four times, and twice for minor-party candidates. Two of the candidates for whom I voted are on my list of worst presidents.

Pragmatism, strong character, vision, political skill, a basic integrity, and the ability to communicate with the American people are generally listed as the qualities for a great or a good president. If so, then the qualities for a poor president are a mirror image of them: bad character, the inability to compromise, a lack of vision, poor political skills, dishonesty, and an inability to communicate. To these, I have added my own basic criterion—*How badly did they damage the nation they were supposed to serve?*

As a result, my list is different from the conventional wisdom. The ground rules under which I made selections are as follows: From the start, I ruled out William Henry Harrison, Zachary Taylor, and James A. Garfield because they were in office too brief a time to have had any great effect. Bill Clinton, as the incumbent when this was written, gets a bye—at least this time around. The reader will also note that I have not included two presidents who have been rated near the bottom in every ranking since 1948: John Tyler and Millard Fillmore. They are yoked together with Zachary Taylor in a pantheon of drab, almost forgotten presidents whose dusty portraits are tucked away in the back corridors of Washington. My guess is that their low ratings are based less upon what they did—or didn't do—in the White House than upon the fact that they were ranked low on the first Schlesinger list and remain there because hardly anyone knows anything about them.

In point of fact, they are not as bad as they are usually portrayed. Both were vice presidents unexpectedly elevated to the White House by the death of their predecessor. Tyler, a diffident Virginia aristocrat who became president after the death of William Henry Harrison, fought off numerous challenges to his authority as the first "accidental president." He refused to allow Congress to brush him aside and take control of the government. By clever management, he brought about the annexation of Texas and presided over the resolution of a major boundary dispute between Canada and the United States—all of which should place him above such nonentities as Benjamin Harrison.

"Honest, commonplace Fillmore," as he was called by historian Allan Nevins, also deserves more respect than he gets. Following the death of Zachary Taylor, he played an important role in the adoption of the Compromise of 1850, which staved off the Civil War by a decade, and dispatched Commodore Matthew C. Perry to open Japan to American trade. My guess is that Fillmore's low reputation is not based upon his presidency but is colored by his decision to run unsuccessfully for president in 1856 on the anti-Catholic, anti-immigrant Know-Nothing ticket. Besides, the name Millard Fillmore seems to generate laughter on its own.

While this book was under way, I was repeatedly asked if I were going to include any contemporary presidents, particularly Reagan or George Bush. Reagan is not included because he came to Washington with two goals—to reduce the influence of "gov'ment" and to destroy the "Evil Empire"—and he accomplished both. Whether one approves of the means he used is open to debate. The key to Reagan's success was knowing where he wanted to take the American people and the ability to convince them to follow him. My guess is that his historical reputation, while not high today, will grow in future years in the same manner as that of Dwight D. Eisenhower, who now stands far higher in the ratings than he did only a few years ago.

As for Bush, he barely misses making the worst list. The creation and management of the alliance that won the Gulf War of 1991 saves him, but lacking vision, he was unable to capitalize on this victory to ensure his reelection. Hoover, although the scapegoat for the Great Depression, does not make it either. In reality, he was the victim of the criminal neglect of previous administrations. The last classical liberal to serve in the White House, Hoover was incapable of dealing with the chilling realities of the economic collapse, but so was everyone else—except for Franklin Roosevelt. I expect the inclusion of Jimmy Carter among the worst presidents will bring howls of protest based upon his postpresidential career. But there is no hiding that he was a poor president.

One thing that emerges from this book is the truly undistinguished nature of most presidential candidates—winners and losers alike. America can survive, and make progress, even with bad presidents. But the country needs—and should have—good presidents. The American people must find and elect men and women of high moral character, as well as intelligence and experience. Character and conduct are clearly linked, and the personal weaknesses of a president can often turn out to be public liabilities. Teapot Dome, Watergate, and Whitewater all have their roots in the character flaws of Warren Harding, Richard Nixon, and Bill Clinton.

For the most part this book has been excavated from standard sources, but I have put my own spin on what I have found. I expect brickbats and dead cats as a result of some of my selections. But as the English historian J. A. Froud said, "Historical facts are like a child's box of letters. You have only to pick out such letters as you want, to spell any word you want." If you disagree with my choices, get your own box of letters.

CHAPTER I

JIMMY CARTER

On New Year's Eve, 1977, as Jimmy Carter's first year in the White House was ending, the president was in Teheran, the guest of honor at a glittering state dinner given by the Shah, Mohammad Reza Pahlavi. Raising his glass in a toast, Carter declaimed: "Iran, because of the great leadership of the Shah, is an island of stability in one of the most troubled areas of the world." Seeing only what he wished to see, Carter completely ignored a rash of violent anti-Shah, anti-Western demonstrations that had exploded earlier that day in this "island of stability."

Within little more than a year, Islamic radicals sent the Shah into exile, never to return, attacked the U.S. embassy in Teheran, and seized fifty-three Americans, who were held hostage for 444 days. Carter's handling of the hostage crisis reinforced an aura of ineptness and ineffectiveness that already hung about him, and it consumed his energies, his credibility, and his administration. He left office in 1981 the most unpopular president of the century with the possible exception of Herbert Hoover, who was saddled with the blame for the Great Depression. Only 13 percent of those Americans polled expressed confidence in Carter as his term ended. Even the disgraced Richard M. Nixon had better numbers when he was forced to resign.

It was Carter's misfortune to become the nation's thirty-ninth president at a time when a free-floating gloom hung over the country. The American people were disillusioned by the mediocrity and mendacity of their own government as shown by Watergate, panicked by the abrupt end of the post–World War II economic boom, and helpless before inflation, mushrooming drug use, racial strife, and the blackmail of terrorists and Arab sheikhs who restricted oil production and raised prices. Equally disturbing was a pattern of defeats and embarrassments around the globe. Vietnam and Cambodia had fallen to the Communists in 1975, underscoring the futility and waste of the war in Southeast Asia.

No leader could have resolved all these problems, and Carter's supporters argue that his presidency was the victim of bad luck and of forces beyond his control. Nevertheless, he made his predicament infinitely worse by a style of leadership—or lack thereof—that invited hostility and derision. Some leaders have used setbacks as challenges, but Carter failed to seize the opportunity. While he was one of the most intelligent and quick-witted men to serve in the White House, he never articulated a sense of purpose or overall direction beyond his strong and frequently expressed moralism. "Carterism does not march and it does not sing," said historian Eric Goldman. "It is cautious, muted, grayish, at times even crabbed."[1]

Out of office, Carter has been admirable in the role of ex-president. Like John Quincy Adams, William Howard Taft, and Hoover, he proved there is life after the White House. Rather than lending lip service to housing the homeless, he has donned jeans and pounded nails to build homes for them. He has not merely preached about comforting the afflicted but has worked to eradicate poverty and disease in Africa and other impoverished areas. He has not talked about extending democracy but has supervised elections and used his prestige to promote peace all over the world, even though his efforts have sometimes been ridiculed or not welcomed.* By the standards of American politics, the post-presidential Jimmy Carter qualifies for sainthood.

On the basis of this performance, revisionists argue for an upgrade of his historical reputation. But a former president's post–White House activities cannot excuse or redeem his missteps while in the presidency. Bad luck and naïveté may indeed have contributed to Carter's failures, but the overarching problem was that having run a brilliant campaign

---

*Critics were particularly bothered by Carter's freelance diplomacy in dealing with the dictatorial regime in North Korea and have suggested that his goals are not completely altruistic. They charge that he has been maneuvering for years to win the Nobel Peace Prize as a capstone to a campaign to restore his reputation.

for the Democratic nomination in 1976 and narrowly defeated Gerald R. Ford, Nixon's handpicked successor, he had no clear idea of what he wanted to do when he became president. He lacked a strategic view, and the American people were ultimately convinced that he was not in control of matters that most directly influenced their lives.

"Carter was an idealist, a good-government moralist, who had trouble connecting ends and means and converting his high-minded goals into politically salable programs," wrote Hedrick Smith of the *New York Times.* "He had so many priorities that he seemed to have none. . . . Whenever I would ask White House officials for Carter's top priorities, the list would run past a dozen items."[2]

Like Bill Clinton, another Southern governor who became president, he was better at campaigning than governing. Carter's predicament recalls the final scene of the movie *The Candidate.* Having unexpectedly won election to the U.S. Senate, Robert Redford turns to an aide and plaintively asks, "What do we do now?"

Carter best summed up his own record. On the eve of the 1980 election in which he was beaten by Ronald Reagan, he told CBS that his presidency deserved a B or C+ on foreign policy, a C on domestic affairs, and "maybe a B" on overall leadership. But as the historian James McGregor Burns has pointed out, "For a president, B and C are failing grades."[3]

On his long march to the White House, Carter presented himself as an "outsider" and representative of ordinary citizens alarmed and disgusted by the wheeling and dealing of the Washington establishment. "I am not a lawyer," Carter proclaimed. "I am not a member of Congress, and I've never served in Washington." Even his sunny facade—an open face creased by a toothy smile, a hairstyle that looked both rustic and stylish, a quick, buoyant manner—set him apart from the gray men who usually prevailed in American politics.

Carter played upon the widespread resentment of big government in Washington and the desire of many Americans for a less activist, less involved foreign policy. He promised no more Watergates, no more Vietnams, and a government "as idealistic, as decent, as competent, as compassionate, as good, as its people." Invariably he pledged, "I'll never tell a lie."

It was all flimflam but the voters bought it. Paradoxically, the American people regard the presidency as the only job in the country in which experience is a liability. While they would never think of hiring an attorney who had not tried a case or permit an untrained surgeon to operate on them, they readily elect presidential candidates such as Carter and Ulysses S. Grant whose main virtue is that they don't know anything about the job they are seeking.

What Carter was *for* was less certain. He was a genius at maintaining a blurred image—a protean figure poised between opposites: a wealthy agribusinessman from a poor section of the nation; a sympathizer with blacks who had been elected governor of Georgia by courting racists and segregationists; a born-again Christian in a nation where charismatic religious beliefs are suspect. People read into him what they wanted. Some saw him as a populist, others a bearer of Rooseveltian New Deal humanism. Still others viewed him as a cool technocrat cast in the mold of that other engineer in the White House—Herbert Hoover. Some even professed to see in Carter a promise of the vitality and excitement offered sixteen years before by John F. Kennedy. In truth, Carter was basically a centrist who sometimes gave his views a conservative bounce with calls for fiscal restraint and jeremiads against big government.

Carter's administration—to use an oxymoron—replaced the realpolitik of the Nixon-Ford-Kissinger years with a rather naive idealism. Human rights, the quality of the environment, nuclear arms control, and the search for peace and justice were the proclaimed priorities. Unlike his Democratic and Republican predecessors, Carter was unconvinced that the ultimate intentions of the Soviet Union were hostile and repeatedly said the United States had become too fearful of the Communists while giving too little attention to the greater dangers of the arms race and its support of repressive right-wing dictatorships. America's enemy should be not simply Communism but tyranny in general.

Although Carter took firm and sometimes courageous stands on individual issues, he failed to demonstrate any understanding of the linkage between them. Some of his proposals contradicted others. While he pledged to pare down the government, he begot two bureaucratic behemoths—the Department of Energy and the Department of Education—with thousands of employees and billion-dollar budgets. Far from making progress in eliminating nuclear weapons, he increased the nation's nuclear arsenal at the same rate as Nixon and Ford.

Even his vaunted human rights policy had its contradictions. It caused a resentment in the Soviet Union that contributed to his failure to secure arms reduction and détente between the superpowers while damaging this nation's relations with its allies. "The Carter administration has managed the extraordinary feat of having, at one and the same time, the worst relations with our allies, the worst relations with our adversaries, and the most serious upheavals in the developing world since the end of the Second World War," huffed Henry Kissinger.[4]

On matters of substance, whether energy policy, the economy, taxes, or health care, the Carter regime was in constant disarray. Lurching from crisis to crisis, it was, in the words of *Wall Street Journal* columnist Alan Otten, "spectacularly inept" with "the evidence of botched endeavors . . . everywhere."[5] This apparent lack of purpose helped to make Carter a target from almost every quarter. No political faction could be certain that he was an ally, and none owed him any loyalty. As a result, he was unable to organize coalitions. Carter also faced an aggressive and truculent Congress, which having recently deposed a president was arrogantly assertive of its powers. Even though controlled by his fellow Democrats, it paid little heed to the president's program or to supporting his initiatives.

Carter was not without his successes, however, especially in the field of international affairs, even though he was, in the words of Henry L. Trewhitt, the diplomatic correspondent of the *Baltimore Sun*, "a local and regional politician with no global experience" who was "squeamish . . . even naive—about the use of power."[6] He fought doggedly for the Panama Canal treaty that is to turn full sovereignty of the Canal Zone over to Panama as of December 31, 1999, thereby healing a running sore in the nation's relations with Latin America. Carter's greatest triumph was the brokering of the Camp David accords in which Egypt and Israel ended their long state of war, raising hopes for peace in the Middle East. On the other hand, having naively disregarded warnings of Soviet intentions, he was surprised and embittered by the Soviet invasion of Afghanistan in 1979. And there was Iran.

In mind and character, Carter reminded most observers of Woodrow Wilson. Both were Southerners and had a sanctimoniousness and arrogance that invited anger and resentment. People wryly noted that his initials were not J.C. for nothing. Hugh Carter, a cousin, saw him as a "lay missionary" who was in harmony between his own ambition and larger spiritual and political purposes.[7] Like Charles de Gaulle at the time of the fall of France in 1940, he offered himself to the nation. "He was and is a moral leader more than a political leader," comments Hendrik Hertzberg, a onetime Carter speechwriter. "He spoke the language of religion and morality far more, and far more effectively, than he spoke the language of politics."[8]

Carter's outsider image and calls for a spiritual awakening played well during his campaign for the Democratic nomination in 1976. The voters were turned off by artifice, insincerity, and Madison Avenue packaging—anything that smacked of manipulation and lies. Evidence abounded that, behind Carter's smile and promises not to lie to the American people, he was a shrewd professional politician not above using half-truths and untruths to win. But his seeming simplicity, his lack of bombast, even his Sunday-school-teacher awkwardness were appealing.

Carter's religious fervor was so strong that on occasion he was moved to perform what Dr. Ethel Allen, a black Philadelphia surgeon, called his "Jesus bit." "He comes up to me, puts his hand on my shoulders like he's giving me his blessing or something. Another time he'd cup my face with his hand, ever so gently, like he was the Messiah. It drives me crazy. I got real itchy when he did that. The thing is, it works. Most black people think it's fantastic."[9]

Dr. Allen was not alone in objecting to the mixture of strenuous religiosity and outward candor projected by Carter. Reg Murphy, who as political editor and then editor of the *Atlanta Constitution* was an early observer of his political rise, noted, "Jimmy Carter was one of the three or four phoniest men I ever met. I don't think he has any human warmth in him, and so I just can't imagine anybody being led by him. I can imagine him sounding good to people for a day or two; I just can't imagine him sounding very good to them for four years. . . . I also believe that leadership demands more than just cold-eyed ability to calculate where the votes are."[10]

Unhappily, Murphy's jaundiced appraisal turned out to be only too correct.

Electing Jimmy Carter president was as close as the American people have ever come to picking a name out of the phone book and giving him the job. When he first announced in December 1974 his intention of running for president after only a single term as governor of Georgia, the proposition seemed so outrageous that even his mother, Lillian Carter, exclaimed, "President of what?"[11] No one numbered him among the leading contenders, and when he went on the television show *What's My Line*, he was so obscure that none of the panel knew who he was. "Jimmy who?" everyone asked.

Eight generations of Carters had lived in Georgia before the future president was born in Plains, in the southwest part of the state, on October 1, 1924.[12] For the most part, they were yeoman farmers and small merchants and a sturdy, restless, and somewhat hotheaded lot. Two were shot and killed in brawls, including William Archibald Carter, Jimmy's paternal grandfather. James Earl, his younger son, finished the tenth grade—the most advanced education of any of the Carter men until then—and went to work in a store owned by a relative.

Following brief service in World War I, Earl returned to Plains and sank his meager savings into an icehouse and then a laundry and cleaning establishment. Prospering, he branched out into farm- and timberland and dabbled successfully in several businesses. In 1923, he married Lillian Gordy, a free-spirited nursing student at the local hospital, whose family was prominent in southwest Georgia. Lillian's grandfather Jim Jack Gordy held the postmastership of nearby Richland for thirty-three years, through four presidential administrations, proof of his nimble political footwork. Earl was twenty-nine when they married; Lillian twenty-five.

Their first child, James Earl Jr., was born the following year in the hospital at Plains—making him the first president born in a hospital.

Small and plump, he was called Baby Dumpling after a cartoon character. He was followed by Gloria in 1926, Ruth in 1929, and by Billy, who was born when Jimmy was thirteen. When Jimmy was four, the family moved to a farm in Archery, a small, mostly black community about two miles west of Plains.

It was pretty country, with the green of the pines, oaks, and young pecans contrasting vividly with the red-clay earth, but living conditions were primitive. Like most rural homes of the period, the Carters' modest clapboard cottage had no indoor plumbing or electricity. The four-hole privy was out back, water was drawn from a well by a hand pump on the rear porch, and meals were cooked on a wood-burning kitchen stove. Later, Carter made Archery sound as if Tobacco Road were a paradise by comparison.

"My life on the farm during the Great Depression more nearly resembled farm life of fully two thousand years ago than today," he declared. "The thing that sticks in my mind the most about my boyhood is hard work . . . shakin' peanuts, pickin' cotton, totin' water, hoein' cotton . . . in the sun."[13] This was sheer hyperbole according to "Miss Lillian," who bridled at her son's tales of poverty. "I know Jimmy writes how poor we were, but we were never poor," she declared. "We didn't feel poor and we always had a car. We had the first radio in Plains. We had the first TV set."

Although sometimes strapped for cash, Earl Carter eventually accumulated several thousand acres of farm- and woodland on which as many as two hundred black sharecroppers raised peanuts and cotton. He also acquired an insurance business, opened a peanut brokerage in which he bought peanuts from the surrounding farmers and sold them in bulk to large processors, and shrewdly made money from New Deal farm programs although he detested Franklin D. Roosevelt and all his works. By the standards of Plains, Earl was well-to-do and was influential in the community, serving on the Sumter County School Board and in the Georgia legislature.

Carter's father and mother were a study in contrasts. Earl was stolidly conservative, tightfisted, and a staunch upholder of traditional Southern values. Lillian was a counterweight to her husband. People thought her fun to be around, and she was one of those salty, high-spirited women whom the rural South often produces.* In terms of her place and times, she was considered a liberal. As a registered nurse, she ministered to whites and blacks with equal compassion—sometimes as midwife—and often without pay. She forbade her children to use the word *nigger* and insisted they treat blacks with consideration. Earl, however, was the family disciplinarian and was regarded by the children as the more influential of their parents.

Growing up in the country, Jimmy played mainly with black children. "We . . . rode mules and horses through the woods, jumped out of the barn loft into huge piles of oat straw, wrestled and fought, fished and swam," he recalled.[14] But the blacks knew their place. When it came time for the children to go to school, Jimmy rode a bus to the all-white consolidated school in Plains, while his black playmates trudged along the red-clay, backcountry roads to a segregated one-room schoolhouse.

In his campaign autobiography, Carter recalled how these unwritten social rules operated. On the night of the second fight between Joe Louis and the German boxer Max Schmeling, in June 1938, the Carters' black workers asked if they could listen in on the family's battery-powered radio. The radio was propped up in a window of the house and everyone sat about on the grass. Louis nearly killed his opponent in the first round, much to the disappointment of the senior Carter. Except for a polite "Thank you, Mr. Earl," the blacks didn't make a sound. Once they returned to their own shacks on the other side of the railroad tracks, they shouted whoops of joy at Louis's victory. "But all the curious, accepted proprieties of a racially segregated society had been carefully observed," Carter noted.

The boy was a model student, well behaved, eager to learn, and an omnivorous reader. A classmate recalled that in addition to being a good student, Jimmy ingratiated himself with everyone. "When you're short, red-haired, and freckled, all you can do is grin," she remarked. His favorite courses were English and history; Julia Coleman, his English teacher, had the greatest influence upon him. She drew up reading lists for him and, when he was twelve, introduced him to *War and*

*Miss Lillian also had a biting wit. When a woman journalist (a Yankee) asked her to explain what she meant by saying her son told "white lies," she offered an example: "When you came here and I said how pretty you are—that was a 'white lie.' "

Peace. Jimmy was disappointed to find that it was about Russian aristocrats and not about cowboys and Indians as he had expected.

Upon his graduation from high school in 1941 at the age of seventeen, Carter's goal was to enter the U.S. Naval Academy at Annapolis. One of his uncles, Tom Gordy, was a navy enlisted man, and his postcards from distant ports had whetted the boy's appetite for foreign travel and a naval career. While waiting for his father to arrange for the local congressman to appoint him to the academy, Jimmy attended Georgia Southwestern, a junior college in Americus, and then Georgia Tech. There, he joined the NROTC and took the mathematics and chemistry courses that had been unavailable in high school. In June 1943, midway in World War II, he entered the Naval Academy.

Carter adapted well to the regimen at Annapolis. The four-year course had been compressed to three years to provide more junior officers for the wartime fleet and had been stripped down to naval and engineering subjects. Except for the choice of a foreign language—he took Spanish—there were no electives. Midshipman Carter had little trouble with his studies, although a rebellious streak brought him more than the average number of demerits as well as special treatment from upperclassmen. War had not suspended the hazing of plebes, and during his first year he was whacked on the rear with a long-handled serving spoon for failing to wipe that irrepressible grin off his face, and again for refusing to sing "Marching Through Georgia," the anthem of Sherman's troops as they swept across the state.* In the summer of 1944, he saw duty on the outmoded battleship *New York* on East Coast convoy patrol, where he was assigned to cleaning the heads.

None of Carter's classmates saw any signs of future greatness in him. They viewed him as an ever-smiling "nice guy" who got good grades without being a "slash" or grind. "Studies never bothered Jimmy," reports his class yearbook, *The Lucky Bag.* "In fact the only times he opened his books was when classmates desired help on problems."[15] Carter graduated in June 1946, ranking sixtieth in a class of

---

*Years later, when Carter was on the campaign trail, a high school band in Phoenix, Arizona, greeted the candidate with "Marching Through Georgia." "Doesn't anyone realize that isn't a Southern song?" Carter, who has no sense of the ridiculous, asked impatiently.

820, a creditable performance, but for some reason he later claimed he was fifty-ninth.* Following the graduation ceremony, Lillian Carter and pretty Eleanor Rosalynn Smith of Plains performed the traditional rite of pinning on the shoulder boards with a single gold stripe that designated him an ensign in the U.S. Navy. Twenty-one-year-old Jimmy and Rosalynn, eighteen, were married in Plains a few weeks later.

Miss Lillian was unhappy about the marriage because she apparently thought Rosalynn, although charming and bright, lacked the social standing to marry into the Carter family. Her father, a Plains mechanic, had died when she was thirteen, and her mother worked as a postal clerk and took in sewing. Rosalynn earned spending money by working part-time in a beauty shop, where she washed hair and did other jobs. She was valedictorian of her high school class and attended Georgia Southwestern. A friend of Carter's sister, Ruth, she had known Jimmy slightly, but they were not attracted to each other until he came home on leave from Annapolis in the summer of 1945. When he first asked Rosalynn to marry him after he graduated, she turned him down, but he persisted, and she changed her mind.

Carter's naval career began with an assignment to an old battleship used to test new weapons in Chesapeake Bay. When his two years of mandatory surface-craft sea duty were over, he chose the submarine service as the best opportunity for advancement in the reduced post–World War II navy. Once his training was finished, he was posted to the submarine *Pomfret*, which operated out of Pearl Harbor. On a voyage to the Far East, the boat was struck by a storm while running on the surface, and Carter was swept off the conning tower by a huge wave. Fortunately, he managed to grab the barrel of the five-inch deck gun and held on until rescued.

When the navy began building nuclear-powered submarines, Carter applied for the nuclear training program and was accepted after a rigorous interview with Admiral Hyman G. Rickover, its hard-driving, irascible chief. "He always looked right into my eyes and never smiled," Carter later related. "I was saturated with cold sweat." Finally, Rickover

---

*Stansfield Turner, the brigade commander and a Rhodes Scholar, was the class star. When Carter became president, he named Turner, by then an admiral, director of central intelligence.

asked for Carter's class standing at Annapolis, and the young officer proudly gave it and awaited the older man's congratulations—which never came. As Carter recalled, "Instead, the question was, 'Did you do your best?' I started to say 'Yes, sir,' but I remembered who this was, and recalled several of the many times at the academy when I could have learned more. . . . I finally gulped and said, 'No, sir, I didn't *always* do my best.' He looked at me for a long time, and then turned his chair around to end the interview. He asked me one final question, which I have never been able to forget—or to answer. He said, 'Why not?' I sat there for a while, shaken, and then left the room."[16]

This interview had a profound and lasting effect upon Carter. "Why not the best?" would be the theme of his drive for the presidency and the title for his campaign biography. He developed an extravagant admiration for Rickover and later stated that the admiral had more effect on his life "than anyone except my own parents." Rickover's larger-than-life image haunted Carter long after he left the navy. Even as governor of Georgia, he would break out in a cold sweat when told Rickover was on the telephone waiting to speak to him.

Carter was assigned as engineering officer of the *Sea Wolf,* one of the navy's first nuclear submarines, which was still under construction. Awaiting her completion, he was sent to Schenectady, New York, where the boat's reactor was being built. There, he underwent training and took a one-semester, noncredit course in nuclear physics at Union College, upon which, without the slightest embarrassment, he later based a claim to be a nuclear physicist. Carter's career now seemed settled. He was a seasoned submarine officer with the rank of lieutenant and was on the fast track. He was the father of three sons, John William, James Earl III, and Donald Jeffrey. Both he and Rosalynn liked navy life—the work, the succession of new experiences, and the camaraderie that existed among the officers and their families—and he expected to remain in the service.

But in 1953, he received word that Earl Carter was dying of cancer. Father and son had drifted apart after Jimmy had departed for Annapolis, but while visiting Earl in Plains, Jimmy regretted the break with his roots. Following his father's death, he went through a midlife crisis. "I began to think about the relative significance of his life and mine," Carter remarked. "He was an integral part of the community and had a wide range of varied but interrelated interests and responsibilities. He was his own boss, and his life was stabilized by the slow evolutionary change in the local societal structure."[17] The more he compared his life with that of his father, the more he was convinced that his father's way was the more satisfying. Over the objections of Rosalynn, who resisted returning to Plains and the control of her mother-in-law, he left the navy after seven years' service.

Taking over the farm and peanut brokerage business, the Carters—Rosalynn kept the books—steadily expanded and improved the enterprise. Carter claimed to have made only a $200 profit the first year, but this, too, was another "white lie" because the business was owed $90,000 for seed and equipment, which was paid the following year when the crop came in. Carter Warehouses soon became one of Georgia's largest peanut wholesalers, and by the early 1970s, Jimmy Carter was a millionaire.* Like his father, he was active in church and community affairs, serving as deacon of the Plains Baptist Church, on various planning and development commissions, and the Sumter County School Board.

Carter's membership on the board coincided with the upheaval throughout the South caused by the Supreme Court's 1954 ruling ending segregated schools. For the most part, he simply went along with the existing racial patterns and avoided taking a public position on the issue. This was possible because in southwest Georgia massive resistance to integration worked at least temporarily, and there was no real mixing of the races until the 1960s—and by then Carter had moved on to state politics. He did, however, spurn an invitation to join the local version of the segregationist White Citizens Councils, and the family stood almost alone against a move by the Baptist church to bar blacks.

In 1962, just before his thirty-eighth birthday, Carter decided to run for the Georgia Senate. He had the support of Sumter County in the Democratic primary, but an adjoining county machine had its own

*With tensions between Rosalynn and Miss Lillian unabated, the elder woman accepted the position as housemother at Kappa Alpha fraternity at Auburn University in 1955, which she held for nearly six years. Jimmy, worried that people might think his mother was working because she had to, bought her a new white Cadillac before she left for Auburn.

candidate and stuffed the ballot boxes to ensure its man a 139-vote victory margin. Carter successfully challenged the outcome in court and was declared the winner. Two years later, he was reelected by a large majority. Foreshadowing his presidency, he was hardworking and moderately progressive and read every bill introduced with a single-minded intensity. In 1965, he was named in a newspaper poll as one of the state's most influential legislators.

Spurred by the desire for higher office, the following year Carter announced his candidacy for the Democratic nomination for governor. He was virtually unknown outside his own district, and pundits gave him little chance to win. Leaving the family business to be run by brother Billy, he crisscrossed the state, campaigning "like a migrant worker hustling for harvest work," said one observer.* By election eve the outlook was so bright, he expected to be in a runoff with either former governor Ellis Arnall or Lester Maddox, an Atlanta restaurant owner who had won national notoriety by standing in the doorway of his business with an ax handle and defying blacks to enter. Carter was shocked when he finished third in the race—Maddox won—and fell into a deep depression, which was relieved only after he found solace in religion.

From the time he was a child, Carter had attended the Baptist church without considering himself devout. But following conversations with his sister, Ruth Carter Stapleton, who had become a faith healer and evangelist, he underwent a religious experience that made him a born-again Christian. No part of Carter's background is more controversial than his religious conversion. When he ran for president, liberals expressed concern over whether his religious convictions would conflict with his civil duties. In his autobiography he took pains to emphasize there was no sudden miracle nor had he undergone a blinding experience like Saul on the road to Damascus. "I formed a very close, intimate, personal relationship with God through Christ," he explained. "That has given me a great deal of peace."[18] He read his Bible daily and volunteered for missionary work in the Northeast—"witnessing for Christ" as it was called—establishing the pattern for his postpresidential activities.

---

*Miss Lillian had, in the meantime, joined the Peace Corps at age sixty-eight and spent two years in India.

Rather than deterring him from politics, Carter's newfound acceptance of Christ only intensified his commitment to public service. He adopted theologian Reinhold Niebuhr's aphorism that "the sad duty of politics is to establish justice in a sinful world." Having made peace with himself, he again ran for governor in 1970. And like Scarlett O'Hara, another Georgian who had suffered defeat, he vowed that he would never again be beaten—no matter what the cost.

Born-again or not, Carter conducted one of the roughest campaigns in the state's history. He attacked his chief foe, the racially moderate ex-governor Carl E. Sanders, for his links with liberal Democrats such as former vice president Hubert H. Humphrey and circulated a photograph in rural areas that showed Sanders celebrating with black baseball players. Open appeals were made to the segregationist and white-supremacist supporters of Alabama governor George C. Wallace; school busing for racial balance was condemned, and Nixon's policy on Vietnam was endorsed. Carter easily beat Sanders in a runoff and then went on to win the general election.

Once in office, Carter reversed his field. Startling his backers, he proclaimed in his inaugural address that "the time of racial segregation is over" and ordered a portrait of the Reverend Martin Luther King Jr. hung in the rotunda of the state capitol in Atlanta. Under Carter, the number of black state employees was increased by 40 percent, blacks were appointed to previously lily-white state boards and commissions, and funding for rich and poor school districts was equalized.

Carter's major goal, the reorganization of the state government, was achieved despite strong opposition that stemmed largely from his own tactical errors. Assuming that those opposed to his programs were acting from selfish motives rather than from their own perceptions of the public good, he stubbornly refused to compromise—again foreshadowing his presidency. All in all, he was a good governor and soon graced the cover of *Time* as an exemplar of the new political leadership in the South.

Two years later, even though he had served only half his term as governor, Jimmy Carter turned his attention toward winning the White House in 1976. Running for president seemed his only option for political advancement. Under Georgia law he could not succeed himself, and it was unlikely that he could win the Senate seat long held by Herman Talmadge. Having met the major possibilities for the Democratic presidential nomination—Hubert Humphrey; Senator Henry M. Jackson of Washington; Governor Wallace; and Representative Morris Udall of Arizona—Carter concluded he was as qualified for the presidency as any of them.

Even though Carter was virtually unknown outside of Georgia, he was encouraged to run by two young aides, Hamilton M. Jordan and Dr. Peter Bourne, a British-born psychiatrist and the governor's adviser on drug problems. They shrewdly recognized what more seasoned politicos had missed: post-1968 changes in the Democratic party's rules had "democratized" the nominating process. Instead of being selected by the professionals, candidates would now be chosen by the ordinary people in a proliferation of primaries. A shift in the country's political temper, mistrust of politics as usual, and the automatic appetite of the media for novelty—or the *new as news*—played into an outsider's hand. And Carter would also be the only moderate among a brace of liberals and the conservative Wallace. Jordan presented Carter with a lengthy memorandum outlining a strategy for victory in 1976 that called for him to run in as many primaries as possible and to mobilize thousands of enthusiastic volunteers rather than rely on old-time political methods to get out the vote.[19]

Beginning in 1974 after his term as governor was over, Carter traversed the country as he had in his first campaign in Georgia, sticking out his hand at everyone he met and saying, "My name is Jimmy Carter and I'm running for president." Being unemployed was an advantage because he could devote full time to campaigning. In his travels, Carter paid particular attention to Iowa, New Hampshire, and Florida, where key early caucuses and primaries would be held. But he remained intentionally vague on the issues. He opposed a constitutional amendment banning abortion, but said he might back a "national statute" limiting abortions. He emphasized family and religious values and exploited the voters' dark, anti-Washington mood.

Even though he had campaigned for Wallace votes in 1970, Carter won the support of Southern blacks, to whom he appealed on the basis of a shared vision of Christian love, forgiveness, and reconciliation. This, in turn, attracted the votes of Northern liberals, who now saw him as a bulwark against the Alabama governor. "Blacks have a kind of radar about white folks," explained Andrew Young, a black Georgia congressman and Carter supporter. "Somewhere along the line, Jimmy passed the test."[20]

Just as Jordan had forecast, the liberal wing of the Democratic party formed its usual circular firing squad, splitting its vote among several candidates and allowing Carter to win a plurality. The first breakthrough came in Iowa, where he won the previously ignored caucus with 27.6 percent of the vote. Less than 10 percent of those eligible participated, but the media, considering only the horse-race aspects of the campaign, dubbed him the "winner." This brought in campaign funds and provided the momentum to win the New Hampshire primary and to narrowly defeat Wallace in Florida and again in North Carolina.

As the delegates to the Democratic National Convention clasped hands and sang the civil rights anthem, "We Shall Overcome," Carter was nominated as the party's presidential candidate—the first true Southerner since before the Civil War. To heal rifts in the party, he selected Senator Walter F. Mondale of Minnesota, a liberal Washington insider and Humphrey protégé, as his running mate. With a lead of thirty points in the polls over Gerald Ford going into the campaign, Carter's victory seemed safely assured.

Unemployment and inflation plagued the nation. Ford had also been severely bloodied in a primary battle with former California governor Ronald Reagan, and despite Ford's efforts to restore integrity to the presidency, he was burdened by the pardon he had given Nixon for any crimes that may have been committed in the Watergate scandal. Ford also committed several goofs, such as maintaining in a televised debate that the Soviet Union did not dominate Eastern Europe.

Yet, as the campaign unfolded, Carter's lead began to melt away. Ford and his razor-tongued vice-presidential candidate, Senator Robert Dole of Kansas, hammered away at his "fuzziness" on the issues. Carter also put his foot in his mouth with an interview in *Playboy* in which, trying to be trendy, he acknowledged that although he loved his wife, he had "committed adultery in my heart many times." Had the election been held a few days later, Ford might have scored an upset, but Carter managed to win with just 50.1 percent of the vote to 48 percent for Ford. Now, he had to show that he could govern.

No inauguration since that of Andrew Jackson had the informality and lack of pomp of that of Jimmy Carter. As he was sworn in at noon on a cold but sunny January 20, 1977, the fifty-two-year-old Georgian wore a business suit instead of formal dress. And in taking the oath of office, he gave his name as "Jimmy Carter" rather than James Earl Carter Jr. To the surprise and delight of onlookers, the new president and first lady bounded from the traditional limousine and strolled hand in hand down Pennsylvania Avenue from the Capitol to the White House with their nine-year-old daughter, Amy, between them. Not long after, emulating Franklin Roosevelt, Carter gave a televised "fireside chat" while wearing a sweater and sitting before an open fire—which perversely sputtered out during the broadcast. And he carried his own garment bag when emerging from the imperial splendors of Air Force One.

In the beginning, these efforts at common-man humility—along with a blitz of legislative proposals—met wide approval. A promised pardon for Vietnam-era draft evaders was signed on January 21. Proposals for stimulating the economy, overhauling the welfare system, abolishing the Electoral College, and providing for public funding of congressional as well as presidential elections rapidly followed. Most met passive resistance in Congress, if not outright opposition. While Gerald Ford had spent his two years in the White House vetoing the actions of Congress, Carter spent much of his presidency being vetoed by Congress. As the traditional honeymoon granted every new president ran out with little in the way of solid accomplishment, Americans began to view the president's "folksy" gestures as hollow substitutes for action.[21]

Carter was much to blame. Lacking the knowledge and experience to deal with the problems facing him, he sorely needed the guidance and support of the Democratic establishment. But having campaigned as an "outsider" with an overriding suspicion of Washington and its denizens, he cavalierly rejected their counsel. Instead, he concentrated all power in his own hands, and all decisions were made by him—increasing the sense of chaos. The president compounded the error by relying for advice upon a close-knit Georgia "mafia" who knew all about campaigning but were as ignorant of foreign and national affairs as their leader. Some of these "good ol' boys" were to cause him much pain and embarrassment and to keep a series of special investigators busy.

Hamilton Jordan, the president's top aide, whose only previous experience in Washington was a patronage job running a Senate elevator, took pleasure in showing contempt for the old-time pols whom he had outsmarted during the campaign. For example, House Speaker Thomas P. O'Neill's guests were given inaugural dinner seats at the last table in the balcony. Tip O'Neill fired back by referring to Jordan, whose name was pronounced "Jurden," as "Hamilton Jerkin." It was hardly the best way to begin relations with the man who had the responsibility of pushing the president's legislative program through Congress.

Basically, the problem was that Carter had goals and espoused policies that were quite different from the agenda of the Democratic establishment. Early on, O'Neill lectured him on the need to separate the rhetoric of the campaign from the reality of the legislative process. "Carter didn't seem to understand," according to the Speaker.[22] Referring back to his experience in Georgia, Carter said he had taken his message directly to the people when the state legislature had blocked his programs. If he faced a similar situation with Congress, he would not hesitate to go over their heads. "I can talk to your constituents easier than you can," he warned—words that did not endear him to the lawmakers.

Unsurprisingly, the president and Congress were soon at loggerheads over a Carter proposal to eliminate a number of the dam and water projects so dear to the hearts of the lawmakers. Carter had also set up an apparatus to identify talent for the hundreds of federal posts that were to be filled. Congressional Democrats had their own candidates for these jobs, and in the ensuing fight over patronage, important positions went unfilled. Relations between the White House and Capitol were even more strained by an unexpected announcement that the administration had rescinded a proposal for a $50 tax rebate to all taxpayers it had originally promised in an effort to energize the economy. Congressional Democrats, who had agreed to support the plan against their better judgment, were left holding the bag.

Carter's handling of the economy was the best illustration of his failure in the domestic sector. With unemployment running at 8 percent and inflation at 10 percent when he took office, he pledged to cut both in half. But as James McGregor Burns has written, he had no blueprint for action: "The White House sent out mixed signals as to what it wanted. Advance preparation was inadequate, follow-through sporadic, lines of communication and delegation scrambled. The normal friction between the executive and legislative branches was exacerbated by exceptionally poor staff work. . . . Above all a clear sense of priorities was lacking."[23]

Aside from the economy, the most pressing matter facing Carter was the energy crisis. Arab oil producers had reduced production and raised prices following the Yom Kippur War in 1973, and the cost of foreign oil had more than doubled. At the same time, U.S. reliance upon foreign sources had increased to over 50 percent of total demand. To reduce reliance on imported oil, Carter urged conservation measures and higher prices to discourage waste and to encourage the development of energy resources at home.

Unfortunately, the energy conservation program produced by the Carter administration was created in secrecy and was unnecessarily complex—it had 113 provisions—and bristled with technical flaws.* Carter, with his usual tendency to apply religious overtones to political matters, called it the "moral equivalent of war."† Not unexpectedly, when the White House finally released the plan, administration officials were so confused they contradicted one another. Critics denounced the package as too complex, and for both going too far and not going far enough. Had Carter brought congressional leaders into its development and sought allies within the energy industry, he might have undercut the opposition. Instead, he blamed his difficulties on the greed of the big oil companies and the pressures of their lobbyists in Congress.

Other efforts at reform fell victim to congressional opposition. A

---

*The Clinton administration repeated the error by developing in secrecy an unnecessarily complex health plan, which it ultimately had to abandon.

†Some jokesters gleefully noted that the acronym for the "moral equivalent of war" was "meow."

major restructuring of the federal welfare system died quietly. An attempt to reform the tax system, one of Carter's major campaign promises, was gutted. Following the $50 tax rebate debacle, supporters of his various policy proposals had the uneasy feeling that he might abandon them at any time if political pressures dictated a different approach. Carter's popularity began a precipitous fall in late 1977 from which it never recovered, and no one had any reason to fear the political consequences of opposing him. Within the flick of an eyelash, he saw adoring smiles replaced by a tight-lipped contempt.

The most important task of a president is to provide leadership—to identify problems facing the nation and then to educate and mobilize public opinion to resolve them. Eloquence is a vital adjunct to this role, but it was foreign to Carter and he was unable to rally the American people behind his policies. In four years he never uttered a sentence—or even a phrase—that was memorable. He never provided a vision, gave a rousing speech, or pounded the bully pulpit. "It is the responsibility of the government, or the president, more precisely, to define the national vision," points out Robert Dallek in his book on the presidency.[24] "If he fails to do so, he ends up dissipating much of the goodwill he holds by virtue of entering office."

While Franklin Roosevelt or Ronald Reagan might have mobilized the nation to deal with a crisis of confidence similar to that faced by Carter, he resisted all chances to show leadership. Instead, he buried himself in details—even taking personal charge of booking the White House tennis court or making lists of the classical records he would listen to each day. In electing Carter, observed the *Washington Post,* the country had chosen "the country's first national city manager." A Pentagon official who dealt with the White House noted that some leaders were "forest men"—seeing the big picture—while others were "tree men." And Carter? "My God, he was a leaf man!"[25]

Persuaded to summon his inner circle into a conclave at Camp David to evolve new policies following a fresh oil-price shock in the summer of 1979, Carter emerged with a televised warning that the country was suffering from "a crisis of the spirit." As usual, the tone was semi-evangelical, with an earnest note of reprimand that seemed to blame the American people for their own misfortunes.* But the real problem, as many saw it, was the president's own inability to formulate and articulate a policy to deal with the nation's difficulties, and the speech backfired. A photograph of the president in a state of near physical collapse while jogging at Camp David evoked not concern but jeers.

Carter's standing with the American voters was also undermined by the forced resignation of his friend Bert Lance, a Georgia banker and former campaign manager, from his post as director of the Office of Management and Budget. Lance came under fire for questionable banking practices before coming to Washington, but the president clung to Lance well beyond the bounds of political prudence. "Bert, I'm proud of you," Carter told him in an unfortunate choice of words. Hamilton Jordan and Tim Kraft, another key aide, were also investigated for purportedly snorting cocaine, but no charges were brought. While of little significance in themselves, these cases raised questions about Carter's often-proclaimed commitment to the highest ethical standards in government.

Billy Carter, the president's alcoholic younger brother, also damaged Carter's reputation. The younger Carter was hardly the first presidential brother to get into trouble: Orville Grant was involved in the selling of Indian-post traderships; Sam Houston Johnson kited checks; Don Nixon was mixed up with Howard Hughes. At first, the nation was amused by Billy's redneck capers, but the laughter died when it was learned he had accepted $220,000 to lobby for Libya's terrorist-sponsoring leader, Mu'ammar Gadhafi.

Foreign policy successes such as the Panama Canal treaty and the Camp David accords gave Carter's popularity a fleeting upward spike, but the charges of drift, ineffectiveness, and incompetence could not be stilled. The final blow came on November 4, 1979—a bleak Sunday morning exactly one year before the next presidential election—when a mob of Iranian "students" seized the U.S. embassy in Teheran and took about

---

*This is usually called the "malaise" speech because Carter supposedly described the loss of faith by the American people as a "national malaise." In fact, Carter never uttered the fateful word. Patrick Caddell, the president's pollster, used it in a press briefing, and it caught the attention of journalists and the public. The common attitude seems to be that even if Carter didn't actually use the M-word, it is what he meant.

a hundred Americans prisoner. While chanting hatred for America and burning American flags, the mob paraded the bound and blind-folded hostages about the embassy compound and demanded that the United States ship the exiled Shah back to Iran to face trial for "crimes against the Iranian people."[26]

Carter was genuinely perplexed by the seizure of the hostages—reduced to fifty-three after women and blacks were released. But trouble had been brewing in Iran ever since 1953, when the CIA had put the Shah back on the throne after he had been dislodged by a leftist-nationalist coup. Under Nixon and Kissinger, Iran had become an American bulwark in the oil-rich Persian Gulf, but anti-Shah, anti-American feeling was intense. Some Iranians were angered by widespread corruption and the brutality of the Shah's dictatorship, while Muslim fundamentalists saw his plans to modernize society as a violation of Islamic law and tradition.

Lulled by the Shah's image as an absolute ruler, American diplomats and intelligence operatives had refused to believe that he could be overthrown by ragtag street mobs pledging loyalty to an aged religious fanatic, the Ayatollah Ruholla Khomeini, who was living in exile in Paris. Moreover, Iran boiled over at a time when the American foreign policy apparatus was already overtaxed by negotiations with the Russians of an arms limitation treaty, by the Camp David accords, and by the normalization of relations with China. The full attention of policy-makers in Washington was not drawn to the crisis in Iran until it was already too late to do anything to save the Shah.

Like most Western political leaders, Carter took for granted the pre-dictability and rationality of events. In dealing with the Iranian crisis, he failed to take into account the irrelevance of Western models of behavior in the Third World. Like his predecessors, he viewed international affairs through the prism of the Cold War and was thrown off balance by a fundamentalist religious revolution that denounced both the United States and the Soviet Union. In particular, Carter failed to recognize that the glue holding together such otherwise incompatible forces as the extreme left, political moderates, and the archconservative Muslim clerics was blended of equal parts of fundamentalism, anti-Americanism, and hatred for the Shah and the dictatorship.

A one-day occupation of the American embassy in Teheran in February 1979 should have been a warning. But instead of reducing the American diplomatic presence to modest levels after this incident, Carter persuaded himself that its quick end meant Iran had returned to "normalcy," and the mission was enlarged. In an effort to improve relations with the Khomeini regime, the ayatollah was portrayed as "some kind of saint," as Andrew Young, then the U.S. envoy to the United Nations, described him.

This approach played into the hands of the Iranian fanatics. With chaos mounting and public enthusiasm running down, they were seeking some way to radicalize the revolution. The decision to allow the terminally ill Shah to obtain medical treatment in the United States—made under pressure from Kissinger and the Rockefeller oil and banking interests, which had ties to him—was merely the catalyst. Over the next 444 days, the Iran crisis festered as newspapers and television focused almost completely on the plight of the hostages, and it became a cancer on the Carter presidency.

Heightened by all-out media coverage, the hostage situation soon dominated almost every aspect of American life, and Carter was consumed by it. He had developed an intense personal commitment to the hostages, probably because he felt guilty at having left them exposed. Sleepless, exhausted, and unable to face public ire over their plight, he became a virtual prisoner in the Oval Office. Not even the death of the Shah brought about the release of the hostages, because his presence in the United States had been just a pretext for holding them. As long as the militants held the hostages, the purifying flames of "the revolution within the revolution" would continue to burn.

Carter would have been wise to disengage and play down the hostage situation because he had no leverage on events. Some critics saw the president as Charlie Brown, a character in the cartoon strip *Peanuts*. The well-meaning Charlie repeatedly allows the mischievous Lucy to hold a football for him as he tries to kick it, even though she unfailingly snatches it away and he takes a resounding pratfall. Tragically, the hostages were a perfect football for the militants. Carter repeatedly tried to negotiate their release, only to have the contemptuous Iranians snatch the ball away at the last minute.

Worried about the effects of the hostage crisis on his chances for reelection in 1980, Carter finally gave the go-ahead for a military rescue mission. But this, too, turned into a nightmare. Well before the rescue team came within striking distance of Teheran, the operation had to be aborted because several of the assigned helicopters broke down. The mission ended in ignominy when one of the craft collided with a transport plane during a hurried nighttime withdrawal and eight crew members were killed in the fiery crash. The last shreds of Jimmy Carter's credibility also perished in the flaming wreckage strewn about the Iranian desert. The hostages were not released until the hour Ronald Reagan took the oath as president.

Jimmy Carter was the victim of the high hopes he had aroused for his presidency. Public expectations had risen to absurd heights, and he was called upon to accomplish far more than was humanly possible. At the same time, the prospects for carrying out even a modest program of change were dimmed by the limitations imposed on his options by a Congress anxious to preserve its prerogatives after ousting Nixon. Moreover, he was buffeted by the conflicting objectives of a raft of newly organized interest groups, each with its own political and social agenda, that had assumed a major role in American politics following the erosion of party discipline.

Carter is certainly a good and moral man—as clearly evidenced by his postpresidential career. Yet, at the same time, he was a failure as president. In his four years in the White House, he was long on good intentions but short on accomplishment. Having come to Washington as an outsider, he never reached an accommodation with the interests and institutions he had campaigned against, but whose support he needed to govern. He was intelligent, honest, and caring, but self-righteously believed in his own moral superiority. He worked diligently for his programs and policies, but failed to educate or influence public opinion in favor of them. Most importantly, he was a president who never adequately formulated a mission for his administration or a purpose for the country.

It was not a formula for a successful presidency.

CHAPTER II

WILLIAM HOWARD TAFT

O ne evening in January 1908, Theodore Roosevelt invited his good friend Secretary of War William Howard Taft and his wife, Nellie, to the White House. Following dinner, the president leaned back in a leather chair, closed his eyes, and pretending to be in a trance, intoned, "I am the seventh son of a seventh daughter. I have clairvoyant powers. I see a man before me weighing three hundred and fifty pounds. There is something hanging over his head. I cannot make out what it is; it is hanging by a slender thread. At one time it looks like the presidency—then again it looks like the chief justiceship."

"Make it the chief justiceship," said Taft.

"Make it the presidency!" cried the ambitious Nellie.[1]

The question of a successor dominated Roosevelt's last two years in office. He came to power in September 1901 following the assassination of President William McKinley and, upon election to the presidency in his own right three years later, had announced that he would not be a candidate for reelection in 1908. Whom would he anoint in his place? Perhaps it would be Elihu Root, who had served him ably as secretary of war and state? Would it be Governor Charles Evans Hughes of New York, who had recently been propelled into the limelight by an investigation of the insurance industry? Or would it be Taft? Unhappily for Roosevelt, Will Taft, and the nation, Nellie Taft got her wish.

Corpulent, lethargic, and slow-moving, Taft projected an aura of fumble, bumble, and stumble. He was the wrong man in the wrong place at the wrong time. The temper of the times was progressive; he was conservative. The nation wanted an activist president; he was the champion of the status quo. Any man who enters the presidency as the leader of a party that controls the White House and Congress and with overwhelming public support and then fritters away his mandate and popularity, barely carrying only two states four years later, certainly belongs on any list of worst presidents. Time has cast a veil over Taft's ineptness, and some writers have tried to rehabilitate him because he was an amiable and even pathetic figure, but the facts speak for themselves.

Taft was far more suited to the bench than for the presidency by personality, temperament, and training. "I love judges, and I love courts," he once declared. "They are my ideals, they typify on earth what we shall meet hereafter under a just God." In 1921, he finally got *his* wish when President Harding appointed him chief justice, and he is the only man to serve as both president and chief justice. On the other hand, Taft detested politics. Campaigning and glad-handing voters were arduous and painful for him. "I don't like politics, especially when I am in it," he said.[2]

Lacking fire in his ample belly, Taft was neither a leader of Congress nor of public opinion. He fumbled the baton of dynamic presidential leadership that Roosevelt had passed to him. Worse, he erred by biting the hand that had put him in the White House, and that hand knocked him out of it. Taft meant well, but he lacked Roosevelt's ability to dramatize an issue and appeal to the average American. He did not have Roosevelt's catlike grace in working both sides of the political street without permanently crossing from one side to the other. Nor did he have the explosive vitality that Roosevelt had used to keep the mutually antagonistic conservative and progressive wings of the Republican party subordinate to his leadership.

Taft's immense bulk had much to do with his style. Weighing in at from 300 to 350 pounds, depending on whether or not he was dieting, he was the biggest man ever to occupy the presidency. The nation exploded with laughter when he got stuck in a White House bathtub. After being pried out, he had a jumbo model installed.* He was an ardent golfer—

---

*It measured seven feet long and forty-one inches wide and weighed a ton. Four average-sized people could use it.

the first in the White House—but was too fat to bend down and place his ball on a tee, so his caddy had to do it for him. While he was governor-general in the Philippines, he cabled Secretary of War Root from Manila after a patch of sickness: "Took long horseback ride today. Feel fine." The sardonic Root at once cabled back: "How is the horse?"[3]

Often, after dining, Taft's head would fall on his chest in midsentence and he would go sound asleep for ten or fifteen minutes, awaken, and then continue the conversation as before. Almost invariably, he fell asleep in church. Once, he dozed off during a funeral while sitting in the first row of mourners and was nudged awake by an aide. While having his portrait painted, he fell asleep standing up. He postponed decisions or left them to be made by others. He forgot the names of political and congressional leaders and the newsmen who covered him daily. He made promises and didn't remember them, creating enemies. He played bridge as papers piled up on his desk, and speeches remained unwritten until just before they were to be delivered. Following his presidency, he confessed he had not accomplished more because of "too much love of personal ease."[4]

Yet, despite his unsuitability for politics, Taft had a remarkable rise—similar to that of George Bush—through appointments rather than election. Except for a run for the Ohio Superior Court, Taft had never gone through an election campaign before running for the presidency. With his usual affability, he later explained that "like every well-trained Ohio man I always had my plate right side up when offices were falling."[5] As a result of his family's political connections, he reached the presidency through an apprenticeship as a judge, administrator, and finally Roosevelt's general troubleshooter.

There is a remarkable resemblance between Taft and Bush. Both men were members of America's upper class and Yale graduates, were uninspiring leaders, and followed activist predecessors—Roosevelt and Ronald Reagan. They found that success outside of elective office was no guarantee of success in the presidency. Neither Taft nor Bush could articulate a vision of America: a broad prospective of the nation's problems and its future. And each was defeated for reelection after a third-party candidate split the Republican vote.

Taft had acquired certain skills and personality traits in his appointive posts that, though appropriate for the confined world of a judge and administrator, were liabilities in an elected leader. Insulated from the press and public, he never found it necessary to develop the political touch or sensitive antennae of the seasoned politician. His accomplishments in office were modest: establishing parcel post (fought by the express companies) and postal savings (opposed by the bankers); creating an independent Department of Labor; extending the civil service; launching more antitrust suits than Roosevelt but losing many cases;* and continuing his predecessor's campaign to conserve America's natural resources. Abroad, Taft promoted dollar diplomacy in which military intervention and diplomatic influence were used to further American commercial interests, especially in the Caribbean and Central America.

The public image of a jolly fat man with a bristling handlebar mustache offers only one insight into a complex personality. For all his lethargy, Taft possessed a well-organized, well-honed legal mind. Major Archie Butt, who served as military aide to both Roosevelt and Taft, made a shrewd appraisal of the latter. "Theodore Roosevelt," he confided, "once said that Mr. Taft was one of the best haters he had ever known, and I have found this to be true."[6] Kansas editor William Allen White, catching Taft off guard, noted that behind the twinkle of his eye could be detected "almost the hint of serpentine glitter."[7]

In his various jobs, he had shown himself as intelligent if not brilliant and a good administrator. Taft and Roosevelt had been good friends since 1890, when Taft was solicitor general under President Benjamin Harrison and Roosevelt was a member of the Civil Service Commission. Taft had supported Roosevelt's policies, both at home and abroad. Taft's perpetual smile and a deep chuckle that often exploded into nearly uncontrollable laughter inspired warmth and trust. When Roosevelt went on a tour of the West, he assured everyone that all would be well in Washington. "I have left Taft sitting on the lid," he declared—a remark that, considering Taft's weight, caused much merriment.

Roosevelt repeatedly offered to appoint Taft to the Supreme Court

*After an attack on the trusts early in his administration, Roosevelt changed his views on the monopoly question and favored regulation rather than trust-busting.

as vacancies occurred, and Taft had been sorely tempted to accept. But Nellie and his older half brother, Charles P. Taft, who bankrolled his career, wished him to remain available for the presidency in 1908. When a family friend asked nine-year-old Charlie Taft if his father was going to be a Supreme Court justice, the boy replied, "Nope."

"Why not?"

"Ma wants him to wait and be president."[8]

Had Taft followed a less dynamic predecessor, his record would probably compare favorably with the average run of American chief executives. But Theodore Roosevelt was an impossible act to follow. He had charged up San Juan Hill into the White House—a name he made official—and the staid old building was never the same again. He grasped the presidency by the nape of its neck and gave it a thorough shaking up. In the years after the Civil War, most presidents had abdicated leadership to Congress. Roosevelt changed all that. He saw the president as the tribune of all the people, not like the members of Congress, who represented sectional or economic interests, and the arbiter between competing interests. Critics, on the other hand, charged him with "executive usurpation of power."

With a fierce joy, Roosevelt brandished a "big stick" abroad and promised a "square deal" at home. The first environmentalist president, he preserved the country's natural resources for future generations, personally settled a coal strike, challenged the trusts, and as the first American leader to play an important role in world affairs, began construction of a long-dreamed-of canal across Panama and won the Nobel Peace Prize for almost single-handedly bringing about a peaceful end to the Russo-Japanese War. "I did and caused to be done many things not previously done by the President," he wrote in a telling passage in his *Autobiography*. "I did not usurp power, but I did greatly broaden the use of executive power. . . . I acted for the common well-being of all our people."[9]

Roosevelt's elevation to the presidency coincided with a revival of the crusading spirit that under different names has periodically swept the country. Progressivism, its latest manifestation, championed clean government and "direct democracy." It targeted the interlocking relationship between big business and government, as exemplified by the trusts that had consolidated industrial production and distribution in the hands of a few corporations. Roosevelt, although basically a conservative, was both the midwife and child of progressivism.

As the time to choose a successor neared, he was reluctant to leave the White House. None of his predecessors had enjoyed the presidency as much as he had. At the age of fifty, he was still comparatively young and craved action. "I make no pretense that I am glad to be relieved of my official duties," Roosevelt told a friend.[10] Moreover, the longer he had remained in office, the further he had drifted away from political orthodoxy and was certain that only he could keep the cause of progressive reform at the top of the national agenda. Had it not been for his unfortunate promise in 1904 to give up office, he would probably have sought a new term.

Left to follow his own instinct, Roosevelt would have chosen Elihu Root as his successor. But Root was too closely identified with Wall Street for such progressive times. The frosty Hughes was both able and progressive, but Roosevelt not only considered him too independent, but cordially disliked him. The faithful Will Taft seemed most likely to continue Roosevelt's program, and he received the president's blessing.

"We had better turn to Taft," Roosevelt told an aide.

Taft's passive attitude toward the presidency and his family's towering ambition should have alerted Roosevelt to his friend's unsuitability for the office, but he ignored these ominous signals. Inasmuch as Taft had been a yes-man, never deviating from the views of his leader, Roosevelt may have believed that Taft would be easy to control, and thus he would be able to retain his authority after departing the White House. As a result, he convinced himself—and the country—that Taft was cut from the same progressive cloth as himself.

Even Taft believed it. "I agree heartily and earnestly with the policies which have come to be known as the Roosevelt policies," he declared.[11] But by instinct, emotion, and ideology, Taft was far more conservative than his benefactor and espoused a different philosophy of the presidency. With his reverence for legalisms, Taft believed Roosevelt had gone too far, too fast in pushing the limits of the Constitution in the name of reform and should not have alienated Republican conservatives.

In securing Taft's nomination, Roosevelt did his work well. He used the weight of the presidential office, including federal patronage, to such advantage that Taft already had 563 delegates before the Republican convention met. Only 491 were needed to nominate. There was one danger, however. Even though the delegates and alternates trooping into the barnlike Chicago Coliseum might be wearing Taft badges, their hearts beat for Roosevelt, and they might renominate him by acclamation if given the opportunity. Alice Roosevelt Longworth, the president's outspoken daughter, who was at the convention, wished "in the black depths of my heart" for such an outcome.[12]

She almost got her wish. Senator Henry Cabot Lodge, the keynote speaker, had only to mention the president's name to ignite a thunderclap of cheering. Someone in the galleries began to bellow, "Four, four, four years more!" and the chant spread from the galleries to the floor. "Four, four, four years more!" Some delegates marched about the hall, carrying portraits of Roosevelt and holding large teddy bears aloft. Worried Taft supporters ordered the band to play "The Star-Spangled Banner" in a fruitless attempt to quell the demonstration.

Back in Washington, Roosevelt sat at a White House telephone with the receiver glued to his ear, a broad grin on his face, during the entire tempestuous forty-nine minutes. Over at the War Department, where Taft and his wife were following the proceedings by telegraph, Nellie was tense and tight-lipped as the demonstration went on and on. She had been convinced all along that Roosevelt had intended to be renominated, and here was the final proof. Finally, Lodge brought the cheering to an end with a declaration that Roosevelt's refusal to seek the nomination was "final and irrevocable."

Taft's nomination the following day brought on a contrived demonstration. Nellie sat in her husband's swivel chair, tightly clutching the edge of the ornate desk. "I only want it to last more than forty-nine minutes," she said grimly. "I want to get even for the scare that Roosevelt cheer . . . gave me yesterday."

"Oh, my dear," clucked Taft. "Oh, my dear!"[13]

In spite of the best efforts of Taft's managers, the cheering faded out after only about twenty minutes, but Taft was, nevertheless, nominated on the first ballot. Roosevelt was playing tennis when he received the news of Taft's victory and pronounced himself *"dee*lighted!"

To quash talk that he would really be running the White House after Taft took over, Roosevelt announced that as soon as his term was up, he was going off to bag big game in Africa and crowned heads in Europe. Meanwhile, Taft campaigned across the country without much energy or enthusiasm. His campaign, said one editor, was "loaded down with calm." For the most part, Taft endorsed Roosevelt's record and seemed content to be his proxy. Never having run for any office but a judgeship, he regarded it as purgatory. He abhorred "buttering people up," and being "exposed to all sorts of criticism and curious inquisitiveness." He hated giving speeches, and most of his major addresses were long, droning affairs delivered with all the passion of a legal brief. One such presentation sent Alice Longworth into such gales of laughter she burst a stitch of an appendectomy incision.

Although Roosevelt made no appearances on Taft's behalf—custom prevented presidents from actively campaigning—he was unable to stand idly on the sidelines and allow Taft to boot away his edge over William Jennings Bryan, the prairie Galahad whom the Democrats had nominated for the third time. He wrote several open letters endorsing Taft and inundated the candidate with avuncular advice. Hit the line hard, old man! Avoid talking about delicate subjects like religion. Stop citing court decisions. Don't have your picture taken playing golf. Stay in hotels rather than private homes so more people can see you. Above all, "you big, generous, high-minded fellow," you must *"always"* smile for "your nature shines out so transparently when you smile."

Roosevelt's concern was misplaced. Taft defeated Bryan by a wide margin in both popular and electoral votes, although he trailed the totals piled up by Roosevelt in 1904.* Triple-chinned and beaming, Taft told a crowd gathered in front of his brother Charlie's home in Cincinnati that his administration would be a "worthy successor to that of

---

*Following his third defeat in 1908, Bryan compared himself to a drunk who tried several times to get into a private club and was thrown out after each attempt. After being thrown out the third time, he picked himself off the sidewalk and said, "They can't fool me. Those fellows don't want me in there."

Theodore Roosevelt." But in the interval between the election and Taft's inauguration on March 4, 1909, relations between the two men began to sour.

The rift first opened when Taft, in writing to Roosevelt immediately after the election, gave the credit for his victory not only to the president but to Taft's brother as well. Roosevelt was taken aback. To be placed in the same category with Charlie Taft and his ever-ready checkbook was hardly what he expected. Newsmen also reported that the Taft family, especially Nellie, thought they didn't owe very much to Roosevelt because "dear Will" would have gotten to the White House on his own. Moreover, Taft had told the president he intended to keep on those members of Roosevelt's cabinet who wanted to stay. Four stated a wish to do so, but after the election, Taft decided they would be more loyal to Roosevelt than to him and decided to name his own team— much to the president's chagrin.

On his last full day in office, Roosevelt expressed his simmering doubts about Taft to Mark Sullivan, a leading journalist of the day. "He means well and he'll do his best," the president declared. "But he's weak. They'll get around him." To illustrate, he pushed his bulk against Sullivan's shoulder. "They'll—they'll lean against him."[14]

If birth can boost a man into the presidency, William Howard Taft was blessed with an auspicious beginning. As the son of Alphonso Taft, a leading Cincinnati attorney, judge, honest secretary of war and attorney general in President Grant's scandal-tainted second term, and later U.S. minister to the Austro-Hungarian Empire and imperial Russia, he was born with an assured social and economic position.[15] The senior Taft was a New Englander who after graduating from Yale with honors read law and headed west to Ohio, where he was immediately successful at the bar and in politics. He married twice. Following the death of his first wife, by whom he had three children, he married Louise Maria Torrey, the daughter of a Boston merchant and seventeen years his junior. William Howard, the oldest of their five surviving children, was born on September 15, 1857.

Will was a cherubic, good-natured boy, already running to fat.

Alphonso Taft was austere, reserved, and disinclined to show his emotions, but the boy had a happy childhood in a home full of love and affection, of easy circumstances and security. The elder Taft insisted, however, that his children exert themselves to the fullest. "Mediocrity will not do, Will," he complained when his son stood fifth in a large class. The boy's mother was strong-willed and efficient, and Taft once observed that she would have made a good railroad president. Later, Louise discouraged her son from going into politics, saying he was ill-fitted for such a life. Before her death in 1907, she endorsed Elihu Root as Roosevelt's successor.

Unlike well-to-do families in the East, the Tafts sent their children to public schools. Will was a good student, usually standing at the top, or near it, in his classes. By the time he entered Woodward High School, he had nearly reached his full height of six feet two inches. The program was heavy with Greek, Latin, mathematics, history, and literature. Taft did well in all his subjects, graduating second in his class, and followed his father and half brothers to Yale in 1874.

Taft performed well at Yale and was fun-loving and popular with his classmates, although he did not smoke and only occasionally drank beer or wine. Despite his size, he was light on his feet and an excellent dancer. He represented the freshman class in the intramural wrestling matches and won. Later, he took prizes in mathematics and public speaking and was tapped by Skull and Bones, the ultimate symbol of success at Yale. Taft singled out William Graham Sumner, the high priest of social Darwinism in America, as his most influential teacher. He graduated as salutatorian in a class of 132 and made Phi Beta Kappa. His parents expressed disappointment that he was not first.

Taft's father and grandfather were both attorneys and judges, so the law was a natural calling for him. Returning home from New Haven in 1878, he enrolled in the Cincinnati Law School and read law in his father's office. He also worked as a part-time courthouse reporter for the *Cincinnati Commercial,* which gave him the opportunity to see how the law was actually administered. In 1880, at age twenty-three, he passed the bar. Turning down an offer to become a full-time staffer on the paper, he secured a post through family influence as assistant prosecutor of Hamilton County, which he fulfilled conscientiously. Taft also made his first political speech that year, for James A. Garfield, the Republican presidential candidate.

Two years later, he was appointed collector of internal revenue for Ohio's First District, but soon resigned after refusing to remove workers for political reasons and formed a partnership with an old associate of his father's. A term as assistant solicitor of Hamilton County followed, a job undemanding enough to allow him to maintain his increasingly profitable private practice and keep up his activities as a young man-about-town. Wearing his success debonairly like a flower in his lapel, he was seen everywhere and could hardly turn down an invitation.

In 1886, Taft married Helen Herron, a pretty and strong-willed young woman everyone called Nellie. They had met several years before at a bobsledding party. He was twenty-eight when they married; she was twenty-five. Nellie's father had been a law partner of President Rutherford B. Hayes, and ever since a stay at the White House as a guest of the first family, she had visions of living there herself. As one of eight children, Nellie had often been forced to fend for herself and, early on, developed a fierce sense of independence as well as a restless ambition for herself and those she loved. To a remarkable extent, she resembled her mother-in-law. Throughout her marriage, she was a goad to her husband, pushing—some said driving—him to the presidency. Nevertheless, their marriage, which produced three children,* was stable and happy.

Upon the couple's return from a three-month honeymoon trip to Europe, Taft was appointed to fill out the unexpired portion of a term on the Superior Court. Pleased with the appointment, he described it as the honor "from which all that I have had since has easily flowed." Eighteen months later, he was elected to a full five-year term of his own. Judge Taft was thorough rather than brilliant, but by citing numerous precedents he gave his rulings an air of erudition. Already, he was casting longing glances at the Supreme Court, but in 1890, President Harrison named him solicitor general instead. Taft was dubious about

---

*The Tafts' eldest son, Robert Alphonso Taft (1889–1953), was elected three times as senator from Ohio and was a leader of the conservative wing of the Republican party. He lost the party's 1952 presidential nomination to Dwight D. Eisenhower.

leaving the bench, but having convinced himself that it was a stepping-stone to higher judicial appointment, he accepted.

In the beginning, Will Taft was not altogether comfortable in his new job, which required him to argue the government's side in cases before the Supreme Court. He felt his knowledge of federal law inadequate, and his arguments failed to hold the attention of the justices. "They seem to think when I begin to talk that this is a good chance to read all the letters that have been waiting for some time, to eat lunch, and to devote their attention to reading proof," he glumly wrote his father.[16]

Not long after Taft's arrival in Washington, he met Theodore Roosevelt, who as a civil service commissioner was flailing away against the evils of patronage and corruption—much to the chagrin of administration insiders. Although totally different in personality—Roosevelt was hyperactive and challenging while Taft was placid and accepting—the two men became firm friends. Their homes and offices were not far from each other, and they often walked to work and lunched together. Roosevelt was restless, caught between alternatives, not quite sure what he wanted next, but the White House, which they passed each morning, undeniably appealed to him. Taft knew exactly what he wanted: a seat on the Supreme Court, preferably as chief justice.

In 1891, Congress created nine new appeals courts to break a logjam of litigation in the federal courts, and Taft lobbied for a seat on one of them. The following year Solicitor General Taft was transformed into Judge Taft of the Sixth Judicial Circuit. "It would be in line of promotion to the Supreme Court, and would be a fine position to hold," he told his father. Nellie was not at all happy with the change. "If you get your heart's desire, my darling," she told him, "it will be an end to all the opportunities you now have of being thrown [in] with the bigwigs."[17]

For the next eight years, Taft was happy as a circuit judge. In addition to his judicial duties, he became a professor and dean of the Cincinnati Law School, where he had been a student, and introduced the case system of teaching law. Over the years, his stature as a jurist grew, and he won a reputation among lawyers for fairness and strict interpretation of the law.

Following the election of William McKinley to the presidency in

1896, Taft lobbied his fellow Ohioan for the appointment of Theodore Roosevelt as assistant secretary of the navy. McKinley was reluctant. "For the truth is, Will," said the president, "Roosevelt is always in such a state of mind."[18] Eventually McKinley gave in and named Roosevelt to the post in which he played a leading role in preparing the navy for the war with Spain in 1898. Part of the fallout of the "splendid little war" was the American occupation of the Philippines and a nasty guerrilla war with the Filipinos who wanted their independence. It also enabled Will Taft to return to the wider world of politics and power he had left for the judicial cloisters.

In 1900, McKinley dispatched Taft to the Philippines, originally as head of a commission to establish civil government in the islands and then as governor. Initially, Taft was reluctant to accept the appointment because he opposed American overseas expansion, but Nellie, who was bored with Cincinnati, urged him to take it. McKinley also sweetened the offer with the promise of appointment to the Supreme Court once the task was completed. In Manila, Taft frequently clashed with General Arthur MacArthur, the military commander,* over the army's harsh treatment of the Filipinos. Taft argued that the Americans should regard them as "little brown brothers," which caused the troops engaged in savage fighting against the *insurrectos* to compose the verse:

> He may be a brother of Big Bill Taft,
> But he ain't no friend of mine.

Taft soon became convinced the Filipinos would be unready for independence for decades, but cleaned up corruption, improved health conditions, established schools, made harbor and road improvements, and negotiated the transfer of Catholic Church lands to small farmers. The portly fellow in a tentlike white suit became a familiar and trusted figure in the islands. Upon two occasions, he refused offers from Roosevelt, who had succeeded to the presidency, to name him to the Supreme Court, saying he wished to carry out his reforms in the Philippines. Finally, in 1904, he accepted when Roosevelt asked him to become secretary of war.

---

*Father of General Douglas MacArthur.

Amoebic dysentery was threatening his health, Filipino affairs would still be in his charge in the War Department, and Nellie would be able to return to Washington.

For the next fours years, Taft served not only as secretary of war but as Roosevelt's all-around fix-it man. He supervised the construction of the Panama Canal and personally inspected the project. Sent to Japan, he worked out an arrangement in which the United States recognized Japanese suzerainty of Korea in exchange for Japan's promise to keep her hands off the Philippines. He filled in for ailing Secretary of State John Hay until Elihu Root was appointed in Hay's place. And for a third time, under the prodding of Nellie and Charlie Taft, he refused an offer by Roosevelt to appoint him to the Supreme Court. They had their eyes firmly fixed on the White House.

On Inauguration Day, March 4, 1909, Will Taft awoke to find Washington had been battered by one of the bitterest snowstorms in many years. "I always said it would be a cold day when I got to be president of the United States," he joked to Theodore Roosevelt.[19] Only a thin crowd of stalwarts turned out to cheer the new president as he rode up hastily cleared Pennsylvania Avenue in an automobile—the first used by a president to go to his inauguration—to take the oath of office in the crowded Senate chamber rather than on the Capitol portico. Once back at the White House, the new chief executive threw his bulk into an armchair, stretched out his legs, and announced to the world, "I am president now and tired of being kicked around."

Few presidents have come into office with a backlog of more goodwill than Taft. He appeared to be that rare bird among politicians: a leader acceptable to everyone. Progressive reformers believed that as Roosevelt's handpicked successor, he was one of them. On the other hand, conservatives, overjoyed at getting rid of the "mad messiah," knew Taft as a warm defender of laissez-faire and a man with a punctilious regard for the constitutional process who would do nothing rash.

Yet Taft, despite his excellent prospects, seemed to have difficulty adjusting to his new station. A few days after the inauguration, when a friend asked him how he liked being president, he replied that he didn't really know. "When I hear someone say 'Mr. President,' I look around expecting to see Roosevelt." Often he would refer to Roosevelt as "the president," much to Nellie's anger, and once she pointed out tartly that he meant "the ex-president." "I suppose I do, dear," Taft replied, "but he will always be the president to me, and I can never think of him as anything else." And to Roosevelt himself, he wrote, "I do nothing in the Executive Office without considering what you would do under the same circumstances."[20]

Without his predecessor's sure hand to guide him, Taft soon blundered into political quicksand. The 1908 Republican platform had pledged tariff revision, which was generally understood to mean a reduction in the high levels established in 1897. Roosevelt had carefully avoided tinkering with the tariff because he realized it was a volatile issue that could only split the Republican party between conservatives, who supported a high protective tariff, and the progressives, who thought it the mother of trusts and monopolies. Taft, long an advocate of tariff reform, promptly called a special session of Congress to fulfill his campaign promise. Unhappily, tariff reform quickly became entangled with progressive efforts to overthrow the arbitrary rule of "Uncle Joe" Cannon, the conservative Speaker of the House.[21]

In the last two years of Roosevelt's presidency, progressivism had developed such volatility that the old guard could not contain it. Insurgents, mostly from the Midwest, formed a bloc of fourteen seats in the Senate, with Robert M. La Follette of Wisconsin as their leader, and thirty in the House. Although elected as Republicans, the insurgents defied party discipline in their determination to put an end to social injustice. Cannon, a rapacious little man with a foul mouth who had represented Illinois in Congress as long as anyone could remember, typified all that they opposed. Through his tight grip on the committee system, he controlled the flow of legislation, decreeing what should become law, and the insurgents were determined to trim his power.

Cannon and his ally, the Senate majority leader, Senator Nelson Aldrich of Rhode Island,* made Taft an offer. In return for his help in blocking the anti-Cannon coup, they agreed to move the tariff bill to

---

*Aldrich had married the daughter of John D. Rockefeller and was the grandfather of Vice President Nelson Aldrich Rockefeller.

the floor. Taft had his predecessor's example before him. Roosevelt had maintained an uneasy truce with the Speaker and had advised Taft to "make peace with Uncle Joe." Although he detested Cannon, Taft agreed to support him against the insurgents in exchange for support for tariff reduction. With the president's help, Cannon temporarily survived the attempts to curtail his power, but Taft was now suspect among the progressives.*

In keeping with the promise made by Cannon, the House promptly approved a bill introduced by Rep. Sereno E. Payne of New York that reduced customs duties on a number of important items. Once it came before the Senate, however, the bill was at the tender mercies of a large bloc of protectionist senators. The Payne-Aldrich Tariff emerged with 847 changes from the House version—most of them upward. An inheritance tax that had been included in the House bill was also struck out. "The Republican party has been thrue to its promises," observed a caustic "Mr. Dooley," the fictional Irish saloonkeeper–political philosopher created by newspaper writer Finley Peter Dunne. "Look at th' free list if ye don't believe it. Practically iverything necessary to existence comes in free. Here it is. Curling stones, teeth, sea moss, newspapers, nux vomica, Pulu, canary bird seed . . . Th' new tariff bill puts these familyar commodyties within' th' reach 'iv all."

Led by Senator La Follette, the angry insurgents attacked the changes item by item—exposing the links between the protective tariff and the trusts. They expected Taft to support them. Roosevelt had encouraged them to believe Taft was a progressive, and besides, they were fighting for his tariff reform program. Taft was in a quandary. Should he go along with the Republican reformers who agreed with him? Or should he support the Old Guard, the party's dominant conservative wing? Without Roosevelt to do his thinking for him, he veered from one side to another.

Taft's problem lay in the fact that he was a progressive—but only up to a point. And that point had been reached. Wracked by self-doubt and unable to sleep at night, he wandered about the White House in his size fifty-four pajamas. To add to the president's misery, Nellie, who was the

---

*The insurgents succeeded in stripping Cannon of his powers the following year.

real politician in the family and upon whom he depended for guidance, suffered a stroke, which affected her ability to speak.

Taft had neither the will nor the stomach to get his own way in this kind of battle. Unlike Roosevelt, he lacked the skill to use patronage to buy his way out of his difficulties or to apply pressure to his opponents by threatening to go directly to the people. Like Bill Clinton, he shifted from one side to the other so often that eventually no one believed he had any convictions at all. He finally decided for the sake of party unity to stick with the Old Guard rather than "have personal popularity" by supporting the insurgents. He valued party unity over his own reputation—and lost both.

Taft not only refused to veto the Payne-Aldrich Tariff as demanded by the insurgents, who now accused him of folly, feebleness, and treachery, but became even more dependent upon Aldrich and Cannon. Having been a yes-man in Roosevelt's cabinet, he inevitably became one for the party regulars. Senator Jonathan Dolliver described him as "a ponderous and amiable island completely surrounded by men who know exactly what they want." By 1910, he was so firmly in the conservatives' camp that he tried unsuccessfully to purge some of the insurgents in the Republican congressional primaries that year.

In the African bush, Colonel Roosevelt, as he now wished to be known, kept abreast of the unhappy events unfolding in Washington through weeks-old newspapers and letters from friends. He was disappointed with Taft's handling of the tariff question, he wrote Cabot Lodge, not because Roosevelt favored tariff reduction, but because of the effect of the president's inept handling of the issue upon party unity. Even more unsettling was Taft's tactless praise of Payne-Aldrich in an off-the-cuff speech in Winona, Minnesota, a hotbed of insurgency, in which he called it "the best tariff bill the Republican party has ever passed." Such remarks outraged Midwestern reformers and led to severe losses by the party in the 1910 elections. By the close of Taft's first year in office, newspapers all over the Midwest were saying that the Rough Rider could have the party's presidential nomination in 1912 for the asking. Out of office, Roosevelt had been transformed into an ideal; Will Taft was the unhappy reality.

* * *

Taft's handling of conservation, the keystone of Roosevelt's legacy, helped destroy for good his standing with progressives. Eyebrows had been raised among environmentalists when he named Richard A. Ballinger to succeed a dedicated conservationist as secretary of the interior. Ballinger was a former mayor of Seattle and chief of the General Land Office. Like most Westerners, he was a "boomer" who advocated rapid exploitation of the nation's natural resources. A clash between Ballinger and Gifford Pinchot, the chief of the Forestry Service and watchdog of Rooseveltian conservation, was inevitable. Minor cutbacks ordered by Ballinger convinced Pinchot that all conservation programs were in danger.[22]

Late in the summer of 1909, Louis R. Glavis, a young Interior Department investigator, sought out Pinchot with a disturbing story. Ballinger, he claimed, was conspiring to turn over valuable Alaskan coal lands to be plundered by a Morgan-Guggenheim syndicate. Pinchot immediately sent Glavis to see the president. Taft, angry that they had gone over Ballinger's head and worried about a scandal that would besmirch his administration, accepted Ballinger's denials and fired Glavis. To appease Pinchot, Taft assured him of his continuing commitment to conservation, but the incident kindled a raging prairie fire that eventually consumed Taft's presidency.

Pinchot now courted martyrdom. He orchestrated a campaign by muckraking journalists against Ballinger, which turned up evidence that the interior secretary had previously represented the Morgan-Guggenheim interests as an attorney. Furious at the leaks emanating from Pinchot's office, Taft fired him. He fully realized that this would anger Roosevelt and the insurgents, but Pinchot's calculated insubordination could not be ignored. From a political standpoint, however, it was another blunder. Had he insisted upon Ballinger's resignation as well, he would have appeared evenhanded.

Ten days after Pinchot's dismissal, a native runner brought the news to the Congo, where Roosevelt was hunting the rare white rhino. "I cannot believe it," the Colonel wrote Pinchot at once. It would be "a very ungracious thing for an ex-President to criticize his successor; and yet as an honest man cease to battle for the principles [for] which you and I . . . stood." Taft, in an effort to show his continuing commitment to conservation, replaced Pinchot with the director of the Yale School of Forestry and, after Ballinger resigned a year later, named a confirmed environmentalist as interior secretary. But the affair widened the gulf between the Old Guard supporters of the president and the progressives linked to Roosevelt. Moreover, the relationship between the two men was never again the same as it had been.

Toward the end of June 1910, Roosevelt, who had returned home only a week or so before to wildly cheering crowds, visited Taft at the summer White House in Beverly, Massachusetts. Upon Roosevelt's arrival in New York, he had resolved to maintain his silence about politics, but his home at Oyster Bay on Long Island quickly became a mecca for progressives who were urging the Rough Rider to seek the Republican nomination in 1912 or to run as a third-party candidate. Roosevelt had pleaded the press of family business in turning down an invitation to the White House upon his return, but used the thirtieth reunion of his Harvard class in nearby Cambridge to call on Taft. It was their first meeting in sixteen months.

"Ah, Theodore, it is good to see you!" exclaimed Taft, stretching out both hands in greeting.

"How are you, Mr. President?" replied Roosevelt affably. "This is simply bully."

"See here, now, drop the 'Mr. President,' " said Taft, playfully punching his visitor on the shoulder.

"Not at all. You must be Mr. President and I am Theodore. It must be that way."[23]

For an hour or so, they chatted on the porch, getting a renewed feel for each other. There was much banter and laughter as Roosevelt regaled Taft with stories of his adventures in Africa and amid European royalty. Following the meeting, Roosevelt insisted that he had no intention of returning to active politics and cautioned his supporters against attacking Taft. But this truce did not last long. Roosevelt became involved in several political controversies in New York State and detected what he believed was underground opposition from Taft and his backers. Furious with the president, he charged that he had "completely twisted around the policies I advocated and acted upon" and, within a month of his return, was off on a sixteen-state speaking tour of the Middle West. Nellie Taft, who had partially recovered from her stroke, made an accurate assessment of these events. "I suppose you will have to fight Mr. Roosevelt for the nomination, and if you get it, he will defeat you," she told her husband.[24]

With the unrestrained fury of a Kansas twister, Roosevelt swept across the plains, stirring the crowds who gathered under a broiling sun in dusty town squares, in baseball parks, and at picnics with a militant call for reform. He attacked the Supreme Court as a barrier to social justice and advocated checks on the power of the judiciary to void legislative acts. If Taft had become more conservative in office, Roosevelt had grown more radical out of it.

In Osawatomie, Kansas, he outlined a set of principles that he labeled the New Nationalism. Social justice could be obtained, he declared, only through the vigorous effort of a federal government that assumed responsibility for reforms previously off-limits under the sacred doctrine of laissez-faire. If this was not frightening enough to the Old Guard, Roosevelt backed it up with a grab bag of "radical" proposals that foreshadowed the welfare state: graduated income and inheritance taxes; workers' compensation; child and women's labor laws; tariff revision; and strict corporate regulation. Informed while on the golf links of Roosevelt's attack on the judiciary, the normally placid Taft was so outraged he angrily flung a club across the course.

Under the strain of his breakup with his old friend, Taft put on even more weight. "He looks terribly," said Archie Butt. "His flesh looks like wax, and his lips are thin, and he is getting those unhealthy bags under his eyes."[25] On another occasion, a reporter found the president with his head in his hands. Looking up, he said in a despairing voice, "Roosevelt was my closest friend." Unable to control himself any longer, he burst into tears.[26]

On February 22, 1912, Roosevelt announced his candidacy for the Republican presidential nomination. With the Old Guard in control of the party machinery, he knew he had little chance of winning but pressed ahead anyway. Personal ambition, a lust for power, boredom, the wish to implement the reforms unveiled at Osawatomie, anger at Taft—all these figured in the decision. But the key factor was his sense of duty. Realizing that he was responsible for much of the progressive sentiment in the Republican party, Roosevelt believed he could not betray his principles and those who were fighting for these principles.

Taft had been so unhappy in the White House that he might not have sought a second term had it not been for what he regarded as Roosevelt's betrayal and open challenge. "I am afraid I am in for a hard fight . . . but I am going to stay in anyhow," he wrote a friend. "I believe I represent a safer and saner view of our government and its Constitution than does Theodore Roosevelt." And in a memorably unfortunate remark, he added, "Even a rat in a corner will fight."[27]

Roosevelt won most of the primaries and arrived at the convention in Chicago convinced he was the choice of the party's rank and file. The nomination turned upon 254 contested delegates; Roosevelt needed about 100 of the disputed seats to clinch the nomination. But the Old Guard controlled the Republican National Committee, which ruled on credentials, and it gave all but 19 to Taft. Storming out of the convention, Roosevelt's angry supporters organized the Progressive party with the Colonel as its nominee. But after the Democrats nominated Woodrow Wilson, the progressive governor of New Jersey, Roosevelt was under no illusions about his chances for victory. Nevertheless, he approached the battle feeling "fit as a bull moose"—giving his party its enduring name—and campaigned vigorously on a platform embodying a full array of reforms.

The exchange between Roosevelt and Taft was vitriolic and personal. Roosevelt referred to his successor as a "fathead" with "brains less than that of a guinea pig"; Taft branded his opponent "a demagogue" and "a man who can't tell the truth." But the election settled down to a two-man race between Roosevelt and Wilson, and they all but ignored the president. Taft, resigned to defeat, delivered a few desultory speeches and lapsed into silence. "There are so many people in the country who don't like me," he said plaintively.

The results in November were as predicted. Roosevelt and Taft split the Republicans while Wilson held on to Democratic voters and won with 42 percent of the votes. The victory returned the Democrats to the White House for the first time in sixteen years. Roosevelt ran second and Taft a poor third. He carried only two states with eight electoral votes, Utah and Vermont, the latter by only 235 votes. It was the worst defeat ever suffered by an incumbent president. Significantly, nearly three-quarters of the voters, both Republican and Democratic, pre-ferred progressive candidates.

Yet, despite this rejection by the voters, Taft was not depressed. "I have one consolation," he said. "No one candidate has ever been elected ex-president by such a large majority."[28] Happy to be relieved of the burden of the White House, he felt a sense of well-being such as he had not experienced in years as he awaited Wilson's inauguration. Offered a professorship of law at Yale, he accepted it with almost as much eagerness as if he had been named to the Supreme Court.

Few ex-presidents had a more productive career after the White House than Will Taft. He was popular with his students at Yale, where he taught government and international law, and was repeatedly cited as their favorite professor. He gave speeches and wrote books and arti-cles about the presidency. The American people tended to assign the president responsibility "for all the sins of omission and of commission of society," he remarked, but "the president cannot make clouds to rain, he cannot make the corn to grow, he cannot make business to be good."

Someone asked the former president about the possibility of a return to politics, and he had a ready answer: "I am now in a respectable pro-fession." When the United States entered World War I, he served as joint chairman of the National War Labor Board. Taft and Roosevelt were both critical of Wilson's conduct of the war, and it led to a resump-tion of their correspondence. Once again, it was "Dear Will" and "Dear Theodore," although they had not met in person since before the ill-starred 1912 election.

One day in May 1918, Taft checked into the Blackstone Hotel in Chicago and learned that Roosevelt was in the dining room. Locating the Colonel alone at a table, Taft walked over to him. Roosevelt was intent on his meal and a book, but sensing a sudden hush, he looked up and saw Taft's beaming face looming over him. Immediately throwing down his napkin, he leaped to his feet, hand extended. Both men shook hands vigorously and eagerly slapped each other on the back. The other guests applauded, and suddenly realizing they had an audience, the two ex-presidents bowed and smiled. Then they sat down and talked animatedly for a half hour.[29]

Taft's plate was again right side up in 1921 when Warren Harding, who had given Taft's nominating speech at the 1912 convention, fulfilled the ex-president's lifelong ambition by naming him chief justice of the United States. The next nine years were the happiest of his life. Taft's geniality helped reduce friction between the rigidly conservative majority and the liberal justices, Oliver Wendell Holmes and Louis D. Brandeis, which made it possible for the court to swiftly clear a clogged docket, maintaining a steady flow of decisions and some degree of collegiality among the brethren.

In contrast to his lethargy as president, Taft was an activist chief justice and wrote 253 opinions, about a sixth of all the decisions handed down while he was on the bench. The crowning achievement of his tenure was obtaining congressional approval for a new home for the Supreme Court. Fittingly enough, the marble temple was built on what had been the site of the Old Capitol Prison, where during the Civil War prisoners were held without access to writ of habeas corpus. In February 1930, at the age of seventy-two, poor health forced Taft to leave his beloved court. A month later, he died and was laid to rest on a graceful slope in Arlington National Cemetery, the first president to be interred there.*

Not long after becoming chief justice, Taft was given an honorary degree by Oxford. While in London, he was introduced to various dignitaries, including the Prince of Wales, later and briefly King Edward VIII. "By the way," allowed the rather dim prince, "haven't you been made a secretary or been put in the cabinet or something?"[30]

---

*John F. Kennedy is the only other president buried at Arlington.

CHAPTER III

BENJAMIN HARRISON

Shortly after Benjamin Harrison was elected America's twenty-third president in 1888, he turned to Senator Matthew C. Quay and, taking his hand, piously intoned, "Providence has given us this victory." Quay, the irascible Republican boss of Pennsylvania, who really knew who had been responsible for the win, was aghast. "Think of the man!" he snorted afterward. "He ought to know that Providence really hadn't a damn thing to do with it." Harrison would "never know how many men were compelled to approach the gates of the penitentiary to make him president."[1]

Although the 1888 election does not come close to that of 1876, in which the Republicans probably stole the presidency for Rutherford B. Hayes, it exudes a ripe odor. Fraud, vote buying, and ballot-box stuffing on a major scale provided Harrison with his margin of victory over President Grover Cleveland. In fact, Cleveland outpolled Harrison by nearly one hundred thousand popular votes only to lose in the Electoral College. He was robbed of reelection by shenanigans in Harrison's home state of Indiana and in Cleveland's own New York, where a bribed Tammany Hall, unhappy with the president's reformist tendencies, ordered its stalwarts to "cut" him.

Harrison's principal claim to fame was that he was the grandson of William Henry Harrison, the nation's ninth president, and it was enough to make him president in an age of puny politicians without ability or imagination. The first Harrison died of pneumonia at sixty-eight, a month after he had insisted upon delivering an inaugural address nearly two hours long while standing in the March rain and sleet without hat, gloves, or overcoat. Harrison II served a full four-year term as president—he took the precaution of wearing chamois underwear at his swearing-in—but cynics sneered that he had no more impact on the office than "Old Tippecanoe." He is hardly mentioned in most textbooks, and one popular 685-page history of the United States omits him altogether.*

Glacially formal, colorless, and dour, Harrison had, said a visitor, a handshake "like a wilted petunia." He was not a bad president in the sense that Richard Nixon or James Buchanan were bad presidents. Instead, he was a study in inaction, with a limited view of the parameters of his office. He neither proposed nor disposed. Less the leader than the led, he served as a high-minded figurehead for an alliance of Republican bosses and big businessmen who actually ran the country. "When I came to power, I found that the party managers had taken it all to themselves," he later lamented. "I could not name my own cabinet. They had sold every place to pay the election expenses."[2]

Harrison's presidency was frustrating for both himself and the nation, for several reasons. He cherished privacy and disliked the public pressures placed upon him and his family in the White House, and had an adversarial relationship with the press. In view of his belief in congressional supremacy in legislative matters, he had no agenda of his own for which to fight. The voters, by giving Cleveland a popular majority, had made it clear that they hadn't really wanted him. And then Cleveland came back to defeat him by a landslide in 1892, so his lackluster term in office was sandwiched between the two terms of an abler chief executive. Harrison's famous name also turned out to be a double-edged sword. While it helped get him elected, his family had a long history of service to the nation and it aroused great expectations that went unfulfilled.

"Damn the president!" snapped an angry Theodore Roosevelt, who lent window dressing to the Harrison administration as a civil service commissioner, after the chief executive failed to support his version of reform. "He is a cold-blooded, narrow-minded, prejudiced, obstinate, timid old psalm-singing Indianapolis politician."[3] For his part, Harri-

*Allan Nevins and Henry Steele Commager, *A Pocket History of the United States* (New York: Washington Square Press, 1986).

son tartly observed that Mr. Roosevelt "wanted to put an end to all the evil in the world between sunrise and sunset."[4]

Harrison was known as Little Ben—not out of affection, but because of his height. Only five and a half feet tall and with a red-tinged beard and a potbelly perched on spindly legs, he resembled nothing so much as a medieval gnome. Because of his relationship to Harrison I, the Republicans campaigned with the slogan "Grandfather's hat fits Ben." The Democrats countered with cartoons showing Little Ben as a pygmy almost lost in the shadow of his grandfather's beaver hat. They also dubbed him Kid Gloves because of his dandified clothes and aloofness.

Harrison was not without talent. He was intelligent, a leading light of the Indianapolis bar, a Presbyterian elder who taught Bible class on Sundays and had risen to the rank of general during the Civil War. A bombastic orator, he was an accomplished waver of the "bloody shirt" of rebellion and twister of the tail of the British lion. His speeches resonated with references to Civil War battlefields "wet with the blood of loyal men" and to the "grasping avarice" of British diplomacy.[5]

Yet he was miserably unsuccessful when dealing with individuals. Both friendly observers and critics agreed that "he could charm a crowd of twenty thousand . . . but could make them all enemies with a single handshake." Friends said he seemed icy because he set high standards not only for himself but for others and was intolerant of those who failed to measure up. "Don't think he means to insult you," one acquaintance warned a group of people before introducing them to Harrison. "It is his way."[6]

Out campaigning by train, Harrison made several speeches at various stops that aroused great enthusiasm from his audiences. But each time, people came away silent and downcast after shaking hands with him. Noticing this, one of his managers began pulling the cord to start the train as soon as Harrison had finished his speech. Chided for rushing the candidate away before he could meet the voters, the man replied, "Don't talk to me. I know my business. Benjamin Harrison had that crowd red-hot. I did not want him to freeze it out of them with his handshaking."

Harrison's administration coincided with the shift of the United States from an agrarian to an industrial economy. While he was proud of the nation's industrial growth, he had, like most national leaders of the day, little understanding of the effect of these changes upon the ordinary working man. Sheltered from the economic realities and consequences of industrial capitalism, he lacked knowledge of the growing impersonality of relations between employee and employer, the intense competition for subsistence-level jobs, and the grinding boredom of most unskilled work. He had no policies to alleviate the class tensions, economic dislocations, anguish, and conflicts of the day.

To refurbish Harrison's reputation, some recent writers have credited him with a key role in the passage of red-letter legislation regarding trusts, tariffs, and finance during his administration. In fact, however, he had little more to do with these measures beyond affixing his signature. Even a favorable biographer concedes that he "seems to emerge greater as a man than as a president."

Benjamin Harrison entered the White House as the American political system was undergoing revolutionary changes. The spoils system, which in Andrew Jackson's day seemed a radical innovation, had become a bulwark of conservatism and was now under attack by reformers.[7] Party leaders resisted with the claim that patronage was the mother's milk of politics. Unless the bait of jobs was dangled before the faithful, it would be impossible to muster the armies of workers needed to drum up votes. Each party boss marshaled a force of postal clerks, federal jobholders, and state, city, and county workers who labored for candidates endorsed by their leaders. They were judged not on job proficiency but on how well they procured votes. Contributions levied on their salaries also filled the war chests of the parties. Realists like New York boss Roscoe Conkling charged that the reformers with their unceasing demands for "snivel service" utterly failed to understand that "parties are not built up by deportment, or by ladies' magazines, or by gush."

Nevertheless, following the enactment of the Pendleton Civil Service Act in 1883, an ever-increasing number of federal jobholders were covered by the merit system, which resulted in fewer party hacks available for campaign work. Laws protecting public employees from shakedowns also meant the parties had to find new sources of revenue. At the same time, the costs of conducting campaigns were taking a quantum leap. The rapid growth of the country and the corresponding expansion of the number of eligible voters required a much more vigorous effort to shape public opinion. Such operations required vast infusions of money, so the politicians turned increasingly to sympathetic tycoons for cash to keep their machines oiled.

Soon, the donations of such giant entities as American Sugar, Standard Oil, and the New York Central Railroad vastly exceeded the revenues that had previously been raised from kickbacks from jobholders. Political leaders now thought in terms of economic interests rather than the old-fashioned sectional politics of the antebellum and immediate post–Civil War years. They regarded "sugar," "iron," and "railroads" as entities deserving representation in the highest councils of the nation and embraced the widespread but unspoken belief that America was a huge profit-making concern. The primary task of government was to assist business in maximizing profits and seeing that these were distributed with as little interference as possible. While businessmen worked with party bosses such as Matt Quay of Pennsylvania and Tom Platt, Conkling's successor in New York, the crasser forms of graft were no longer the immediate goal. The party in power in Washington could bestow favors far more valuable than the boodle of an earlier day.

The protective tariff was foremost among these benefits. Big business regarded high tariffs as an integral part of the "American system," and necessary for the continued growth of the economy. The tariff, it was said, not only protected infant industries but was patriotic because it encouraged domestic prosperity and ensured a high standard of living. William McKinley, an Ohio congressman and mouthpiece of his state's manufacturing interests, cast scorn upon the idea of cheap foreign imports. "*Cheap* is not a word of hope," he declared. "It is not a word of inspiration. It is the badge of poverty; it is the signal of distress."

If any politician embodied the values—or lack of them—of the Gilded Age, it was James G. Blaine of Maine. Member of Congress, Speaker of the House of Representatives, ranking senator, secretary of state, and a perennial presidential hopeful, the "Plumed Knight" was a dominant figure in Republican councils and in the affairs of the nation.* A magnetic leader with eyes that seemed to flash sparks and a voice that hypnotized the galleries, he pursued the voters up and down the byways of the Republic for nearly thirty years.

Year after year, election after election, his name echoed across the land like a drumbeat: "Blaine! Blaine! James G. Blaine!" But he could never convince a majority of Americans that he was not a crook. Blaine's contribution to the art of politics lay not in the laws he drafted or in the bills he shepherded through Congress. Instead, he cemented the alliance between the Republican party and big business, and it became the party of bankers and manufacturers, of the Eastern cities, rather than the party of the agricultural Western states that it had been originally.

In 1884, Grover Cleveland had narrowly defeated Blaine to become the first Democrat to be elected president since before the Civil War. Reform Republicans, worried about their nominee's mottled reputation, had bolted to Cleveland.[8] Just as his term was ending, the president, ignoring the advice of Democratic insiders, unexpectedly called for a reduction in the prohibitively high tariffs. He argued that the Chinese wall of tariffs was not only costly to consumers, but also contributed to the growth of trusts. "Our present tariff laws, this vicious, inequitable, and illogical source of unnecessary taxation, ought to be at once revised and amended," he declared. Moreover a high tariff had created a government surplus, which was a temptation to Congress to go on a spending spree.

Cleveland's surprise proposal for tariff reform was a windfall for the Republicans. They immediately branded him a free trader who favored British manufacturers over American industrialists and workers alike. "There's one more president for us in protection," exulted Jim Blaine—and there was no doubt whom the Plumed Knight had in mind. But there was considerable unease among party leaders about his public reputation, and he thought better about seeking the nomination. Instead, he chose to play kingmaker—and while looking about for a harmless

---

*Blaine appears as the corrupt Senator Ratcliffe in Henry Adams's unsigned novel, *Democracy*.

nonentity upon whom to bestow his apostolic blessing, his appraising eye focused upon the diminutive figure of Benjamin Harrison.

Service to the nation was in Harrison's genes. The first of the clan in America—also named Benjamin—settled in 1632 in Virginia, where he became a member of the House of Burgesses and one of the colony's largest landowners.[9] Later Harrisons were also prominent in Virginia affairs, among them Benjamin V., who signed the Declaration of Independence. His son, William Henry Harrison, was the victor over the Indian chief Tecumseh at the Battle of Tippecanoe in 1811 and became a national hero. He served in Congress, as U.S. senator from Ohio, and as minister to Colombia before being elected to the presidency.

John Scott Harrison, the fifth child of William Henry Harrison, was born in Vincennes, Indiana, in 1804, while his father was serving there as an officer in the U.S. Army. Prospering as a farmer in Ohio, the younger Harrison was from 1853 to 1857 a Whig member of Congress and opposed all measures to extend slavery. He had married in 1824 and, upon the death of his first wife, married Elizabeth Irwin in 1831, by whom he had six children who lived to adulthood, including the future president.*

Benjamin Harrison was born on August 30, 1833, at the home of his paternal grandfather in North Bend, on the Ohio River just below Cincinnati. Not long after, the family moved to The Point, a six-hundred-acre estate downriver provided by the elder Harrison, who was elected president when the boy was seven. As soon as he was old enough, Ben was assigned chores about the farm, and the rest of his life he professed to admire rural rather than city life. There was no school, so Scott Harrison had a one-room log schoolhouse built on the farm for his children and those of his neighbors. Harriet Root, the school's first teacher, said Ben was "terribly stubborn" and determined to get ahead in everything.

*Scott Harrison had a rather macabre end. Following his death in 1878, his body was stolen by grave robbers, who sold it to the Ohio Medical College in Cincinnati, where it was dissected by medical students. One of his sons had business at the school and found to his horror the cadaver dangling by the neck from the end of a rope in one of the classrooms. DeGregorio, *The Complete Book of Presidents,* 139.

Although his father suffered financial reverses, Harrison attended a private academy in Cincinnati from 1847 to 1850, where he began a lifelong interest in history and politics. There, he developed the following insight: "The manner by which women are treated is a good criterion to judge of the true state of a society. If we knew but this one feature in a character of a nation, we may easily judge of the rest." Harrison entered Miami University in Oxford, Ohio, as a junior, and graduated after two years near the top of his class. A deeply religious young man, he was torn between the law and the ministry—and the law won out. Over the next two years he studied in the Cincinnati offices of Storer and Gwynne, one the city's leading law firms, and was admitted to the bar in 1854.

The year before, Harrison had married his college sweetheart, Caroline Lavinia Scott, the daughter of the headmaster of a female academy in Oxford. She was twenty-one; he was twenty. The young attorney decided to settle in Indianapolis, then a fast-growing Western town, but clients came slowly. "They were close times. . . . A five-dollar bill was an event," he recalled. Over the years, he built one of the most prosperous law practices in Indianapolis. A neighbor remembered Harrison as "kindly, agreeable, and studious, reserved even then. . . . I do not think he ever had an acquaintance with anyone that ripened into the hottest kind of friendship."

In 1856, Harrison joined the newly organized Republican party and campaigned for John C. Fremont, its first presidential nominee. Despite a warning from his father to avoid the "temptations" of politics, the young man was elected Indianapolis city attorney the following year. He became state supreme court reporter and by the outbreak of the Civil War had achieved a reputation for ability and integrity.

In July 1862, Harrison was offered command of a regiment of Indiana volunteers and accepted although he was the father of two children. The newly minted regimental commander lacked military experience, but he managed to whip his men into a semblance of soldiers—whether they liked it or not. Some men can apply stern discipline and retain the affection of their troops, but Harrison was not one of them. His icy demeanor and abruptness made him unpopular with his officers and men, but during Sherman's Atlanta campaign, he was cited several times for bravery and promoted to brigadier general. For the rest of his life, his wife and supporters referred to him as General Harrison.

At war's end, Harrison resumed his post as supreme court reporter and then returned to the practice of law. Aided by his war record, his political contacts, and his knack for making simple presentations of complicated issues, he soon became one of the most sought-after attorneys in Indiana. Nevertheless, he was intense, uncomfortable in social situations, hated small talk, and his chilly manner did not court familiarity. With a mass of confused and complicated facts churning in his mind, he would often pass acquaintances in the street without seeing them or returning their greetings. Away from the pressures of business, however, he seemed a different man. "When he's on a fishing trip, Ben takes a drink of whiskey in the morning just like anyone else," noted a friend. "He chews tobacco from a plug he carries in his hip pocket, spits on his worm for luck, and cusses when the fish gets away."[10]

Harrison supported the Radical Republicans during Andrew Johnson's ill-fated administration and campaigned for various candidates, but did not actively seek office until 1876, when the party nominated him for governor. Following a hard-fought race against Jim "Blue Jeans" Williams, a farmer who affected a Lincolnian simplicity, Harrison ran ahead of the rest of the ticket but was defeated by a little more than five thousand votes. At the Republican convention in 1880, he supported his fellow Union general James Garfield for the nomination and, after Garfield won the presidency, was offered a seat in the cabinet. Harrison refused, however, having already been elected to the U.S. Senate by the Indiana legislature.

In the Senate, Harrison played an unobtrusive role, generally following the orthodox party line, but only to the extent that he regarded it as "reasonable." He was a monument to reason. He supported a reasonable protective tariff, reasonable labor legislation, reasonable railroad legislation, and reasonable pensions for Union veterans. Unlike many conservative Republicans, he was sympathetic to the problems of the Indians and the homesteaders and voted against a bill excluding Chinese immigrants, apparently on constitutional grounds.

Harrison's search for the reasonable led him down strange byways. While he favored the Pendleton Civil Service Act, he opposed laws designed to prevent government employees from being shaken down for political contributions. Everyone, he claimed, had a right to use their property as they wished. He was willing to spend federal funds to improve the navigation of the Mississippi River but opposed flood control and reclamation projects. He filled page after page of the *Congressional Record* with "learned nonsense," interpreting the Constitution to support these arguments.[11] Unhappily for Harrison, the Democrats won control of the state legislature, and in 1887, he was defeated for reelection by a single vote. But it was of no matter. The following year, Jim Blaine picked him as his candidate for the Republican presidential nomination.

In the 1888 campaign, President Cleveland, who had been renominated by the Democrats, declined to actively campaign, believing that it was beneath the dignity of his office. Harrison, on the other hand, conducted a "front porch" campaign from his comfortable home in Indianapolis. Special trains deposited groups of voters—veterans, blacks, railroad workers, German-Americans—on the candidate's doorstep, where they were rewarded with brief homilies. "I have a sincere respect for, and a very deep interest in, the colored people. . . . You have signaled the Republican train to go ahead. . . . My German-American friends, you are a home-loving people." And so it went.[12]

While Harrison mouthed platitudes, Tom Platt and Matt Quay and the other Republican bosses set about electing him. Cleveland's assault on the protective tariff represented a challenge to the large corporations, and big businessmen flocked to support the Republican ticket. If they needed further encouragement, Levi P. Morton, one of the nation's leading bankers, was named the GOP vice-presidential candidate. John "One Price" Wanamaker, the Philadelphia merchant prince, who wished to crown his career with a prominent political office, went to work "frying the fat" out of the fat cats. As finance chairman of the Harrison committee, he enjoyed phenomenal success by applying business methods to politics. One of his first moves was to summon ten prominent Philadelphia businessmen to a meeting at which each agreed to contribute at least $10,000 to the party's coffers. Wanamaker himself sweetened the pot by kicking in a $50,000 donation.

Wanamaker informed America's leading industrialists of the benefits they could expect by returning the Republicans to the White House, and they were expected to subscribe a percentage of their earnings to guarantee Harrison's victory. The country was organized into districts to make collections more efficient. In western Ohio, a Cleveland businessman named Marcus Alonzo Hanna quickly raised $100,000. In New York, Platt called in the moneymen and came away with a neat pile of $10,000 checks. So much money was raised—close to $4 million, a phenomenal sum at the time—that the election of 1888 was known as the Boodle Campaign. The Democrats managed to gather less than a quarter of that. The marriage of the Republican party and big business had turned out to be a bonanza for all.

What was done with this huge amount of money? There were, of course, the usual costs—printed propaganda, buying editorial support, and travel expenses for bringing the voters to the candidate. The Republicans pounded away at Cleveland for his stand on the protective tariff, his plans to return captured Confederate battle flags to the Southern states, and his veto of a bill to spend the federal surplus on increased pensions for the veterans. The Republicans had a former British citizen write the British minister to the United States, Sir Lionel Sackville-West, soliciting his advice about whom to vote for and drew the desired response from the duped diplomat: Cleveland. The Republicans distributed copies of Sackville-West's note, and the very idea of a British official advising an American how to vote so enraged normally Democratic Irish voters that they defected in substantial numbers to Harrison.

But a sizable portion of these funds were earmarked for less publicized operations, such as vote buying.[13] Even here, the business politicians added a thrifty touch. In the old days, "floaters," whose votes were for sale to the highest bidder, and "repeaters," who voted early and often, were paid in advance. Now, they were not given their pay until they could show they voted.

The situation in Indiana, Harrison's home state, was particularly lurid. Quay was said to have dispatched trainloads of loyal supporters of his Pennsylvania machine to that pivotal state to ensure a Republican victory. And Colonel W. W. Dudley, a one-legged Union veteran who was both boss of the Indiana machine and treasurer of the Republican National Committee, marshaled his force of floaters for action. The floater vote in Indiana was estimated to run as high as twenty thousand, and each cost $15 in gold or $20 in greenbacks. To his lieutenants, Dudley wrote: "Divide the floaters in blocks of five and put a trusted man with the necessary funds in charge of these five and make him responsible that none get away and that all vote our ticket." Such arrangements were so common that no one raised an eyebrow when a ward heeler shouted across a police line on election day, "Are there any more repeaters out there who want to vote again?"[14]

Dudley's men provided the margin of victory for Harrison in Indiana. After upward of $700,000 had been expended, he carried the state by a mere 2,300 votes. New York, another key battleground, was won by Harrison by only 12,000 votes out of 1.3 million ballots cast after Platt had the foresight to buy the votes of Tammany Hall. Between them, these two states provided Harrison with a margin of victory in the Electoral College even though Cleveland had beaten him in the popular vote.

Forty-eight years to the day after his grandfather had become president of the United States, Benjamin Harrison took the oath of office as president on March 4, 1889. Head uncovered in a relentless rain, small, erect, and looking something like a pouter pigeon, he delivered an hour-long inaugural address in which he spoke of a nation "so magnificent in extent, so pleasant to look upon, and so full of generous suggestion to enterprise and labor." But the army of Republicans who swarmed into Washington in his wake took a more elementary view of the national panorama. "God help the surplus!" observers declared.

In their eagerness to return to the public trough, the Republicans had made promises to every wing and section of the party: higher tariffs to the Eastern capitalists, liberal pensions to Union veterans angered by Cleveland's vetoes, inflated farm prices to the agricultural areas, extension of civil service to the reformers, and jobs for spoilsmen. Payoff time was at hand.

Newspaper cartoonists were soon portraying John Wanamaker, the new postmaster general, with a tape measure over his arm calling out "Cash!" as if he were holding a bargain sale of post office jobs in his store.

Although Harrison had proclaimed his intention to enforce the Pendleton Act "fully and without evasion," open season was declared upon Democratic jobholders. In all, Wanamaker removed some thirty thousand fourth-class postmasters and replaced them with deserving Republicans. As a sop to the reformers, these new appointees were placed under civil service, ensuring that they could not be thrown out by the Democrats when they returned to power. A collision between Wanamaker and Theodore Roosevelt, who had been appointed to the Civil Service Commission,* was inevitable, and most of Harrison's term was bedeviled by the infighting between them.

Wanamaker was not the only rich man to join the cabinet. Representatives of business and industry took such a prominent place in Harrison's administration that his cabinet was known as the "businessman's cabinet." Jim Blaine claimed the post of secretary of state and assumed the role of gray eminence in the administration. Redfield Proctor, the marble king of Vermont, was named secretary of war. William H. H. Miller, a Harrison law partner, became attorney general. Tom Platt wanted to be secretary of the treasury, but Harrison bridled at that. As a consolation prize, Platt's law partner, Benjamin F. Tracy, was made secretary of the navy. Inconsolable, Platt said he would never again "trust men from Ohio"—where the president was born.[15]

Business leaders were no longer satisfied with mere representation in the cabinet and took over the actual seats of power. Wealthy men held so many Senate seats that the body became known as the Millionaire's Club. Kansas newspaper editor William Allen White observed that a senator now represented "something more than a state, more even than a region. He represented principalities and powers in business." It was made possible by the tight boss control of the all-too-venal state legislatures, which until 1913 elected U.S. senators. Nelson Aldrich of Rhode Island was the spokesman for entrenched Eastern wealth and the protective tariff. George Hearst represented the silver-mining interests first and California second. Chauncey Depew was the envoy of the

---

*Originally, Roosevelt had wanted an appointment as assistant secretary of state as a reward for having campaigned for Harrison. Blaine, who knew his man well, said if he gave him that post, he would be unable to sleep at night because Roosevelt might do something impetuous while Blaine was not looking, and turned him down.

Vanderbilt railroad interests. Matt Quay made certain that Pennsylvania's manufacturers were heard. By the turn of the century, over two dozen business and industrial magnates occupied seats in the Senate chamber.

With the Republicans in control of the presidency and both houses of Congress for the first time in fourteen years, the legislators immediately went to work on the surplus. Mindful of the promises made to the "boys in blue," Congress awarded pensions to any disabled Union veteran regardless of whether his disability was service-connected. Widows, orphans, and dependent parents were also given pensions. Pension expenditures spiraled over a single year from $98 million to $157 million. River and harbor improvements, coastal defenses, new public buildings, and other pork-barrel measures also got their share, and the surplus melted away like snow in the April sunshine. All over Washington, Republicans raised their glasses in a familiar toast: "The old flag and an appropriation."

The Fifty-first Congress was dubbed the Billion Dollar Congress because of its lavish spending. But as the newly elected Speaker of the House, Thomas B. Reed, cheerfully remarked as he presided over the doling out of immense sums and the auctioning of public privileges of even greater value, America was "a billion-dollar country."

Reed is one of the most fascinating figures in American politics. Well over six feet tall and weighing about three hundred pounds, he had an enormous, clean-shaved baby face that gave him the air of a New England Buddha. He was the ablest debater in Congress and was noted for his cool sarcasm. When one member proclaimed that he would rather be right than president, the Speaker quietly observed, "The gentleman need not be disturbed; he will be neither." And when another member haltingly proclaimed, "I was thinking, Mr. Speaker, I was thinking," Reed expressed the hope "that no one will interrupt this commendable innovation." When the Democrats tried to block Republican bills by refusing to be recorded on roll calls, preventing a quorum, "Czar" Reed coolly had their names recorded as "present and refusing to vote."[16]

President and Mrs. Harrison found that the White House had the air of a seedy, second-rate commercial hotel and was several cuts below their home in Indianapolis. The physical arrangements were so haphazard that servants carrying cleaning materials and potted plants from the conservatory passed in front of visitors. The acoustics were so poor that the Marine Band almost deafened guests at receptions. First Lady Caroline Harrison spent most of her first year in Washington fighting a losing battle with rats. Hordes of them had taken over the place and all but ate with the family. She secured a $35,000 appropriation from Congress, and the floors and walls of the kitchens were torn out and replaced in an attempt to deal with the rats and insects.* New plumbing was installed along with electricity, but the Harrisons were afraid of it and left the lights on until a butler turned the switch.

Since he lacked human warmth and the common touch, Harrison's strongest suit as president was administration, which he preferred to the give-and-take of politics. He was a master of bureaucratic detail and eagerly soaked up information about new styles of penmanship in the various departments, filing methods in the Pension Bureau, and personnel procedures. But the only bills composed in the executive offices were minor.

Visitors to the presidential office were seldom asked to take a chair, lest they stay too long, and the president clearly showed his irritation with those he felt were wasting his time—a bad trait when dealing with congressmen. He greeted one senator, watch in hand, gestured toward a pile of reports on his desk, and announced, "I've got all these papers to look after, and I'm going fishing at two o'clock." Snapping his watch shut, he waited stonily for the man to state his business.[17]

This obsession with minor detail, inability or unwillingness to delegate authority, and a tendency to overwork, compounded by personal intolerance and curtness, all combined to undermine any efforts at leadership Harrison may have made. He would grant a request, but "in a way which seemed as if he were denying it," said one observer, while Blaine could refuse one as if he were conferring a favor.[18] "The president is not popular with the members of either house [of Congress],"

---

*The rats remained a problem, and during Cleveland's second administration a servant discovered that "a great rat had forced his way into [a canary's cage and] had just killed the poor little canary." Billings, "Social and Economic Life in Washington in the 1890's," *Records of the Columbia Historical Society of Washington, D.C.*, 1966–68.

noted Solicitor General William Howard Taft. "His manner of treating them is not at all fortunate, and when they have an interview with him, they generally come away mad."

Neither of the Harrisons was socially inclined and they only entertained when required by their official positions. The president preferred to use his leisure strolling around the White House gardens, inspecting the stables, walking in Lafayette Square, or looking into shop windows along Pennsylvania Avenue. Tourists spotted him in the street, usually wearing a tightly buttoned Prince Albert, with brown kid gloves and furled umbrella, but he rarely took notice of their greetings.* Upon returning to the White House, he would nod to the columns and declare, "There is my jail."[19]

While Harrison exercised little leadership, his administration witnessed the passage of three significant pieces of legislation. Public pressure had been growing for government action to curb the power of the monopolies and trusts that were taking over the American economy, and Congress passed the Sherman Antitrust Act in 1890. It declared illegal any business combination in restraint of trade or any attempt to organize a monopoly, and gave the power of enforcement to the federal courts. But like the Interstate Commerce Act, which had been passed a few years before to regulate the railroads, the business politicians regarded it as a sop to the malcontents that was not to be strictly enforced. Paradoxically, the Sherman Act became an effective weapon in the hands of business in its fight against labor organizations. As Mr. Dooley, the fictional Irish saloonkeeper-philosopher, asserted, "What looks like a stone-wall to a layman is a triumphal arch to a corporation lawyer."

Congress also dealt with the money question by passing the Sherman Silver Purchase Act. (John Sherman, an elderly Ohio senator and brother of General Sherman, had a talent for getting his name attached to important legislation.) Farmers and debtors had been pressing for years for inflationary measures such as the free coinage of silver to punch up the economy. This would increase the amount of money in

---

*In contrast, as a college student in Washington, I remember seeing President Truman on his early-morning strolls. He always answered greetings of "Good morning, Mr. President" with a cheery "Good morning!" and a jaunty wave of his walking stick.

circulation, thereby reducing the value of the dollar and facilitating the repayment of mortgages and other debts in cheaper money. The "free silverites" had the support of the silver mine operators, but believers in "sound" money rejected their arguments as dangerous radicalism.

The Silver Purchase Act, which directed the government to buy a stipulated amount of silver each month and to issue legal tender notes redeemable in gold or silver, was a compromise measure, but it had little effect on the economy. It was designed at least in part to win the support of reluctant Western congressmen for an increase in the protective tariff that was to repay those who had given of their "fat" for Harrison in 1888.

Introduced by Ohio's William McKinley, the "Napoleon of Protection," the proposed tariff offered a new concept: it not only protected American industry but was also an instrument of exclusion. Duties were fixed so high that some foreign goods could not even enter the country. Infant industries were not only protected, but prohibitive rates were set for products, such as tin plate, that were not even produced in the United States, to allow investors to establish a new industry without fear of foreign competition. Thus the McKinley Tariff was a free lunch for monopolists.

Ironically, Secretary of State Blaine was one of those who protested against the protective wall erected by the tariff. Blaine's handling of foreign affairs, particularly relations with Latin America, was the one distinguished aspect of a largely undistinguished administration. Despite his earlier protectionist views, he now wished to expand foreign trade and was a leader in organizing the International Bureau of the American Republics—later the Pan American Union and now the Organization of American States.

Protesting that the removal of hides from the free list would damage trade with South America, Blaine warned that the few votes gained from cattlemen would hardly recompense for the lost votes of consumers, who would pay higher prices for shoes. "Such movements as this for protection will protect the Republican party into retirement," he warned.[20] Blaine turned out to be prescient. Prices immediately started to rise after the McKinley Tariff was approved, arousing a storm of protest that resulted in a political revolution in the midterm elections of

1890. Only 88 Republicans were returned to the new House, as against 235 Democrats. In the Senate, the Republican majority was reduced to eight unstable votes from the Far West. William McKinley was among those swept from office.*

Halfway through his term, Harrison had already been discredited. While the McKinley Tariff received much of the blame, the president was also out of harmony with the popular mood and had failed to provide leadership in a time of political and social unrest. Falling prices, drought, overproduction, the tariff, and high interest rates had aroused the anger of Southern and Western farmers and ranchers, and the stage was set for the creation of a party of revolt—the Populist party.

Nothing like it had been seen before. Populism also embraced other dissidents besides the farmers: socialists, woman suffragists, single-taxers, and free silverites. There was even an attempt to reach across racial lines to blacks, which sent a shiver down the spines of Southern bourbons. In 1890, the new party swept a dozen Western and Southern states—and loomed as a major element in the upcoming 1892 presidential election.

Harrison's political fortunes sagged along with those of his party. With the Democrats in control of the House, there was no chance for wide-ranging legislative initiatives, although lavish spending on pork-barrel projects continued. Moreover, the president was at odds with Platt and Quay over patronage, so they worked behind the scenes to dump him. "No threats are made," noted an observer. "No open opposition [is] shown, but the President suddenly discovers that the wheels are not turning. . . . Nominees are not confirmed . . . departments don't function. . . . There is an inertia that . . . creeps over everything like an incoming tide."[21]

One of the deepest blows to Harrison's credibility was the defection of Charles W. Eliot, the president of Harvard, to the Democrats. He cited the tariff, the pension largesse, and a comparison of Cleveland's and Harrison's records on civil service as his reasons for switching par-

---

*Among the casualties of the McKinley Tariff was an effort by the administration to secure passage of a bill taking the offensive against restraints on black voters in the South. But it was traded for Southern votes for the tariff.

ties. Harrison had planned to retire at the end of his term, but the opposition to his renomination caused him to stubbornly announce his candidacy or "forever wear the name of political coward."[22] The ailing Caroline Harrison was surprised. "Why, General?" she asked. "Why when it has been so hard for you?"

Although Harrison won the nomination on the first ballot, a significant vote for Blaine and McKinley made it clear that he was in trouble. The Democrats renominated Grover Cleveland, and the election was anticlimactic. Cleveland won by about four hundred thousand votes. The Populist candidate amassed a million votes—mostly in the South and West. Two weeks before the election, the president suffered another blow when his wife succumbed to tuberculosis.

In his last annual message to Congress, Harrison spoke glowingly of the prosperity attained under the McKinley Tariff. "A comparison of the existing conditions with those of the most favored in the history of the country will, I believe, show that so high a degree of prosperity and so general a diffusion of the comforts of life were never before enjoyed by our people." Six months later, the nation plunged into the worst economic depression since the Civil War.

Fifty-nine years old when he left the White House, Benjamin Harrison was still vigorous but was devastated by the death of his wife. Returning to Indianapolis, he slowly shook off his despair and resumed the practice of law. In 1896, the former president again married, this time to the thirty-seven-year-old Mary Scott Lord Dimmick, a widow and niece of his first wife's. In protest, Harrison's grown children from his previous marriage refused to attend the wedding, but the couple had a child, a daughter, of their own.

From 1897 to 1899, Harrison served before an arbitration panel in Paris as legal counsel for Venezuela in a dispute with Britain over its border with British Guiana. In a prodigious display of energy and mastery of detail, he filed an eight-hundred-page brief and presented twenty-five hours of oral argument over five days. The panel, however, awarded 90 percent of the disputed territory to the British. Two years later, after a bout of pneumonia, Harrison died, on March 13, 1901. Mrs. Harrison survived him by nearly fifty years.

Back in 1896, some Republicans had suggested that Harrison run for president again, but he had had enough. "Why should a man seek that which to him will be a calamity?" he asked. While his presidency was not calamitous to the nation, it was characterized by an absolute lack of leadership and vision as well as a wild raid on the Treasury surplus. This was hardly a fit of testament to the scion of a family notable for its high standards of dedicated public service.

CHAPTER IV

CALVIN COOLIDGE

C alvin Coolidge had all the virtues of a small-town New England
bank clerk. He was honest, thrifty, punctual, taciturn, conscientious, frugal, cautious, conservative, and moral. A true Puritan,
he put his faith in a righteous God and double-entry bookkeeping.
Even his coming to the presidency fitted this flinty Yankee image.
Coolidge, then vice president, was at the family homestead in Vermont
when he was awakened shortly after midnight on August 3, 1923, to
hear the news of the sudden death of his predecessor, Warren Gamaliel
Harding. Stunned but not shaken, he was sworn in as president by his
father, a notary public, in the flickering light of a kerosene lamp. The
symbolism was perfect because America's thirtieth president was a
reluctant refugee from the nineteenth century.

Americans wanted nothing done during the time Coolidge was president "and he done it," someone once said. He assiduously followed the
maxim that the government that governs least governs best. Upon
entering the White House, the new president placed a rocking chair on
the elegant portico and sat there rocking and contentedly puffing on a
cigar for the next five years and seven months while the world passed
by.* He slept more—nine hours a night plus a two-hour afternoon
nap—and did less work than any other president in history. One
evening he went to the theater to see *Animal Crackers,* and Groucho
Marx, the star of the show, spotted him in the audience. "Isn't it past

*Coolidge smoked fifty-cent Coronas; White House guests were offered nickel stogies.

your bedtime, Calvin?" he slyly inquired from the stage.[1] "Nero fiddled while Rome burned, but Coolidge only snored," said H. L. Mencken.[2]

As Coolidge snoozed through a long summer of prosperity, brokerage houses were crowded with men and women staring fixedly at the ticker tapes that proclaimed record highs on the New York Stock Exchange. Most Americans had bought their first bonds in the Liberty Loan drives of World War I and, hypnotized by booming stock prices, had turned to more speculative issues. "Anyone not only can be rich but ought to be rich," proclaimed John J. Raskob, a General Motors millionaire who voiced the unqualified optimism of the day.

Most of this speculative wave of stock buying was on margin, with investors putting up as little as 5 percent of the value of their shares, while their brokers advanced the rest by borrowing from the banks. Janitors put their savings into Montgomery Ward; gas-station attendants had margin accounts in American Can; nursemaids eavesdropped on their employers in hopes of picking up hot tips on the market. U.S. Steel was at 261¾, Anaconda Copper at 130⅞, AT&T at 302, General Electric at 395. Stock prices were no longer rooted in productivity or real earnings or worth. Holding companies and investment trusts were pyramided one atop the other, and the entire structure rested on a quagmire of unrestrained speculation.

Coolidge prosperity was not evenly distributed and did not touch the lives of millions. Farm prices had never recovered from a recession that followed World War I. Radiant statistics about wage growth, rising industrial production, and employment cloaked the fact that distribution of income was growing progressively worse each year. Nearly half of America's families made only $1,500 or less annually, even though government statistics said a family of four required $2,500 a year to maintain a "decent" standard of living. "I can't understand where all this . . . money [for speculation] comes from," lamented Justice Louis D. Brandeis. "I think we must be exploiting about eighty percent of Americans for the benefit of the other twenty percent."[3]

In October 1929, the bubble burst and the United States and the rest of the world hurtled down the slope into the Great Depression and ultimately World War II. While Coolidge cannot be blamed for the crash, his failure to curb speculation was an important contribution to the debacle. Queried about the rising volume of brokers' loans, he brushed them off as "a natural expansion of business." Had Coolidge been more alert, more interested in what was occurring about him, more willing to exercise the authority of his office, the cataclysm might have been fended off—or its worst effects diminished. But, then, if he had, he would not have been Calvin Coolidge.

Fate threw Coolidge into a situation beyond his talents and imagination. Most of the other presidents on my worst list are there because of something they did. Only he and Benjamin Harrison make it for doing nothing. Coolidge transformed stasis into an art form. "Mr. Coolidge's genius for inactivity is developed to a very high point," said Walter Lippman, the political commentator. "It is far from being indolent inactively. It is a grim, determined, alert inactivity."[4] Coolidge encapsulated his philosophy in a single sentence: "Four-fifths of all our problems in this life would disappear if we could only sit down and keep still."[5] Critics raged at this "genius for inactivity," but Coolidge was the symbol of a prosperity thought to be perpetual—and most Americans were satisfied as long as it lasted.

Herbert Hoover, the secretary of commerce, who succeeded Coolidge in the presidency, later stated that as early as 1925 he was concerned about the "fever of speculation." Over the months and years that followed, this concern gradually changed to premonition and then to alarm. But every effort to restore a semblance of sanity to Wall Street was frustrated by Coolidge, Treasury Secretary Andrew W. Mellon, and the Federal Reserve—all passionate advocates of inaction. Forever afterward Hoover was fond of saying: "The only trouble with capitalism is capitalists. They're too damned greedy."[6] Ironically, they escaped blame for the crash while it cost Hoover his office and his reputation.

At the core of Coolidge's policies were minimal government interference with business, supply-side tax cuts, balanced budgets, low interest rates, economic nationalism, and hostility to immigration. There was more than a whiff of his views in the 1996 Republican platform. No knight in shining armor riding forth to tilt at assorted wrongs—indeed, the only horse at the White House in his time was a mechanical steed for exercise—Coolidge was the high priest of the status quo. Under his hand, whatever remained of the progressivism of Theodore Roosevelt and

Woodrow Wilson was quietly chloroformed. "The business of America is business," Coolidge intoned. He believed "the man who builds a factory builds a temple," and the "man who works there worships there."

Coolidge was an odd figure to preside over the White House during the hyperactive Roaring Twenties, and Kansas editor William Allen White dubbed him a "Puritan in Babylon." With his sharp nose, thin, pursed lips, and Vermont twang—it was said he pronounced the word *cow* with three syllables—Coolidge seemed embarrassingly out of place in the world of flappers, get-rich-quick schemes, bootleg booze, and easy sex. He appeared so austere that Alice Longworth, passing on a joke she had heard, said he "looked like he had been weaned on a pickle."[7] But to a nation rocked by the scandals of the Harding years, Coolidge stood for rectitude. In the midst of political cynicism and spiritual doubts, he signified old-fashioned piety. Many Americans found him an ideal leader at a time when they were pushing the outer limits of self-indulgence, yet feared that traditional values were being lost.

Coolidge's political career was a shining example of the power of inertia over talent. Harold J. Laski, the British political writer, saw him as "a churchwarden in some rural parish who has by accident strayed into great affairs."[8] From his election to the city council of Northampton, Massachusetts, in 1898, three years out of Amherst College, until he departed the presidency in 1929, he was hardly out of office. He served as city solicitor, clerk of the court, as a member of the state legislature, mayor of Northampton, state senator, lieutenant governor and governor of Massachusetts. Uninspired and unheroic, he showed no special distinction in any of these positions, yet was catapulted onto the national scene by a widely publicized—and unearned—role in crushing the Boston police strike of 1919.

Coolidge was nominated by the Republicans for vice president on the 1920 ticket with Harding only through accident. The cabal of party leaders who engineered Harding's nomination in the famous "smoke-filled room" had wished to balance the ticket with a modestly liberal vice-presidential candidate and had tapped Senator Irving Lenroot of Wisconsin for second place. But Lenroot was not popular with the rank and file. When Lenroot's name was presented, one delegate shouted,

"Not on your life!" In the tumult, an Oregon delegate, acting on his own, placed Coolidge's name in nomination, and he won on the first ballot by a landslide 674 to 146 votes.

The age of ballyhoo and public relations was just dawning, and Coolidge made political capital out of two traits uncommon for a president—he was tight-lipped as well as tightfisted. Reporters and comedians told stories about these characteristics, some true, some exaggerated, which transformed this fundamentally colorless man into a national character. "Every time he opens his mouth," noted someone, "a moth flies out of it."[9] Under the cover of public silence, he was, in reality, somewhat garrulous*—as the texts of his press conferences make abundantly clear—but Coolidge joined in the game, shrewdly recreating himself as "Silent Cal"—the sly and laconic Yankee rustic who was cleverer than he appeared.

Newsmen sought him out for comment during the 1924 campaign in which he won the presidency on his own. "Have you any statement?" asked one. "No," replied Coolidge. "Can you tell us about the world situation?" queried another. "No." "Any information about Prohibition?" "No." As they turned away, Coolidge cautioned, "Now, remember—don't quote me."[10] Upon another occasion, he told a press conference that he was going to visit a country fair. Would he speak there? "No," he replied. "I'm going as an exhibit."[11] A typical exchange took place with a White House guest. "You must talk to me, Mr. President," she said. "I made a bet today that I could get more than two words out of you." "You lose" was the reply.[12] Foreign diplomats were told Coolidge "can be silent in five languages." Before leaving office, he gave Hoover some advice on how to deal with long-winded visitors. "If you keep dead still, they will run down in three or four minutes."[13]

Coolidge's silences did not cloak a wide-ranging mind, however. He knew his American history but little of the rest of the world. Reading his bland speeches and *Autobiography* is a sure cure for insomnia. The most interesting thing about them is their uncompromising unoriginality. They are filled with such copybook maxims as "The success

*One reporter went to what he thought would be an interview with President Coolidge, but for two hours he was harangued on everything from trout fishing to the cost of cigars and, even though he tried diligently, never managed to get in a question.

which is made in life is measured almost exactly by the amount of hard work that is put into it. . . . There is only one form of political strategy in which I have any confidence, and that is to try to do the right thing. . . . If society lacks learning and virtue, it will perish."

Coolidge's frugality—or stinginess—was legendary. In Northampton, his family lived in half of a two-family house with a monthly rent of $36. Coolidge's telephone was on a party line, and he did not own a car. He was probably the only president to save money in the White House.* Snooping about the kitchen one day, he complained to the house-keeper about the unwarranted extravagance of providing a half dozen hams for a dinner of sixty people. He expressed annoyance when he gave an aide a dime to buy a magazine and did not get his nickel change. Colonel Edward Starling, his Secret Service bodyguard, recalled that as Coolidge prepared sandwiches for them both in the White House pantry after an afternoon walk, the president grumbled that he had to pay for the cheese.[14] At the end of his presidency, he refused to make the customary purchase of the chair he had used at cabinet meet-ings. Hoover and Mellon bought it for him.†

Coolidge also had a boorish side that showed itself in practical jokes with an undertone of sadism. "Ike" Hoover, the longtime chief usher of the White House, noted that "he seemed always to be watching, rather suspicious lest something be 'put over' on him."[15] Sometimes he pol-ished off his dessert at state dinners and left the table while his abashed guests were still eating theirs. Family members, White House aides, and servants who crossed him were treated to storms of abuse or frosty silence. He intentionally tripped the White House alarm and then hid behind the curtains as the frantic guards searched for the intruder. A Secret Service agent who was asked to bait the president's hook during a fishing trip swore that Coolidge had deliberately snagged him with it. Moreover, when the Mississippi River swept across the Middle West and South in 1927, driving more than a million Americans from their

*Coolidge's estate totaled over $700,000 at the time of his death—a considerable sum considering the fact that he had spent most of his life on the public payroll.

†Not long after he became vice president, Coolidge received a letter from Washington's exclusive Cosmos Club notifying him that he had been elected a member and enclosing a bill for the initiation fee. He declined to pay.

homes, Coolidge, despite repeated personal pleas from local officials, refused to visit the flooded territory.

Following the stock market crash of 1929, Coolidge's reputation went into a free fall but has, in recent years, been on the upswing, notably among conservative advocates of more limited government. Ronald Reagan, who was a teenager when Coolidge came to power, admired him so much that in 1981 he ordered a portrait of Thomas Jefferson removed from the Cabinet Room to make way for one of Coolidge. "Look at his record," said Reagan. "He cut taxes four times. We had probably the greatest growth and prosperity that we've ever known."[16] There was no mention of the day of the locust that followed the Coolidge prosperity. "A job, any job, seemed like the ultimate success," Reagan said of *that* era.[17]

Reagan and Coolidge were alike in many ways, although their personalities differed greatly. Both served as governors—Reagan in California and Coolidge in Massachusetts—and won national fame as advocates of law and order. Reagan sacked striking air controllers. Coolidge received credit for breaking the Boston police strike. Both men were ideologues whose approach to public problems rested on the application of a few broad homilies: America's social and economic orders were sound; its critics were either misguided or dangerous radicals; private enterprise was the backbone of the nation; the role of government should be kept small, especially in regulating business; and the United States, by virtue of its superior institutions and enlightened moral sense, held an exceptional place among the nations of the globe. Unlike Reagan, however, Coolidge opposed adventurism overseas.

John Calvin Coolidge—he dropped the John after graduating from college—was the only president born on the Fourth of July, in his case July 4, 1872, in the living quarters adjoining the family general store in the out-of-the-way hamlet of Plymouth Notch, Vermont. Coolidges had lived in the Green Mountains since the Revolution and, as Yankee yeomen, were only distantly related to the Coolidges of Boston's codfish aristocracy. They were content with what God, in his infinite wisdom, had given them and disinclined to look beyond the next ridge. The future president's father, also John Calvin, was a prosperous farmer, storekeeper, and public official. From him, Young Cal inherited his taciturnity, tightness with a dollar, and interest in public affairs.

Virginia Moor Coolidge, his mother, also a native Vermonter, was a pretty and sensitive but frail woman with a touch of "mysticism and poetry" in her nature. She loved to "gaze at the purple sunsets and watch the evening stars," according to her son. Virginia died at the age of thirty-nine, probably of tuberculosis, when Calvin was twelve. Although the boy badly missed his mother, he and his equally inarticulate father kept their sorrows to themselves. For the rest of his life, Calvin carried Virginia's picture in his watchcase and often talked of her. The care of the boy and of Abbie, a younger sister, devolved upon their paternal grandmother.

Life was not easy in the Notch, although the Coolidges were well-off by the standards of the area. As soon as he was old enough, Calvin had chores to do: tapping the maple trees, mending fences, piling up wood for winter, and plowing by himself by the time he was twelve. "It always seemed as though Cal could get more sap out of a maple tree than any boy I knew," said his father. Although the boy was not often punished, punishment was terrible when it came. He was locked up alone for hours in a dark, cobweb-filled attic. A frail child, he was sometimes seized by sneezing and coughing attacks traced to several allergies. These contributed to congestion of his nasal passages and resulted in an unusual quacking quality in his voice that grated on people's nerves. The famous indolence of his later years may have resulted not from a lack of energy but ill health.

Perhaps because of his odd voice and ailments, he had few friends as a child. Looking back later in life, he recalled, "In politics, one must meet people, and that's not easy for me. . . . When I was a little fellow, as long ago as I can remember, I would go into a panic if I heard strange voices in the kitchen. I felt I just couldn't meet the people and shake hands with them. . . . The hardest thing in the world was to have to go through the kitchen door and give them a greeting. I was almost ten before I realized I couldn't go on that way. And by fighting hard I used to get through that door. I'm all right when I'm with friends, but every time I meet a stranger, I've got to go through the old kitchen door, back home, and it's not easy."[18]

When he could be spared from his chores, Calvin attended the local one-room schoolhouse. In 1886, at the age of fourteen, he was sent to the Black River Academy, a Baptist-supported school in Ludlow, about a dozen miles over the hills from home, which his parents had attended. Shy and lonely, he was an average student and took no part in school activities or athletics. Life picked up when Abbie, now a pretty, vivacious girl of thirteen and an outstanding student, joined him in 1888, when he was in his junior year. But in March 1890, she was suddenly stricken with appendicitis and died during the week. "It is lonesome here without Abbie," Calvin wrote his father not long afterward. For a Coolidge this was an outpouring of emotion.

Calvin was the first of the family to attend college and was influenced toward Amherst, just over the line in Massachusetts, by one of his teachers. He failed the entrance examination, but after a year of preparation, earned his college entrance certificate and entered the school in 1891. The taciturn and withdrawn freshman hoped for acceptance without knowing how to achieve it. Fraternities were important at Amherst, but none bothered to "rush" him. "I don't seem to get acquainted very fast," he wrote wistfully to his father.

By his senior year, Calvin had won a measure of acceptance. A friend who had been pledged by a newly organized fraternity insisted Coolidge be taken in, too. His grades improved and he came under influence of Charles E. Garman, who stressed a doctrine of service in his philosophy course that guided the young man toward a political career. At Amherst he also met two students, Dwight W. Morrow and Harlan Fiske Stone, who were to be important in his rise. Some of his classmates had also become aware of the dry wit that lay below his Vermont-granite exterior, and he was chosen to give the Grove Oration, the traditional Class Day humorous address. He won a $150 gold medal for first prize in an essay contest sponsored by the Sons of the American Revolution and graduated cum laude in 1895.

No soaring ambition filled Coolidge as he faced the world, and he had no desire to move beyond the familiar hills that had always hemmed in his horizon. He considered storekeeping and law as careers and chose the latter. When a friend asked him where he planned to settle, Coolidge tersely replied, "Northampton's the nearest courthouse."

Rather than attending law school, he read law in the primitive tradition of the early Republic with a pair of local attorneys. He sat in the outer office learning to prepare writs, deeds, and wills while reading textbooks in his spare time. He received no salary.

Coolidge spent twenty months there, an unobtrusive, inscrutable, and silent figure. Then, one morning, his table was clear of books and he was gone. He had learned enough to pass the bar examination and, in 1897, using a small inheritance, opened an office of his own. Not long afterward, he began an active role in Republican politics.

Northampton was a town of some fifteen thousand people with its industry tempered by Smith College, which had been founded two decades before. The old-line business and professional class was undeviatingly Republican, but the Irish and French-Canadian millworkers were Democrats and numerically superior. Coolidge, however, had two qualities that were essential to political success. He was inordinately lucky and, for all his taciturnity, had the knack of winning the goodwill of working-class voters. In fact, he felt more at ease with the barber, the cobbler, even the tavern keeper, than with Northampton's elite. Some even abandoned their traditional party loyalty to vote for him.

In 1898, with his election to the city council, Calvin Coolidge—as he now styled himself—began his systematic rise up the Massachusetts Republican escalator. This smoothly running machine could, if the budding politician did what was expected of him, carry him from ward politics to the gilt-domed State House in Boston and then to the blessed security of a bank or life-insurance directorship. Coolidge was no boat rocker, and two years later, he became city solicitor at a salary of $600 a year. He was defeated when he ran for reelection, his only defeat in a lifetime of running for office, but the party took care of its own. He was appointed circuit court clerk and then won election to the state legislature. With his neat black suit, prim manner, and pinched face, some colleagues mistook him for an undertaker.

In the meantime, Coolidge lived a quiet life in a rented room on Round Hill across from the Clarke Institute for the Deaf. Now and then he stopped by a beer garden for a glass of beer, but he spent most evenings reading biography, history, and law in his room. He did not

BENJAMIN HARRISON
"A cold-blooded, narrow-minded, prejudiced, obstinate,
timid, old psalm-singing Indianapolis politician."
(National Portrait Gallery, Smithsonian Institution)

CALVIN COOLIDGE
Otherwise known as Chief Leading Eagle of
the Sioux tribe.
(National Archives)

ULYSSES S. GRANT
If you had his friends,
you'd look glum, too.
(Library of Congress)

ANDREW JOHNSON
His administration was
an object lesson in how not
to generate public trust.
(National Archives)

JAMES BUCHANAN
He had one eye that was farsighted
and one that was nearsighted:
perfect equipment for a politician.
(National Archives)

FRANKLIN PIERCE
Vain, showy, and pliant, he fought
many a losing battle with the bottle.
(Library of Congress)

WARREN GAMALIEL HARDING
Besides the Shriners, Harding was a member of the Kiwanis,
the Rotary, the Masons, the Elks, and the Moose, and
played tuba in his hometown band.
(Library of Congress)

RICHARD M. NIXON
The ultimate Pitchman in Politics.
(Library of Congress)

THOMAS JEFFERSON
"A kind of free-floating icon who
hovers over the American political
scene like one of those dirigibles
cruising above a crowded
football stadium,"
according to one writer.
(Library of Congress)

JOHN F. KENNEDY
Kennedy's most enduring contribution
to national life may have been to raise
the curtain on an age of political imagery.
(National Archives)

dance or play cards and was too shy to approach women. One day in 1904, Grace Goodhue, an attractive, black-haired teacher of lipreading, was watering the flowers outside a school building when she glanced up at an open window of a nearby house. There she saw a strange sight—a man shaving in front of a mirror with nothing on but long underwear and wearing a felt hat—and burst into laughter. Startled, Coolidge caught a glimpse of her as she turned away in embarrassment.

The young man sought a more formal meeting at which he told Grace that he had an unruly lock of hair that got in the way while he shaved and had anchored it by wearing a hat. Like Coolidge, Grace Goodhue was of old Vermont stock but, as the daughter of a Burlington mechanical engineer, was a cut above him on the social ladder. They were attracted to each other, although they made a strange pair. Grace, a Phi Beta Kappa graduate of the University of Vermont, was outgoing and liked by everyone who knew her. Her friends could not understand what she saw in this old-maidish, dry stick of a lawyer. Coolidge tried to please her by learning to dance—not very successfully—and by squiring her to church socials and parties. It was his hope, he joked in his pinched way, "that after having made the deaf to hear, Miss Goodhue might perhaps teach the mute to speak."[19]

Following a prolonged and rather silent courtship, Coolidge proposed in his usual straightforward manner during a walk in the woods. "I am going to be married to you," he declared. Grace accepted him, and he walked on without another word for fifteen minutes. When she asked him if he had anything else to say, he replied that perhaps he had already said too much. Though Grace's mother was opposed, they were married on October 4, 1905. He was thirty-three; she was twenty-eight. Mrs. Goodhue, who never liked her son-in-law, thought he owed most of his later political success to Grace.

The Coolidges rented half of a two-family house on a maple-shaded street in Northampton that was to be home to them and their two sons until they went to Washington. Grace quickly became familiar with her husband's oddities. She learned that all through their courtship, he had secretly been translating Dante's *Inferno* into English. He also had what must have been the largest collection of socks in the state, almost all with holes in them. One day, he gave Grace a bag containing fifty-two pairs to be darned. She asked him if he had married her to get his socks mended. "No," he replied, "but I find it mighty handy."[20]

In 1909, Coolidge was ready for the next move up the political escalator and ran for mayor of Northampton. Suppressing his shyness, he went door-to-door in every ward of the city, introducing himself and saying, "I want your vote. I need it. I shall appreciate it." He even carried the city's normally Democratic working-class areas. Coolidge served two terms as mayor, in which he emphasized honesty, efficiency, and economy.

Upon one occasion, the Coolidges entertained a Baptist preacher who was in town to conduct a revival meeting. The guest ate sparingly, explaining that abstinence improved his ability to preach. After the revival, Coolidge gave Grace a succinct critique of his performance: "Might as well have et."[21]

Three terms in the state senate followed, and during the last, he served as president of the body. With the Democrats in control of the governorship and the lieutenant governor's office, he was the highest-ranking Republican official in the Commonwealth, able to reward his friends and conciliate his enemies. In 1915, he announced his candidacy for lieutenant governor and won again. During this period he acquired the backing of two powerful patrons, Frank Stearns, a wealthy Boston merchant, and Dwight Morrow, an Amherst classmate and partner in the firm of J. P. Morgan.

Traditionally, a lieutenant governor served three one-year terms before moving up to governor. Biding his time, Coolidge was rotated into the governor's chair in 1918, having achieved little in the way of a record in twenty years in politics—but without antagonizing anyone. He was a living embodiment of Woody Allen's observation that "eighty percent of success is showing up."

"What is your hobby?" a newspaper writer asked the new governor. "Holding office," declared Coolidge.[22] In fact, he did little more than that. Do not speak, spend, or act unless absolutely necessary was his guide. Every morning he saw a few visitors and signed letters, had lunch at the Union Club, usually alone, strolled back to the office, leaned back in his chair with his feet on the big desk to smoke a cigar, and read the early edition of the *Boston Transcript*. Then he would doze off for several hours and go home.

This idyll was broken in September 1919, when about 75 percent of the Boston police force, with greater desperation than judgment, struck for recognition of their union and an increase in their miserably low wages.[23] Mayor Andrew J. Peters urged Coolidge to send in the State Guard to maintain order, but the governor passed the buck back to the mayor, contending he lacked the power to intervene in the city's affairs. Coolidge was obviously worried about the effect of a reputation as a strikebreaker upon his chances for reelection. While he held off action, rioting broke out in Boston, and with the press lambasting the strikers as "Bolsheviks" and "deserters," Peters ordered out the local Guard units, which was his legal right. This was sufficient to restore order, although the strike went on. Peters was now in control of the situation, but on the third day of the walkout, Coolidge unexpectedly took it upon himself to order additional state troops into Boston, which broke the back of the strike.

Realizing they had made a serious tactical error, the striking policemen voted to return to work, but Coolidge would not have it. Samuel Gompers, the president of the American Federation of Labor, urged him to reconsider a decision to fire the strikers, but Coolidge refused in ringing tones: "There is no right to strike against the public safety, by anybody, anywhere, anytime." These words were widely hailed throughout the country, and he was propelled onto the national scene. Although Coolidge had in reality only a belated and minor role in ending the walkout, he had managed to win most of the credit. The road to the vice presidency—and the White House—was now wide-open to him.

Someone once asked Calvin Coolidge what his first thought had been upon hearing that Harding had died and he was now the president of the United States. "I thought I could swing it," he replied.[24] Nevertheless, he faced several challenges, and as an "accidental president" had to proceed cautiously. First of all, he had to ensure public confidence in the stability of the government following Harding's death. He also had to deal with the rising stench of the scandals that plagued the administration that were just coming to light. And he had to win the Republican presidential nomination for 1924. With no power base of his own, he had to maneuver among the party's contending factions to gain support for his candidacy. Coolidge accomplished all these goals with a minimum of fanfare.

The new president, the public soon learned, did not drink, play cards, or chase women, and he quickly distanced himself from the excesses of the Harding era. Under Grace Coolidge, who presided over the White House with charm and dignity, the fumigation was complete. The first time Alice Longworth visited the Coolidge White House, she found it as different from the Harding days "as a New England front parlor is from the backroom of a speakeasy."[25] The ablest members of Harding's cabinet—Hoover, Mellon, and Charles Evans Hughes—were asked to stay on. But unwilling as always to antagonize anyone, Coolidge took his time in jockeying the scandal-tarred Attorney General Harry M. Daugherty and Edwin Denby, the navy secretary, out of the cabinet.*

Wary of jeopardizing the Republican party's chances in 1924, Coolidge was reluctant to make a full housecleaning. Some observers called his position "cautious immobility." Eventually, he appointed two special co-counsels to investigate Teapot Dome, but only after congressional Democrats had prodded him into it. And then with the declaration "Let the guilty be punished" he reaped accolades for fighting corruption. As Franklin Roosevelt, the Democratic vice-presidential candidate in 1920, unhappily noted, it was a repetition of the aftermath of the Boston police strike, when Coolidge had cannily obtained credit for the accomplishments of others.

Coolidge consecrated himself to "stability." "Whatever his [Harding's] policies were, are my policies," he told his first press conference, and he pledged to usher in a "new era" in the relationship between the federal

---

*Harlan Fiske Stone, dean of the Columbia Law School, whom Coolidge had known at Amherst and whose ability and character were unquestioned, was named to replace Daugherty. He, in turn, fired William Burns, chief of the Bureau of Investigation, who was believed to have conspired with Daugherty in the various scandals. Burns was replaced by J. Edgar Hoover, the ambitious and zealous head of the Bureau's intelligence division. The agency was also formally designated the Federal Bureau of Investigation.

government and business. By stressing economic stability he conveyed a need for political stability—which meant a new term for himself. Higher profits for business was his recipe for national prosperity, so he cut federal spending to diminish the need for increased taxes. "I am for economy," he declared. "After that, I am for more economy."

The White House set an example for what the president called "orderly retrenchment." Unnecessary lights were turned off; paper drinking cups were replaced by old-fashioned glass tumblers; the number of towels in the lavatories was reduced; news correspondents were told to buy their own pencils. Critics pointed out, however, that Coolidge kept the presidential yacht, *Mayflower,* in commission for weekend cruises on the Potomac while its half-million-dollar annual cost was concealed in the Navy Department budget by classifying the vessel as a warship. Otherwise, spending on the military was slashed.

Until the Harding administration, wryly observed Lincoln Steffens, the aging "muckraker," the federal government was merely the kept woman of business. Now, Wall Street and Washington had married.[26] Most Americans who went to the polls in 1924 gave the nuptials their blessing. With the Harding scandals receding, the economy going into high gear, and no foreign or domestic crisis in sight, Coolidge easily won the Republican nomination on the first ballot—and his victory in November was foreordained by savage infighting among the Democrats.

The Democrats had hoped to exploit the Harding scandals, but whatever chance they had to win was dashed by Coolidge's seeming rectitude and their own internal divisions. This split was based on regional rivalries and conflicting moralities. One faction was urban and Northeastern, of immigrant stock, opposed to Prohibition and heavily Catholic. The other was rural, native born, dry, and largely Protestant. These differences were aggravated by racial and religious bigotry that fed on rural America's fear of cultural dominance by the immigrant rabble of the cities. Such hatreds provided fertile breeding ground for the resurrected Ku Klux Klan. By 1924, the Invisible Empire had spread its tentacles beyond the South and was a powerful political force in Oregon, California, Oklahoma, Kansas, and Indiana.

The candidacy of New York's governor, Al Smith, was a lightning rod for all these animosities. With his Catholicism, ever-present brown derby, cigar, and rasping accent, he symbolized everything that rural America hated and feared, and the countryside supported William G. MacAdoo, Woodrow Wilson's son-in-law, for the nomination. The convention in New York City's Madison Square Garden deadlocked, with neither Smith nor MacAdoo about to muster a two-thirds majority. This was the first convention to be broadcast, and for two weeks the nation listened in as the Democrats tore themselves to pieces amid shouted threats, curses, and fistfights.[27] Finally, on the 103rd ballot, the now worthless nomination was given to John W. Davis, an ultraconservative Wall Street lawyer who had been Wilson's solicitor general.

Probably no Democrat could have won in 1924 after the party's raucous convention, but Davis offered little in the way of an alternative to Coolidge. Sometimes, he even sounded more like the Republican candidate than did Coolidge. The real opposition was offered by Senator Robert M. La Follette, of Wisconsin, candidate of the Independent Progressive party. An alliance of insurgent Republicans, Socialists, the Farmer-Labor party, and the railroad unions, the Progressives charged that the two major parties had turned their backs on the farmer and working man.

As expected, Coolidge sailed to an easy victory, but the triumph was clouded by the sudden death of his sixteen-year-old younger son, Calvin Jr. The boy blistered a toe while playing tennis on the White House lawn in sneakers without socks, and blood poisoning set in. Coolidge was devastated by his son's death and later lamented, "When he went, the power and the glory of the Presidency went with him. . . . I don't know why such a price was expected for occupying the White House."[28]

"I don't anticipate to change very much," Coolidge said soon after his election to the presidency in his own right.[29] "The country does not appear to require radical departures from the policies already adopted as much as it needs a further extension of those policies." Believing little needed to be done, he did little. It seemed to work because America appeared to be moving ever closer to what Coolidge called the "the age of perfection." Between 1925 and 1929, 22,800 new manufacturing establishments opened for business. Industrial production rose by 26 percent and the number of new jobs kept pace. Consumer demand for cars, radios, and other goods spiraled upward. If workers complained that their wages lagged behind economic growth, they could console themselves with relatively stable prices.

The stock market also began to leap ahead. At the end of May 1924, the *New York Times* average price of twenty-five industrial stocks stood at 106. By December the average had jumped to 134. A year later, it had climbed to 181. A similar blend of greed and gullibility fueled a Florida land boom. Hundreds of thousands of Americans enticed by the prospect of having their own place under the swaying palms put their life's savings into home sites in developments that existed only on paper or were still alligator-infested mangrove swamps. In the Marx Brothers movie *Cocoanuts,* Florida real estate developer Groucho announced, "Buy a lot! You can have any kind of house you want! You can get wood or brick or stucco—oh, boy, can you get stucco!" And thousand of Americans got "stucco" when the boom collapsed as unexpectedly as it had begun.

Both the stock market and Florida booms were stoked by the cuts in corporate and personal income taxes pushed through by Andrew Mellon, who was hailed as "the greatest secretary of treasury since Alexander Hamilton." Surtaxes on the highest incomes were cut in half, while taxes on incomes under $4,000 were reduced only from 4 to 3 percent. Inheritance and gift taxes were also abolished. Further reductions were made in 1925, 1926, and 1928, and loopholes allowed some wealthy individuals to pay no taxes at all. At Mellon's behest, the commissioner of internal revenue sent him a memo for his own use that outlined various ways to avoid paying taxes.

Coolidge left in place high tariffs, which picked the pockets of consumers. He tried to give away valuable natural resources, such as Muscle Shoals on the Tennessee River, to private developers but was blocked by public-power proponents in Congress.* He vetoed a bonus for World War I veterans to be paid in 1945, which was overridden, and a general increase in benefits for all veterans, which was sustained. Cheeseparing economies eviscerated the regulatory agencies, resulting in fewer food,

---

*Muscle Shoals later became the nucleus of the Tennessee Valley Authority.

drug, and meat inspectors. Farm relief legislation was twice vetoed because business interests claimed it was too expensive.

Coolidge also had strong views on race. "Biological laws shows us that Nordics deteriorate when mixed with other races," he declared. He gave lip service to the passage of antilynching legislation without doing anything to push it through Congress, and his record on control of the Ku Klux Klan and the appointment of blacks to office was bleak. When the governor of Oklahoma, where the Klan had all but seized control of the state, asked for federal troops to keep order, Coolidge ignored him. "America must be kept American," he claimed as he supported the Immigration Act of 1924, which was aimed at curbing the flow of immigrants in general and immigration from Southern and Eastern Europe in particular. Japanese immigrants were excluded altogether, worsening already tense relations between the United States and Japan.

Coolidge "did not have an international hair on his head," remarked one observer, and his basic foreign policy concern was to collect the $10 billion in World War debts owed the United States by its allies. To his small-town New England mind, payment of a debt on schedule and in full approached religious dogma. But the debtor nations claimed they were unable to pay because their gold reserves were low and impossibly high tariffs prevented them from selling goods in the United States. So they sought cancellation of the debt, arguing that the wartime loans should be considered part of America's contribution to the Allied victory. Coolidge refused. "Wal, they hired the money, didn't they?" he supposedly drawled.*

Coolidge's penny-pinching refusal to cancel these debts contributed to the rise of Adolf Hitler. To meet the American claims, France and Britain insisted on wringing payment from Germany of the $33 billion in reparations leveled against her by the Versailles Treaty. Wild inflation and a crippled economy sent Germany into default, and the French seized the Ruhr Valley in retaliation, aggravating the unhappy nation's plight and helping Hitler and his Nazis crawl out of obscurity. Over the next decade, several plans for dealing with the debt and repa-

---

*This statement is not found in the transcripts of his press conferences, and some authorities believe it apocryphal, but it sounds like vintage Coolidge.

rations were announced and failed. In the end, the Americans got little of their money—along with Hitler and World War II.

Traditionally, the United States is portrayed as isolationist during the Coolidge years, but Americans were willing to have contact with the rest of the world—as long as it was on their own terms. Like Harding, Coolidge wished to have nothing to do with the League of Nations but supported adherence to the World Court. The Senate eventually approved American membership, but with so many restrictions that the other member nations refused to accept the United States. The major diplomatic accomplishment of Coolidge's term was the Paris Peace Pact of 1928. Under this agreement, negotiated by Secretary of State Frank B. Kellogg, sixty-two nations pledged themselves to refrain from war as a national policy in a feeble attempt at collective security. Yet, without any means of enforcement except the good intentions of the signatories, the treaty was about as effective as the pledge made by Americans to swear off drinking during Prohibition.

With prosperity reaching its crest, had Calvin Coolidge wanted another term in the White House, he could have had it for the asking. But he did not ask. On August 2, 1927, during one of his typically long summer vacations—this one in the Black Hills of South Dakota—he took time off from trout fishing to call the press together. He handed each reporter a small slip of paper with twelve words upon it: "I do not care to run for President in nineteen twenty-eight." Shocked, the newsmen clamored for further comment, but Coolidge's steel trap of a mouth snapped shut and he went to lunch. It was one day short of the fourth anniversary of his accession to the presidency. Neither his wife nor any of his advisers knew the announcement was coming.

Numerous reasons have been advanced for Coolidge's decision to turn down certain reelection. Did he sense what lay around the corner? Mrs. Coolidge was later quoted as telling friends that "Poppa says there's a depression coming."[30] But this indicates a degree of prescience that Coolidge had never shown before. More likely, he no longer found the presidency a novelty and had grown tired of the job. Never energetic, he was worried about his health and that of his wife, who did not flourish in Washington's erratic climate. Moreover, he had been deeply depressed since young Calvin's death. "There were no thrills while he reigned, but neither were there any headaches," wrote Henry Mencken upon his departure. "He had no ideas, and he was not a nuisance."[31]

Coolidge's fabled luck held and he escaped from the White House just as a final orgy on Wall Street was getting under way. Yet cracks in the system's foundation were already evident to those who looked closely. Of course, the farmers, coal mining, and textiles had been in trouble for years, but tremors were now being felt in other segments of industry. Purchasing power lagged, unemployment was creeping upward, and production was falling. Unsold radios filled the store shelves; cars were piling up in dealers' garages; construction was off; bank failures averaged two a day. Coolidge saw none of this. "The country can regard the present with satisfaction and anticipate the future with optimism," he declared shortly before leaving office. Six months later, the stock market crashed and the long slide into the Great Depression began.

From his retirement in Northampton, the ex-president, already a spectral figure receding into the shadows of history, looked on as factories shut down, banks collapsed, and people lost their jobs, their savings, their hopes. After a bank in Northampton failed, he found his former law partner slumped at his desk with his head in his hands. Coolidge left a check for $5,000 beside him and slipped away.[32] In the darkest days of the crisis, he unburdened himself of the following wisdom:

> Our banking system is not yet perfect.
> Public officials are not infallible.
> The future may be better or worse.
> Raising tax rates does not now seem to be popular.
> The final solution for unemployment is work.[33]

On January 5, 1933, Calvin Coolidge suffered a heart attack while shaving in the bathroom of his Northampton home and collapsed. When the writer Dorothy Parker was told that he was dead, she replied, "How can they tell?"

CHAPTER V

ULYSSES S. GRANT

Some years ago, Bill Moyers asked a distinguished historian why Ulysses Simpson Grant appears so sad in all of his pictures. "If you had his friends, you'd look glum, too," came the reply. Grant was saddled with the misdeeds of a grasping family and rapacious and unsavory friends who made his administration one of the most scandal-ridden in presidential history. The old soldier had played a magnificent role in preserving the Union, and the hero-worshiping American people thrust upon him their greatest accolade, for which he was entirely unsuited. Like Grant, they regarded the presidency as a reward rather than a responsibility—and it became a curse.

"I did not want the presidency, and have never quite forgiven myself for resigning command of the Army to accept it," Grant said after leaving office. "But it could not be helped. I owed my honors and opportunities to the Republican party and if my name could aid it I was bound to accept."[1]

Grant's frank appraisal was supported by Woodrow Wilson, one of Grant's abler successors: "This honest, simple-hearted soldier had not added prestige to the presidential office. He himself knew that he had failed . . . that he ought never to have been made president."[2] Grant was manipulated by the managers and operators of a post–Civil War spoils system that subordinated every facet of the federal government to their own devious ends. Grant merely presided at the White House during the height of the Gilded Age while the spoilsmen and big-business moguls not only ran the country, but ran off with most of the gilt.

Grant was an ignorant and confused president, and during his eight long years in blunderland, he was surrounded by mediocrities, self-seekers, and out-and-out rascals who made his administration into a high-priced tollbooth for government favors. Worst of all, he failed to protect the rights of the newly freed blacks, who loyally supported him. Over Grant's tomb high above the Hudson River in New York City are inscribed the words "Let Us Have Peace," which marked his formal entry into politics in 1868. They might also have been the murmured prayer of relief that accompanied his departure from the White House.

How could a man so brilliant in war commit such follies as president? There is no easy answer. Perhaps the best is that the horse-loving Grant had no political horse sense, no experience with civilian office, and no grasp of politics. He had voted only once for president—and that was in 1856 for James Buchanan, a Democrat—before becoming president. He had no real comprehension of the duties and powers of the office, already muddied by the prolonged struggle over Reconstruction between his predecessor, Andrew Johnson, and Congress. He knew nothing of law or even the Constitution and had no interest in learning anything about them. He called cabinet meetings and forgot to appear. Lackadaisical and irresolute, he left important state documents unread upon his desk and refused to answer letters that interfered with his frequent vacations. Most of all, he lacked vision and the true politician's zest for people. There was a persistant strain of nativism in his views and even when he supported state and federal aid for the public schools, it was couched in anti-Catholic tones.* Nevertheless, millions of Americans found comfort in Grant's political unsophistication. Twice he was elected president and then was almost successful in breaking the two-term tradition.

The voters who elected Grant in 1868 were weary of politics. For more than a decade, the nation was torn by civil war and then by the tensions of Reconstruction. The unsavory political scheming surrounding the impeachment of Johnson had aroused genuine disgust. It was a relief at last to get away from the petty politicians and turn to a man already enshrined in a misty Valhalla of tattered battle flags held

*In 1862, he had issued an order expelling all Jews "as a class" from his military department on grounds that they were speculating in cotton. President Lincoln quickly reversed the so-called "Jew order."

high and far-off bugle calls. Grant was regarded by the people as a man of decision and integrity, a strong, simple, silent soldier who would bring dignity, efficiency, and reform to Washington. They were to be woefully disappointed.

In recent years, some historians have challenged the conventional view of the post–Civil War era as an age of unparalleled corruption.[3] They suggest that graft was little worse than usual and contend there was so much talk about it because Grant and others were seriously trying to make improvements. Grant has received such bad press, it is argued, because an extremely articulate band of reformers painted a lurid portrayal of the Gilded Age. Perhaps. But even if these mitigating factors are taken into account, there was still plenty for the reformers to complain about.

Yet it would be a mistake to blame everything on Grant. The war had given the North not only victory, but unprecedented power and prosperity. The Southern plantocracy, which had played a key role in running the nation and setting its standards since Thomas Jefferson's day, was swept away. A new class of men replaced them—pushing, cynical fellows who had made fortunes by selling shoddy goods to the government, by speculating in necessities, and by other schemes in which the public pocket was picked. At war's end, this crew entered into an alliance with grasping politicians and operated with the same ruthlessness and greed as before. Somehow the "poor man's fight" of the Civil War had become the rich man's peace. "Every man at present may be said literally to live by his wits," observed Edwin L. Godkin, editor of *The Nation*. "The result is a kind of moral anarchy."[4]

The deterioration of morals perceived by the reformers was not limited to Washington, however. The capital was merely a faithful mirror of the nation as a whole. Charles Darwin's new theory of evolution of species, with its emphasis on struggle and the triumph of the strongest species, was transformed into the doctrine of Social Darwinism. This psuedoscientific dogma caused the successful to believe their accomplishments were both meritorious and socially acceptable. Moreover, Americans were heartily sick of great causes such as the crusade against slavery before the war, the fight to maintain the Union during the war, and the struggle to reconstruct the nation after the war. The inability to solve the problems of sectionalism and race produced a general disillusionment that led many Americans to mistrust idealism in any form.

On the surface, society was governed by a severe Victorian moral code, but passion raged behind the scenes. Piety seemed to walk hand in hand with double-dealing. The Reverend Henry Ward Beecher, the country's leading divine and self-appointed keeper of public morals, was discovered to have had astonishing success in seducing his female parishioners. Senator Roscoe Conkling of New York conducted a long-time love affair with Kate Chase Sprague, the comely wife of one of his colleagues, which ended on an absurd note when the lady's aggrieved husband ran Conkling off with a shotgun. Commodore Cornelius Vanderbilt gleefully cheated his son, William, in a manure-hauling contract and shipped his wife off to an insane asylum for several months to still her objections to moving to a new home. And the paragon of business morality was Daniel Drew, who, it was said, knew more Scripture and less charity than any other man on Wall Street. Fittingly, he left his money to found a theological seminary.

Corruption was confined to no one party or region. The Southern states, alternately at the mercy of carpetbaggers and the Ku Klux Klan, were only the most obvious example of excess. State treasuries across the South were looted. Legend places the blame upon the uneducated former slaves who supposedly dominated local governments after the war. In reality, the worst crimes during Reconstruction were committed by white carpetbaggers and their Southern scalawag allies. Political thievery was also rampant in the large cities of the North, where New York City was held captive by the Tweed Ring, and the Gas House Gang had a stranglehold on Philadelphia. In Iowa, some light-fingered soul made off with the entire treasury of the State Agricultural College.[5] "Isn't everybody corrupt there?" Europeans asked American visitors.

Such extreme conditions required a president of considerable moral stamina to keep his administration on the straight and narrow, and Grant was not up to the task. Whatever fires that had raged within him during the Civil War seemed to have flickered and died by the time he entered the White House. "The progress of Evolution from President Washington to President Grant was alone evidence enough to upset Darwin," observed Henry Adams.

* * *

Hiram Ulysses Grant, as he was originally named, was born on April 27, 1822, in a two-room cabin at Point Pleasant, Ohio, about twenty-five miles up the Ohio River from Cincinnati.[6] His father, Jesse Root Grant, was a verbose and grasping tanner and dresser of hides who prospered, amassing the then considerable fortune of $150,000. Hannah Simpson Grant, his mother, was just the opposite: silent, reserved, and deeply religious. Not long after the boy's birth, the family moved to Georgetown, Ohio, where he and his five younger siblings were raised.

Young Grant received a rudimentary education in the local schools and later, away from home, in boarding schools. He liked mathematics and performed acceptably in other subjects. Shy and reticent, he received little affection from his rather remote parents and had few friends. The boy developed a phobia against retracing his steps; if he walked past a destination, he would continue on until he came to a crossroad and work his way back to his original target rather than turn back.

From an early age, he demonstrated a marked talent for handling horses and assumed all the chores requiring their use. He hauled wood, cleared and plowed fields, and carried passengers—anything to keep from being put to work in his father's tannery, where the blood-caked hides made him sick. Paradoxically, in view of his later career, Grant could not stand the sight of animal blood. He did not hunt, even as a boy, and, nauseated by rare steak, insisted his meat be served well done. In Mexico, he was sickened by a bullfight.

Without consulting him, Jesse Grant, in 1839, arranged for his son's appointment to West Point by Rep. Thomas L. Hamer. Young Grant, fearing failure, did not wish to leave home, but finally ended his resistance, undoubtedly to escape an unappealing future in the tannery. The elder Grant looked with favor on a West Point education for his son because it was free and would provide him with a job after graduation.

Before Grant's departure, someone had the bright idea of putting his initials on his trunk with tacks, but when he saw the result—H.U.G.—he was appalled and reversed the first two letters and went off to West Point bearing the name Ulysses Hiram Grant. By mistake, however, Congressman Hamer had enrolled him as Ulysses Simpson Grant. Always willing to go along, the youth raised no objection, and that, henceforth, was his name. To his fellow cadets, he was known first as Uncle Sam and then as Sam.

West Point had no appeal for the diffident youngster, and he became even more withdrawn. He did not excel in any subject, although he did his best work in mathematics and was a good horseman. Always homesick, he later confessed that he had frequently prayed that a talked-of plan in Congress to abolish the academy would pass. Some authorities claim that because of his lack of social graces, he also developed a sense of inferiority to the more polished members of his class, especially those from the South, that persisted throughout his life. In his four years at West Point, he never went to a dance, had a date with a girl, or was a guest in a private home.

Grant numbered among his friends and acquaintances fifty cadets who later served as generals in the Civil War. Knowing the strengths and weaknesses of these men, both friend and foe, helped him in battle. But he had no interest in a military career. "The truth is I am more of a farmer than a soldier," he told Otto von Bismarck during a glittering review staged at Potsdam in the touring ex-president's honor. "I take little or no interest in military affairs." Earlier, upon meeting the son of the Duke of Wellington, he innocently observed, "They tell me, my Lord, that your father was also a military man."[7]

Following his graduation in 1843, twenty-first in a class of thirty-nine, newly minted Second Lieutenant Grant proudly returned to his home in Ohio in full uniform with a sense of accomplishment. He was crestfallen to find the stableman at the village tavern strutting about with cotton stripes sewed down the sides of his blue pantaloons in obvious imitation of the young officer. From then on, his uniform meant little to him, and eventually he was known for the slovenliness of his dress.

Grant had requested service with the cavalry in view of his skill with horses, but with typical military logic, he was detailed to the Fourth Infantry, at Jefferson Barracks near St. Louis. The young officer developed a friendly relationship with the family of Fred Dent, his West Point roommate, who lived on a nearby plantation called White Haven. The senior Dent, a slaveholder and self-styled "colonel," prided himself on his hospitality. But the main attraction for Grant was eighteen-year-old Julia Dent. She was bright, vivacious, and an excellent horsewoman, and the bashful Grant, who scarcely noticed a slight crossing of her eyes, was captivated.

Out driving in a buggy one day, the young couple came to a bridge flooded by a suddenly swollen creek. Julia was reluctant to cross but Grant assured her it was safe. Unconvinced, she grasped his arm, saying, "I'm going to cling to you no matter what happens." After crossing safely, Grant turned to her and asked, "How would you like to cling to me the rest of your life?"[8] Julia accepted the proposal and they embarked on a four-year engagement that included a separation caused by the Mexican War.

"I do not think there ever was a more wicked war than that waged by the United States on Mexico," Grant wrote later. "I thought so at the time, when I was a youngster, only I had not moral courage to resign." Nevertheless, he did creditable service as a regimental quartermaster and participated in most of the war's battles. But he failed to win the distinction gained by Robert E. Lee and others and emerged from the struggle still only a lieutenant. Once the war was over, he returned to Missouri, where he and Julia were married. James Longstreet, one of Grant's army comrades, was best man. Throughout the years ahead, from poverty to riches and then back to poverty again, the couple remained in love—often holding hands in public, a shy, prosaic pair whose romance was the only passion of their lives.

Grant had hoped for an appointment as a mathematics instructor at West Point but was sent, instead, to a series of dreary garrison posts, finally in Oregon and northern California, where Julia and their growing family could not accompany him. Lonely and depressed, he took to the bottle. The evidence indicates that he was not the heavy drinker of legend.* Apparently, he had a weak head and little more than a sniff of the cork would make him drunk. Although Grant had been promoted to captain, in 1854, his commanding officer gave him the choice of

---

*There is no truth to the story that Abraham Lincoln dismissed reports of Grant's drinking during the Civil War with the famous retort: "Well, I wish some of you would tell me the brand of whiskey that Grant drinks. I would like to send a barrel of it to my other generals." It was invented by a reporter for the *New York Herald* and appeared there for the first time on November 26, 1863. Lincoln flatly denied ever having made the remark. Except for a monumental bender during the most frustrating stage of the Vicksburg campaign, Grant seems to have been mostly abstemious throughout the war.

resigning from the army or a court-martial because of his drinking. He resigned. It was a squalid end to his military career and left him penniless at the age of thirty-two.

Bitter failure dogged Grant over the next seven years. He tried farming a plot of land near St. Louis given him by Julia's father and, to provide cash, peddled firewood in the streets of the city. Many people later recalled him as a shabby, mud-spattered figure in an old army overcoat and the beginnings of a beard. The Dents despised him and were reluctant to continue supporting the couple's growing brood of children. Old friends from whom he had borrowed money avoided him. One Christmas, he was reduced to pawning his watch to buy presents for his family. Finally, in 1858, Grant acknowledged his failure as a farmer and abjectly accepted a $50-a-month clerkship in his father's leather and hardware shop in Galena, Illinois.

The Civil War gave Grant a new start in life. Upon the outbreak of hostilities, he sought to retrieve his commission but heard nothing from the War Department. Years later, the letter was found tucked away unread in a dusty file. Instead, he was taken on as drillmaster of a regiment of newly mustered Illinois volunteers. Stumpy, badly shaved, and with only a part of a uniform, Colonel Grant did not inspire confidence at first sight, but he hammered the raw farm boys into a semblance of soldiers. Somehow, this nondescript fellow who had never wanted to be an officer and always disliked soldiering was good at it.

Near the end of his life, Grant would open his memoirs with these lines: "Man proposes and God disposes. There are but few important events in the affairs of men brought about by their own choice." Chance certainly played a role in his life because within a month he was recommended to the War Department as one of the four volunteer brigadier generals to which Illinois was entitled. Resolute and dogged rather than brilliant, he showed a reluctance to retreat in the face of adversity—perhaps a throwback to his schoolboy superstition about retracing his steps—that was in vivid contrast to most Union generals.

Grant's response to a request from General Simon Bolivar Buckner* for surrender terms at Fort Donelson, which controlled the Cumberland

---

*Buckner, an old army friend, had, in 1854, lent Grant the fare to get home to his family.

River—"No terms except an unconditional surrender can be accepted. I propose to immediately move upon your works"—captured the imagination of the dispirited North at a time when it desperately needed heroes. "U.S." now stood for "unconditional surrender." Newspapers reported the coolness with which he had prepared to attack, cigar clenched between his teeth, and admirers sent him some 10,000 boxes of cigars. Some he gave away; the rest he smoked at a rate of twenty a day—laying the groundwork for the throat cancer that eventually caused his death.

Grant's capture of Vicksburg, the last rebel bastion on the Mississippi, cut the Confederacy in two. Following the fall of Chattanooga, which opened the way for an invasion of Georgia, Lincoln called him to Washington in March 1864 to take command of all Union troops. Possessing an overwhelming preponderance in men and armaments, Grant ground down the Confederates in a relentless war of attrition that produced such heavy casualties that the Northern press branded him "Grant the Butcher." But all was forgotten when General Lee surrendered at Appomattox on April 9, 1865. In victory, Grant was magnanimous and offered lenient terms that treated the defeated with dignity. It was his finest hour. Had fortune been kind to him, he, not Lincoln, would have been killed at Ford's Theater five days later.*

It was an incredible rise. Only a few years before, Grant had been all but down-and-out. Now he was engulfed by a tide of adulation. Congress named him the first full general since George Washington. Wealthy and powerful men sought his friendship and opened their bankrolls to him. The grateful citizenry of Galena, who had not long before taunted him as "Useless Grant," gave him a new home; a group of New Yorkers presented him with a check for $105,000; Philadelphia provided a lavishly furnished mansion; and "fifty solid men of Boston" bought him a $75,000 library—a real extravagance because he rarely read anything. Horses, carriages, and other expensive gifts poured in. Having known poverty, Grant and his wife partook of the good life with unrestrained

---

*Grant and his wife were invited by the Lincolns to attend the theater that night, but Julia disliked Mrs. Lincoln and they declined, saying they had already decided to go to Burlington, New Jersey, to visit their children, who were in school there.

pleasure. "Since Richmond's capitulation the stern soldier has spent his days and eked his nights in conjugating the transitive verb *to receive*," grumbled the *New York Tribune*.

The taciturn Grant had little to say in response to the cheers that greeted him everywhere, being "entirely unaccustomed to public speaking and without the desire to cultivate the power." Once, when a crowd clamored for a speech and the general was his usual tongue-tied self, his son, seven-year-old Jesse Grant, leaped into the breach by reciting "The Boy Stood on the Burning Deck."[9]

Such popularity inevitably carried Grant into politics. Originally, he brushed off talk of the presidency with the comment, "I should like to be mayor of Galena long enough to build a new sidewalk from my house to the depot." Others purported to see through these pleasantries. Gideon Welles, the crusty secretary of the navy and no admirer of Grant's, confided in his diary that he had found the general "very ambitious, has low cunning, and is unreliable."[10]

Much against his will, Grant was drawn into the vicious political struggle between Lincoln's successor, Andrew Johnson, and Congress over the reintegration of the former Confederate states into the Union. Johnson—after an initial phase of bitterness toward the South—followed a lenient policy that would, in effect, have quickly turned these states over to the white leaders who had ruled before the war. But Republican congressional leaders, called Radicals, regarded this as outright abandonment of the freed slaves and a betrayal of all for which the war had been fought. Moreover, they saw a plot by Johnson, a onetime Democrat, to restore the Democratic power base in the South that had dominated national affairs before the war.

No one quite knew where Grant, the army's ranking officer, stood as this witch's brew boiled over—probably not even Grant himself.[11] At first, he seemed to side with Johnson, and then, convinced the president's policies were resulting in the sacrifice of all for which so many had died, he supported the Radicals. Johnson later claimed he had been betrayed by Grant's shiftiness. The career officer's traditional view that Congress is the boss in the American system may have been the determining factor in Grant's decision.

Orders come from the executive, but Congress confirms or rejects promotions, passes appropriations bills, and declares war. Everything in his background and experience told Grant that Congress must be the final authority. For him, the struggle between Johnson and the Radicals provided an object lesson in what can happen when a president and Congress are at odds, and it governed his view of the role of the president when he got to the White House. It also presents an enduring illustration of the riskiness of putting a professional soldier in the presidency—paradoxically, not because he will try to assume too much authority, but because he may hesitate to use the authority he has. Dwight Eisenhower's presidency is a prime example of this phenomenon.

In May 1868, as the Senate sat in solemn judgment on President Johnson, the Republicans were having their convention in Chicago to nominate their presidential candidate.* The Senate acquitted Johnson of "high crimes and misdemeanors" in a parliamentary cliff-hanger, while on the first roll call, the Republicans embraced U. S. Grant—"the strong, silent man from Appomattox"—as their nominee. Compared with the other possibilities, he seemed cloaked in innocence, perhaps because he was innocent of any ideas. More in keeping with the temper of the times was the vice-presidential choice: Schuyler "Smiler" Colfax, a sticky-fingered Indiana congressman and Speaker of the House who, it was said, brought new meaning to the word *vice*.

Once Grant had accepted the nomination with a brief speech of which nobody remembered anything except the final words—"Let us have peace"—he retired to his gift house in Galena and said nothing, maintaining the image of the simple soldier awaiting the call of duty. Now the politicians and the spoilsmen swung into action. Such "fat cats" as A. T. Stewart, the merchant prince, and "robber barons" Collis Huntington, William B. Astor, Commodore Vanderbilt, and William B. Dodge were squeezed for campaign expenses. The discredited Johnson tried to win the Democratic nomination, but New York governor Horatio Seymour was chosen instead. Seymour, who had opposed the draft during the war, and his party were tagged as supporters of secession and treason. With the backing of black voters in the South, Grant

*The details of Johnson's impeachment are in chapter 6.

carried all but eight states. Andrew Johnson angrily refused to attend his inauguration.

At forty-six, Grant was the youngest man yet to become president. Vigorous and at the height of his popularity, he took the oath as the nation's eighteenth president on March 4, 1869, amid hope that his would be an administration of conciliation and reform. As a national hero, he owed the politicians nothing. Thus, it was reasoned, he would have a free hand to surround himself with able men rather than spoilsmen and to establish policies in the spirit of Appomattox. Like many others, the youthful Henry Adams expected great things from the new president. "Grant represented order. He was a great soldier, and the soldier always represented order," he wrote. "A general who had organized and commanded half a million or a million men in the field must know how to administer."[12]

The announcement of Grant's cabinet brought instant disillusionment. Without qualifications for his office, the new president's only hope for success lay in the wisdom and integrity of his advisers. Instead, most of the places went to friends from Galena, Army cronies, and wealthy men who had financed his campaign or given him lavish gifts. Their names "had the singular effect of making the hearer ashamed, not so much of Grant, as of himself," for hoping the new administration would do better, said Adams. With the exception of a few men of ability—and Grant soon broke with them—his choice of advisers seemed based mostly on the desire to have no one about who would overshadow him.

Over the next eight years, cabinet officers came and went with unsettling rapidity—and the abler they were the faster they went. With the exception of Hamilton Fish, a Knickerbocker aristocrat who became secretary of state and stayed the course, Grant was largely surrounded by an array of nonentities and downright crooks. Few had any experience in government or politics, nor were they known for talent or intellect. Although a leader of men, Grant was not a good judge of them. Starved for affection in boyhood and the victim of thirty years of failure, he looked hungrily for friendship wherever he could find it. He was an easy mark for men who flattered him, told him what he wanted to hear, and filled his mind with their own pet schemes.

Like most Americans, the president was dazzled by the new "captains of industry," the promoters and go-getters. A. T. Stewart was named secretary of the treasury but the appointment had to be withdrawn because of rampant conflict of interest. Adolf E. Borie, the head of the fund drive for Grant's Philadelphia house, was appointed secretary of the navy. Borie found the job claimed more of his time than it warranted and resigned after only three months. General John Rawlins, Grant's former chief of staff, became secretary of war. Rawlins died before the year was out, and it was discovered he had accepted $28,000 in bonds from a lobbyist who represented a Cuban revolutionary junta that was seeking U.S. support against Spain.

Grant's legislative team also gave off a certain aroma. Senator Roscoe Conkling, New York's flamboyant Republican boss—who favored white flannel trousers, florid vests, and a "turkey-gobbler strut"—became the administration's spokesman in the Senate. Michigan's facile Senator Zachary Chandler managed its backroom operations. They were assisted by Senator Oliver Morton of Indiana, a masterful practitioner of the politics of spoils. Simon Cameron, the Pennsylvania boss who had been dropped from Lincoln's wartime cabinet on grounds that he was a crook, was one of Grant's favorite companions. Cross-eyed Ben Butler, whose incompetence and scrupulous dishonesty during the war had aroused Grant's ire, was now forgiven his trespasses and welcomed into the inner circle.

Regarding the White House as his rightful prerogative, Grant, who as a candidate had murmured support of civil service, lost no time in doling out jobs to family members. Fred Dent, his brother-in-law, became the chief White House usher. His father-in-law, "Colonel" Dent, hung around the place drinking juleps and sounding off about the damn Yankees. Old Jesse Grant and the president's brother Orvil came to town to sniff out deals. A cousin, Silas A. Hudson, an Oregon cattle trader, was made minister to Guatemala, and the Reverend M. J. Cramer, a brother-in-law, became consul in Leipzig. Julia's brother-in-law, James F. Casey, was named to the lucrative post of collector of customs in New Orleans. In all, some forty relatives of either the president or first lady were scattered about the government or earned large fees from influence peddling. "No president was ever 'got in the family way' so soon after the inauguration," observed John Bigelow, a New York newspaper editor. Grant's mother was his only relative who never set foot in the White House.[13]

Grant was neither hardworking nor conscientious. He "does not intend to labor like a drudge . . . does not propose to study public affairs, has no taste for books or intellectual employment," observed Gideon Welles. Faced with an aggressive Congress and believing in the theory that it best expressed the will of the people, Grant was content to let the legislature determine the policies that he was to administer.

Usually, Grant began his working day at 10 A.M. and ended it at 3 P.M. He would then visit the presidential stables where he would relax in the company of his horses. He was the first president to take long vacations—usually at the expense of rich friends. Julia, now at the top of the social heap after so many lean years, entertained lavishly in the ostentatious style of those she and her husband admired. Soon, the Grants thought nothing of sitting down with thirty-six guests for a dinner of twenty-five dishes and a different wine with every third course.

Phlegmatic at best and haunted by years of poverty and humiliation before the war, Grant froze up in the presence of men of talent, learning, and culture.* These men, awed in turn by his reputation and position, found it almost impossible to break down the barrier, and an uncomfortable standoff usually resulted. On one occasion, Mark Twain, then still largely unknown, was introduced to Grant. Grant maintained his usual taciturnity after they shook hands, and Twain couldn't think of a word to say. At last the writer stammered, "General, I'm embarrassed. Are you?"[14]

Grant's presidency was not a total loss. In some ways, he accomplished a good deal—enough for him, at least, to look back on his record in the White House with pride. The economic wreckage of the war was largely cleared away. Inflation was brought under control and a stable currency created. A major financial panic was overcome, and the West was opened to settlement by the completion of the transcontinental rail-

---

*Nor did he have an ear for music. "I know only two tunes," Grant once said. "One is 'Yankee Doodle.' The other isn't."

road. The South was reintegrated into the Union—although at the cost of the fundamental rights of the ex-slaves. And under the steady hand of Hamilton Fish, all the outstanding claims against Britain resulting from the depredations of the *Alabama* and other British-built Confederate commerce raiders were liquidated with the award of $15.5 million to the United States.[15]

Yet these successes are overshadowed by the corruption that besmirched Grant's administration. While most of the scandals that gave his regime its notoriety were not exposed until he was well into his second term, scandal was an early caller at the White House and made itself comfortably at home. Only a few months into his term, Grant found himself, as a result of his ethical obtuseness, assisting Jay Gould and Jim Fisk, an unsavory pair of financial buccaneers, in a conspiracy to corner the gold market and scoop in millions for themselves.[16]

To make certain that the government would not foil their scheme by selling gold from the Treasury reserves if things got tight, the pair employed another of Grant's ubiquitous brothers-in-law, a shady Wall Street operator named Abel R. Corbin, to exert his influence upon the president. In exchange for a $25,000 fee and a promised share of the swag, Corbin tried to persuade Grant that higher gold prices would be good for American farm exports. Gould and Fisk also arranged to be seen entertaining the president, spurring speculation that not only Grant but Julia and some White House aides were in on the deal. Had Grant any sense of the propriety of his office, he would never have allowed himself to be seen with such malodorous characters.

Puffing on his usual Havana—and probably mystified by all this talk about the price of gold—Grant said nothing. But a few days later, he ordered the Treasury not to follow its usual practice of selling gold to stabilize the price. Word apparently leaked out—possibly from General Daniel Butterfield, another presidential crony who was in charge of the subtreasury in New York and was in on the scheme—and Gould and Fisk bought gold with a will. The price was driven up from $135 an ounce until it reached $163.50 on September 24, 1869, a date known in financial annals as Black Friday. Panic raged on Wall Street, and the stability of the nation's commerce was threatened. Appalled and tardily realizing that he had been duped, Grant ordered the Treasury to sell

$4 million in federal gold reserves, which sent the price plummeting back down to $133 in only fifteen minutes.

Gould and Fisk went off to other financial adventures, but the affair hung around Grant's neck like a golden albatross. A House investigating committee looked into it, but the Republican majority adroitly fended off the question of presidential involvement and blocked Democratic demands for testimony from the president and his wife. Few believed that Grant was guilty of overt wrongdoing, but his unthinking association with Gould and Fisk raised questions about his judgment. "Everyone dreaded to press [the] inquiry," commented Henry Adams, because they "feared finding too much."

Also in 1869, Grant was deeply involved in a bizarre effort to annex what was then called Santo Domingo.* The project was originally cooked up by a pair of Yankee fortune hunters and the bankrupt Caribbean nation's president with the hope of reaping a rich monetary harvest from the takeover. Powerful financial and commercial interests were also involved, along with such ethically challenged figures as John Rawlins, Ben Butler, and Grant's personal secretary, Colonel Orville E. Babcock. Grant, who desired a naval base at Samaná Bay at the eastern end of the country, was an enthusiastic supporter of the proposal. Moreover, he had a visionary plan both to end racial tensions in the United States and do justice to the ex-slaves by resettling them on the island where several all-black states could be established.

To the end of his days, Grant thought this dubious scheme one of the best ideas he had ever had—which should make clear the quality of his ideas. Nevertheless, he went about it in such an amateurish way as to doom any chance for success. Rather than have Secretary of State Fish negotiate a treaty of annexation, Grant dispatched Babcock to Santo Domingo to work things out. He returned to Washington with a treaty in his pocket, which, despite the evil odor surrounding it, was duly submitted to the Senate for ratification. Grant, however, had antagonized Senator Charles Sumner, the imperious chairman of the Senate Foreign Relations Committee—for one thing Grant had absentmindedly referred to him as chairman of the Judiciary Committee—and the

*Now the Dominican Republic.

agreement was voted down. After that, Grant never passed the Massachusetts senator's home without shaking his fist.*[17]

The gold conspiracy and the Santo Domingo affair were of little importance in themselves, but they revealed just how easily Grant could be manipulated by dubious characters. Although the full measure of the corruption that honeycombed his administration was unknown as his first term ended, enough was suspected to outrage reformers and liberals. "It looks as though the Republican party is going to the dogs," said former senator James W. Grimes of Iowa. "It has become corrupt and I believe that it is today the [most] corrupt and debauched political party that ever existed."[18]

When the regular Republicans nominated Grant for a second term in 1872, the reformers, unable to stomach him for another four years, broke ranks and chose Horace Greeley, the editor of the *New York Tribune,* as the candidate of the Liberal Republican party. Despite Greeley's antislavery record, the Democrats also nominated him with the forlorn hope of avoiding four more years of Grant. A Greeley victory was thought unlikely, but about six weeks before the election, the nation was rocked by the Crédit Mobilier scandal, which should have improved his chances.[19]

The Crédit Mobilier was used by the promoters of the Union Pacific Railroad to skim off huge profits from the federal funds allocated for construction. To protect themselves from the possibility of a congressional inquiry, they doled out shares in the company that paid dividends of 350 percent to several prominent members of Congress, including "Smiler" Colfax, then House Speaker; James A. Garfield, his successor as Speaker and later president, and numerous others. Grant was not involved in the scandal, but reformers saw it as one more sign of the easy morality prevailing in Washington. Many people agreed with a cabinet officer—possibly Hamilton Fish—who told Henry Adams, "You can't reason with a Congressman! A Congressman is a hog! You must take a stick and hit him on the snout."[20]

---

*Upon being informed that Sumner did not believe in the Bible, Grant growled, "No. He didn't write it."

Greeley tried to make the most of the scandal, and Colfax was dropped from the Republican ticket,* but most voters discounted the story as one concocted for campaign purposes, just as future generations discounted Watergate and Whitewater. With the assistance of campaign funds from the usual assortment of robber barons, and the votes of the freedmen and former soldiers, Grant buried his opponent in a landslide and looked upon the election as a personal vindication. But a headline in the *New York Sun* told a different story: "Four Years More of Fraud and Corruption."

As if to reinforce the charges of the reformers, as soon as the election was over, Grant was inundated by a rising landfill of allegations of wrongdoing.[21] Almost every department of the government was found to be undermined by corruption. Grant's reaction, like that of chief executives before and since, was to blindly defend his appointees and claim the charges against them were really aimed at him and obviously politically inspired.

Navy Secretary George M. Robeson amassed a fortune of $320,000 by shaking down contractors doing business with his department. Funds for refitting ships went into his pocket, and it was hardly safe to send a vessel to sea in Robeson's day. Columbus Delano, the secretary of the interior, solicited bribes to enter fraudulent land grants in the records. Treasury Secretary William A. Richardson connived with a political sharper linked to Ben Butler to turn the collection of delinquent taxes into a racket. Mrs. Grant's brother-in-law, James F. Casey, looted the New Orleans Customs House and was reappointed to the job by the president despite a House report that found him totally corrupt.

James Watson Webb, the U.S. minister to Brazil, extorted $100,000 from the Brazilian government for a false claim and pocketed it. General T. B. Van Buren shook down American concessionaires at an international fair in Vienna.† Robert C. Schenck, the American minister in Great Britain, touted shares in a fraudulent Utah silver mine that hoodwinked British investors. He wrapped himself in diplomatic immu-

---

*He was replaced by Senator Henry Wilson of Massachusetts, who was also involved in the Crédit Mobilier scandal.

†He was replaced as American representative at the fair by Theodore Roosevelt Sr., the father of the future president.

nity to escape arrest. Attorney General George H. Williams, whose qualifications for his job were questionable, used government money to supply himself with an expensive carriage and liveried servants. Fred Dent listened at the keyhole to cabinet meetings and peddled the information so gained. "What a nasty crew to have about one!" raged Fish. "Drunken, stupid, lying, venal, brainless."

Worse was still to come. The Democrats won the congressional elections for the first time since the Civil War in 1874 and launched a fresh series of investigations with a whoop and a holler. William W. Belknap, the secretary of war, was found to have raked in as much as $100,000 a year by selling licenses to disburse supplies, usually of shoddy quality, to the Indians herded together on government reservations. In short, both the government and the luckless Indians were robbed. The president's brother Orvil was found to have shared in the plunder. Grant tried to block attempts to impeach Belknap by accepting his resignation "with great regret" in a tearful scene in the White House. Did this mean he regretted Belknap's dishonesty? Or the loss of a crony?

The exposure of the "Whiskey Ring" finally brought the dirty linen into the White House. For years, distillers in the Middle West had, with the connivance of federal agents, been robbing the Treasury of millions of dollars in unpaid liquor taxes. In St. Louis alone, the take was $1.2 million a year. In 1874, Grant himself was lavishly entertained there by the Ring's chief for ten days and accepted the gift of a matched team of horses and expensive harness. Despite these favors the president righteously proclaimed, "Let no guilty man escape," when an inquiry into the Ring's activities began. But he quickly changed his tune upon learning that his favorite, the ineffable Colonel Babcock, was deeply involved.

Only with some difficulty was Grant restrained from racing halfway across the country to testify in his aide's behalf. Instead, he did everything he could to ensure that Babcock would escape conviction. Federal attorneys were instructed not to follow the usual practice of offering immunity to small fry to get at the main offenders, and Grant made a sworn deposition used at Babcock's trial that testified fulsomely to the defendant's integrity. Despite the overwhelming weight of the evidence, Grant's deposition and his obvious eagerness for the acquittal of his aide had great influence with the jury. Babcock was the only one of the 110 persons charged in the whiskey frauds to be found innocent although most people thought him guilty.

Grant's greatest failure, however, was in protecting the rights of the former slaves, who had voted for him in overwhelming numbers. Throughout the South, white supremacists systematically organized campaigns of intimidation aimed at black voters. Legal efforts to enforce civil rights legislation in the courts also failed. In some cases, black political rallies were disrupted and people were killed. In September 1875, the Republican governor of Mississippi appealed to Washington for federal troops to restore order, but Grant refused. Although angered by the murders, he was reluctant to send troops out of fear of the greater bloodshed of a race war. As a result, the white counterrevolution succeeded—ending black hopes and aspirations in the South for a century.

Finally, it was all over, but Grant did not go quietly. Having gotten used to the White House and being blind to his ineptitude, he maneuvered for a draft in 1876 that would challenge the hallowed no-third-term tradition. But the House administered a stinging rebuke to the president by passing an anti-third-term resolution by an overwhelmingly bipartisan vote of 233 to 18. And so the Grant years drew to a close with, fittingly enough, the first stolen presidential election in American history.

And why not?

Everything else had been stolen.

The rest of the story can be quickly told. On their own for the first time since 1861, the restless Grants embarked on a two-and-a-half-year world tour. It carried them on an aimless path across Europe, the Middle East, and the Far East, in which they were feted like royalty. Today, it is remembered only for the former president's offhand comment to a young Englishwoman that "Venice would be a fine city if only it were drained."

Newspaper reports of Grant's triumphant tour helped him regain some of his lost luster and, supported by the spoilsmen who were savoring the prospect of "four more years of good stealing," he tried in

1880 to capture the Republican presidential nomination. Although he ran ahead on the first thirty-five ballots, the deadlocked convention eventually stampeded to the dark-horse candidacy of James Garfield, who despite his well-publicized ties to the Crédit Mobilier, won the presidency. In a turnabout, Garfield espoused the cause of reform— but did more for civil service by being fatally shot by a dissatisfied spoilsman than by anything he could have done alive.

Grant's last years were a mixture of tragedy and triumph. There was one more swindle, in which he was the chief victim. He had invested all his savings in the Wall Street investment firm of Grant & Ward in which one of his sons was a partner, but its chief was a crook. The firm went bankrupt in 1884, and Grant found himself broke again at the age of sixty-two. Going through his pockets, he found $80; Julia had $130 in the house—all that was left of their fortune. He also learned that he was suffering from throat cancer. Facing death and the prospect of leaving his wife penniless, Grant began work on his memoirs. Mark Twain, who agreed to publish the book, gave him a contract in which he was to receive an unheard-of 75 percent of all domestic sales.

With the same obstinacy with which he had pounded Lee's army two decades before, Grant raced with death to finish his book. The first part of the manuscript was dictated to a secretary, but as the cancer advanced, the pain became too great. He wrote out the remainder, line by line, page by page, in longhand while sustained by ever-larger doses of painkilling cocaine. The present faded and dissolved and he again saw the lines of muddied blue troops rallying on the bluffs of Shiloh . . . the night ripped apart by shells and rockets as Union gunboats sped past Vicksburg . . . the lines at Lookout Mountain wavering, reforming, and continuing their climb into the clouds . . . And finally, he saw Lee, correct and imperturbable in his best uniform, in the parlor of the McLean House at Appomattox.

From afar, the nation watched with fascination as Ulysses Grant fought his last battle, and its heart went out to him. He died on July 23, 1885, about a week after putting the finishing touches on the manuscript. Through his courage and steadfastness, he had not only won a final victory, but in doing so, had won back the respect and admiration of the American people.

CHAPTER VI

ANDREW JOHNSON

*H*ow say you? Is the respondent, Andrew Johnson, President of the United States, guilty or not guilty of a high misdemeanor . . . ?"

A verdict in the long-running impeachment trial of Johnson was at hand. One by one, the fifty-four senators sitting in judgment upon the president rose as Chief Justice Salmon P. Chase, impressive in his robes, put this question to them. The buzz of excitement among the senators, representatives, newsmen, and spectators packed into the stifling Senate chamber on May 16, 1868, suddenly grew silent. Outside, crowds milled about in the halls of the Capitol and spilled out onto the grounds. The only answers that could be given were "guilty" or "not guilty." Nothing more could be said, and no senator could decline to render a verdict. The clerk began to call the roll in alphabetical order:

"Senator Anthony of Rhode Island."

"Guilty."

This had been expected. As the roll call continued, one observer noted that "men grew pale and sick under the suspense, while such a stillness prevailed that the breathing of the galleries could be heard." It was especially noticeable each time a doubtful senator voted, with the audience holding its breath as the words "Guilty" or "Not guilty" were pronounced. Senator William Fessenden of Maine paused before answering, and in the silence, the tinkle of a woman's earring was plainly heard. He voted not guilty.

In the White House, at the other end of Pennsylvania Avenue, Johnson anxiously awaited the outcome of the polling. Relays of aides periodically arrived with the latest news and rumors. The president seemed coolness itself, but the emotions of his companions rose and fell as waves of optimism were submerged by bleaker reports, only to surface again.

For three years, the United States had been convulsed by a bitter struggle between the nation's seventeenth president and Republican Radicals in Congress. Ostensibly, the fight was over the reintegration of the former Confederate states into the Union and with it the treatment of the 4 million newly freed slaves. Johnson, who had been elevated to the presidency by the assassination of Abraham Lincoln on the night of April 14, 1865, backed a lenient policy that permitted a rapid return of these states to the Union, but it left the former masters in control. Alarmed, the Radicals, who had opposed slavery before the war, insisted that the federal government protect the basic rights of the ex-slaves and advocated a bitter peace—one that treated the rebel states as conquered provinces until full civil rights for the freedmen were assured.

The real struggle, however, was over who was to control the nation. The Radicals saw speedy reconstruction of the Southern states as a plot by the "obstinate, self-willed, combative" Johnson, a Democrat although he had been elected on a bipartisan National Union ticket, to restore the Democratic party's power base in the South and get himself reelected as a Democrat. On the other hand, if Southern whites were disenfranchised and blacks were allowed to vote, the Republicans, who even in 1860 had been a minority, could solidify their control of the government. This had a special appeal to Northern business and industry because it would result in favorable tariff and financial legislation.

The Radicals tried to thwart Johnson, first by encroaching on his power and then by trying to remove him through impeachment. The president fell into the trap laid for him by deliberately testing the Tenure of Office Act by firing the Radicals' ally Secretary of War Edwin M. Stanton. There was no vice president, and if Johnson were ousted, Senator Ben Wade of Ohio, a leading Radical and president pro tem of the Senate, would replace him.

No one was certain of the outcome of the battle. Johnson's opponents could count on thirty-five votes, but with the votes of two-thirds of the senators needed to impeach, they were one short of a conviction. The pressure on the individual members was intense as both sides lobbied to win the key vote or to block the other side from gaining it. Threats of retaliation and physical violence were bandied about. There had even been talk of kidnapping several of Johnson's supporters to keep them from voting.

When the name of Iowa senator James W. Grimes, partially paralyzed by a recent stroke, was called, the chief justice suggested that he remain in his seat, but the haggard Grimes painfully pulled himself to his feet and voted, "Not guilty."

Up to this point the tally showed twenty-four votes to convict, but it was clear that the impeachers were still one vote short of a two-thirds majority. The outcome would hinge on the uncommitted vote of Senator Edmund G. Ross of Kansas. All eyes were fixed on him. Kansas was a Radical state, and the newly elected Ross had been warned that if he did not vote for conviction, his promising political career would be finished. Throughout the early voting, he sat at his desk abstractedly tearing slips of paper into smaller pieces, and the floor about him was littered with debris. When the clerk finally called his name, he rose and more scraps fluttered from his lap. The question was put, and even the chief justice leaned forward to catch the reply.

"Not guilty," said Ross in a slight, conversational tone.

There was a sound like air being sucked out of the chamber, while groans rose from the Radicals. The final tally was 35 to 19, one vote short of conviction. Seven Republican moderates had joined the Democrats in voting to acquit Johnson, and the first—and only—attempt to remove a president by impeachment had failed. Johnson served out the remainder of his term in a sort of limbo, and when it ended ten months later, he returned home to Tennessee. In 1875, he was elected to the Senate, the first former president to serve there. Johnson saw this as a vindication, but the verdict of history has been less favorable.[1]

No presidential reputation has fluctuated more dramatically than that of Andrew Johnson.[2] In his lifetime and for years afterward, he was regarded with odium and contempt because his pro-Southern Reconstruction policies were seen as a betrayal of all for which the Civil War had been fought. Later, however, scholars refurbished the image of Lincoln's rough-hewn successor into that of a defender of the constitutional principle of separation of powers. A Supreme Court ruling in 1926 overturning the Tenure of Office Act added to Johnson's luster. Also, any means, including violence, were viewed by some observers as acceptable to "redeem" the prostrate South from the clutches of the Radicals, their carpetbagger allies, and the ignorant ex-slaves they were using as pawns.*

But in the wake of the civil rights revolution of the 1960s—called the Second Reconstruction—the pendulum has swung the other way. Now, Johnson is viewed as a white supremacist whose attempts to preserve the South as "a white man's country" undermined Reconstruction and condemned black Americans to a century of racism and repression. Because of this he belongs on my list of America's worst presidents.

Yet, in many ways, Johnson was an admirable man. He rose to the White House from a background even more Dickensian in its bleakness than that of the martyred Lincoln. Born poor, the child of illiterate tavern servants, he was the only president of the United States who never went to school a day in his life. Apprenticed at the age of thirteen to a tailor, he taught himself to read and write. He pulled himself up by the bootstraps through the rough-and-tumble of Tennessee and national politics and rose from alderman, state legislator, congressman, governor, U.S. senator, and military governor of Tennessee to vice president.

Unhappily, Johnson was unfitted by temperament and personality to deal with the monumental responsibilities thrust upon him by Lincoln's death. As Eric Foner, the preeminent modern historian of Reconstruction, has observed, the post–Civil War presidency "required tact, flexibility, and sensitivity to the nuances of public opinion—qualities Lincoln possessed in abundance, but Johnson lacked."[3] Rigid and dour, he was a lonely, suspicious, and stubborn man, intolerant of crit-

---

*The most famous expression of this view was D. W. Griffith's classic 1915 film, *The Birth of a Nation*, which was shown in the White House and supposedly hailed by Woodrow Wilson, who grew up in the post–Civil War South, as "like writing history with lightning."

In 1942, in the movie *Tennessee Johnson*, Van Heflin portrayed Johnson in heroic dimensions.

icism. He lacked Lincoln's political skills and keen understanding of Northern public opinion. Unlike Lincoln, he did not grow in office and was unable to bend to political realities that conflicted with his own ideas and aims. Johnson's presidency is a story of lost opportunities.

Even more important, although Johnson supported emancipation during the war—not out of any sympathy for the slaves but to break the power of the slavocracy—he was an uncompromising racist. Frederick Douglass detected in him "a bitter contempt" for blacks.*[4] For his part, Johnson saw Douglass as a dangerous incendiary. As the self-proclaimed champion of the poor white farmers and workingmen of the South, Johnson condemned the old planter class, upon whom he blamed secession, but saw no role for blacks in shaping Reconstruction or the South's future and suggested they be encouraged to emigrate to other countries. "Damn the Negroes!" he declared. "I am fighting those traitorous aristocrats, their masters!"[5]

While he was undeniably a man of integrity and courage, devoted to the Union and the Constitution as he saw them, Johnson's impatience, rigidity, lack of self-control, ill-temper, and sometime boorishness proved his undoing. Some historians praise the Tennessean for strengthening the presidency by preventing a coup by the congressional Radicals even though he was nearly thrown out of office for his efforts. In reality, he left behind a presidency much weaker than the office he had inherited from Lincoln. The hollow triumph of surviving impeachment hardly compensates for the woes visited upon millions of Americans, white and black, because of his blunders.

Johnson's defenders have created the myth that he was "crucified" in place of Lincoln. Johnson helped midwife this legend himself when he declared in 1866 that "if my predecessor had lived, the vials of wrath would have poured out upon him." Johnson also claimed that his plan was the same as that espoused by Lincoln before his death. Nearly a

---

*Johnson in his December 1867 annual message to Congress insisted that blacks possessed less "capacity for government than any other race of people. No independent government of any form has ever been successful in their hands. On the contrary, whenever they have been left to their own devices, they have shown a constant tendency to relapse into barbarism." Eric Foner calls this "probably the most blatantly racist pronouncement ever to appear in an official state paper of an American President." *Reconstruction*, 180.

century later, President Truman, an amateur historian who had many of the same flinty characteristics as the tailor from Tennessee, rated him a great president. "If Lincoln had lived, he would have done no better than Johnson," Truman declared.[6]

"Nothing could be further from the truth," asserts Hans L. Trefousse, a recent Johnson biographer.[7] While Lincoln might have had trouble with Congress, which was already trying to reassert its power following the end of the Civil War, as a victorious wartime leader and unquestioned head of his party, he would have fared better than Johnson. Johnson was merely an accidental president and not even a member of the Republican party. Lincoln was a shrewd politician and the supreme pragmatist. While adhering firmly to fundamental principles, he was a past master of political maneuvering and infighting. He was hardly likely to have gotten himself impeached.

While it is true that during the war Lincoln had proposed to restore the seceded states to the Union after only 10 percent of their prewar voters pledged to accept the end of slavery and took an oath of allegiance, this was strictly a wartime plan designed to hasten a Union victory. If even only a few states accepted his plan, it would be a blow to the Confederacy, he reasoned. As early as 1864, the Radicals opposed Lincoln's "10 Percent Plan" as too lenient and failing to protect the rights of black Americans.

But the breach was not irreparable. Lincoln and the Radicals worked together for approval of the Thirteenth Amendment, which abolished slavery. Soon after, they cooperated in creating the Freedmen's Bureau, an agency designed to protect the legal rights of the freed slaves and to provide them with assistance during the difficult transformation from slavery to freedom. What Lincoln would have done if he had not been assassinated is an unresolved question. Nevertheless, there are signs that his attitude toward the former Confederate states was becoming more stringent. Just before his murder, he revoked a plan to convene the Virginia legislature to take the state out of the Confederacy and proposed limited black suffrage in Louisiana, which had been occupied by Union troops since 1862.

The two men's views of the freedmen's rights were also at variance. Johnson held the deep-seated antipathy to blacks common to most

Southern poor whites, while Lincoln took a more positive view of the prospects of the ex-slaves. In his last speech, just a few days before his death, he endorsed the idea of giving the vote to literate, responsible blacks and those who had served in the Union army. That he would have allowed the freedmen to be left to the mercies of their former masters seems unlikely. "Johnson had no such inhibitions," notes Trefousse.

Paradoxically, the Radicals originally looked with favor upon Johnson when he assumed Lincoln's place in the White House. Throughout the war, he had strenuously insisted upon stern retribution against the rebel leaders, and the Radicals thought him one of themselves. On April 15, 1865, the new president's first day in office, a group of Radicals led by Ben Wade called upon the new president, who received them cordially.

"Johnson, we have faith in you," Wade declared. "By the gods, there will be no trouble now in running the government."

"Judge of my policy by the past," Johnson told the group. "Everybody knows what that is. I hold this: Robbery is a crime; rape is a crime; *treason* is a *crime* and must be punished. . . . Treason must be made infamous and traitors punished."[8]

Yet within a few months Johnson adopted a more lenient policy toward the South. What inspired this startling change? The answer lies in his experience, personality, and outlook.

"I have grappled with the gaunt and haggard monster called hunger," Andrew Johnson declared in later life, and it was the starkest truth.[9] The son of Jacob and Mary Johnson, both illiterate tavern servants, he was born on December 29, 1808, in a two-room shack in Raleigh, North Carolina. Jacob Johnson came from a family of yeoman farmers in Amelia County in southern Virginia, but they fell on hard times and lost their land. Following a period of aimless wandering, he settled in Raleigh, where he became a porter and odd-jobs man at a tavern. Honest and reliable, he was appointed city constable and rang the town bell for weddings, funerals, and public announcements—but as a poor white was at the bottom of the social ladder.

On September 9, 1801, he signed with his "mark" the bond required to obtain a license to marry Mary McDonough, whom everyone called

Polly, and was a servant at the same tavern. He was twenty-three; Polly was eighteen. Andrew had just turned three when his father died and was buried in the local "citizens' cemetery," which was a potter's field by another name. Left penniless, Polly tried to feed and clothe Andrew and an older brother, William, by taking in sewing and washing. The boys ran wild, for free schools did not exist in Raleigh and there was no money for a private academy. Andrew's lowly position left deep scars upon him. Upon one occasion, he and some other boys were run off land owned by a local aristocrat, who had his black coachman whip the "poor white trash" back to their shanties.

In 1822, Andrew was apprenticed to James J. Selby, a Raleigh tailor to whom William had already been indentured. This, at least, would provide the boy with upkeep until he was twenty-one and teach him a trade. Although deprived of books and schooling, Andrew discovered a zest for learning. Public-spirited citizens came to Selby's shop to read to the tailors as they sat cross-legged busy with needle and thread. One visitor read from a collection of great speeches, which so fascinated the boy that he was given it. Leafing through the book after his fifteen-hour-a-day stints in the shop were over, he slowly taught himself to read.

Two years later, the Johnson brothers got into a scrape with a neighbor and fled Raleigh. Selby ran an advertisement in a local newspaper offering a reward of $10 for the return of Andrew, whom he described as having "a dark complexion, black hair, eyes, and habits." The boys walked fifty miles to Carthage, where Andrew obtained employment as a journeyman tailor. Fearing apprehension, he moved on to Laurens, South Carolina. All the while, Andrew read everything he could get his hands on and taught himself to write. A year later, he returned to Raleigh in an effort to persuade Selby to end the indenture, but the tailor refused. Johnson decided to strike out for the West. With his mother and their few belongings piled into a two-wheel cart pulled by a blind pony, he crossed the Great Smokies into East Tennessee.

For a while, Johnson plied his trade in various towns, including the mountain village of Greeneville, then moved on. In March 1827, after the local tailor had died, he returned to Greeneville, where he rented a shop and posted the sign A. JOHNSON TAILOR over the door. Two months later, at the age of eighteen, he married Eliza McCardle, a pretty brunette two years younger, to whom he had been attracted on his first visit to the town. Eliza's father, a shoemaker, had died, and she and her mother supported themselves by making quilts.

The couple lived behind the shop, and while her husband cut and sewed, Eliza, who had a good elementary education, read aloud and patiently tutored him in reading, writing, and simple arithmetic. The Johnsons had five children, but in middle age Eliza developed "slow consumption" and was a semi-invalid for the rest of her life. Even though they were often separated for lengthy periods, their marriage, which lasted nearly fifty years, was happy. "Two souls and minds merged in one," observed a friend.

Johnson was a skilled tailor, industrious and prompt with deliveries, and his customers soon included some of Greeneville's more affluent citizens. "My work never ripped away," he proudly declared years later. Before long, business was so good he hired an assistant. His thirst for self-improvement was unabated, and he joined a debating society at Greeneville College. Every Friday evening, Johnson locked the door of his shop and walked the four miles to the school, where he pitted his wits against the students in argument over political and philosophical questions. The shop also became a gathering place for some of the younger, more assertive self-employed tradesmen, or "mechanics" as they were then known. Responding to the democratizing changes that led to the election of Andrew Jackson to the presidency, they were dissatisfied with their submerged status in the community.

From these informal meetings and the debating society, it was an easy jump into local politics. In 1828, Johnson was elected alderman with the support of the mechanics, and six years later he was so well regarded by his fellow citizens that he was elected mayor of Greeneville. In 1835, they sent him to Nashville, to represent them in the state legislature, ostensibly as a Democrat but in reality following his own star. There, he blundered for the first time in his nascent political career. Semifrontier East Tennessee was badly in need of improved transportation, but Johnson opposed the extension of a railroad line into the area because it would put small inns and cattle drovers out of business. The people of his district did not appreciate his explanation, and he lost the next election.

Two years later, lesson learned, Johnson was reelected as assembly-man and then, having formally proclaimed himself a Democrat, was elected in 1843 to Congress, where he served five consecutive terms. In Washington, most of his efforts were devoted to passage of a homestead bill that would give 160 acres of the public domain to the head of any family who settled on it for five years. Johnson's fellow Southerners, who opposed the creation of more free states, blocked the proposal. He supported the Mexican War, opposed the abolition of slavery in the District of Columbia, and as a gadfly, denounced what he called extravagant expenditures for the Smithsonian Institution and West Point.

Taking offense, Jefferson Davis, of Mississippi, a graduate of the military academy, sneered on the floor of the House, "Can a blacksmith or tailor construct . . . bastioned fieldworks?" Johnson, proud of having made his own way, responded heatedly: "I do not forget it that I am a mechanic. I am proud to own it. Neither do I forget that Adam was a tailor and sewed fig leaves, or that our Saviour was the son of a carpenter."

By now, however, Johnson was a well-to-do businessman and professional politician rather than a simple tailor. He owned considerable real estate, including a farm where his mother lived, several slaves, and a handsome house on Greeneville's main street, and was addressed as Colonel Johnson, having risen to that rank in the militia. Black eyes, a large head, and thickset shoulders all gave force to a harsh voice when he lashed out at opponents. Often tactless and outspoken in debate, he sometimes got carried away and argued with members of his audience.

Unable to defeat Johnson at the polls, the Whigs gerrymandered him out of his congressional seat in 1852, but the maneuver backfired. He returned home to be promptly elected governor of Tennessee in a spirited campaign in which his opponents accused him of demagoguery—and with good reason. Political combat was personal battle to Johnson. Compromise was alien to his nature. Glorying in his rise from the masses, he was driven by a need to avenge himself against the rich, the well-born, and the educated for the hardships and slights of his boyhood. An opponent described him as a man "who cuts when he does cut not with a razor but a case knife."[10] Appealing to those like himself, whom he called "plebeians," he said they were the true foundation of society, while the overbearing, self-styled upper class in their fine mansions were an "illegitimate, swaggering, bastard, scrub aristocracy."

Johnson assured the small farmers and tradesmen they could count on him to uphold their interests and that the Constitution was the Bible and Jefferson and Jackson the prophets of the only true political religion. Like his mentors, he coupled his devotion to basic democracy with an unshakable belief in the inferiority of black Americans. God himself had created the differences between the races, according to Johnson, and he bitterly denounced the efforts of abolitionists to outlaw slavery, an institution he saw as vital to the Southern way of life.[11]

Johnson's major accomplishment as governor was the establishment of Tennessee's first tax-supported public school system, although for the most part his initiatives were blocked by the Whigs. Nevertheless, he won reelection in 1855, even though he had spoken out against the Know-Nothings and the tide of anti-Catholic prejudice sweeping the nation, hardly a popular move in a state where rock-ribbed Protestant fundamentalism reigned supreme.* Two years later, the Democrats recaptured control of the legislature and awarded him a prize he had long coveted by electing him to the U.S. Senate. The once-penniless runaway was now numbered among the nation's elite.

In the Senate, Johnson preached economy in government, defended slavery, and again championed his homestead bill with the hope that it would propel him into a vice-presidential or presidential nomination. Despite continued opposition from his fellow Southern Democrats, the proposal was approved by both houses of Congress with Northern support, only to be vetoed by President James Buchanan, who was ever ready to please the South. The Homestead Act finally became law in 1862, after Southern opponents had left the Senate.

The secession crisis soon overrode every other issue. As a Southerner opposed to the breakup of the Union, Johnson saw himself as a com-

---

*Nativism, or antiforeign sentiment, was rife in mid-nineteenth-century America as a result of a rising tide of immigration, particularly of Irish Catholics and Germans. Similar to the anti-immigrant hysteria of our own day, it expressed itself in the American or Know-Nothing party—so called because its members, if asked for the party's beliefs, were instructed to answer, "I know nothing." While the party was especially strong in the cities, nativism also overflowed into rural areas.

promise candidate for the Democratic presidential nomination in 1860. The Tennessee delegation at the Democratic convention in Charleston loyally supported him as the state's favorite son for thirty-six ballots, but the convention broke up without selecting a nominee after most of the Southern delegates walked out. Northern Democrats later supported Senator Stephen A. Douglas for president while Southerners backed John C. Breckinridge. Johnson stumped for the latter. But asked what he would do if Southern fire-eaters used the election of Abraham Lincoln, the Republican candidate, as a pretext to secede, he replied, "When the crisis comes, I will be found standing by the Union."

Between Lincoln's election and inauguration on March 4, 1861, Johnson, alone among Southern lawmakers, denounced secession. Although he believed in states' rights and defended slavery, as a good Jacksonian he stood for the indivisibility of the Union. In slashing speeches on the Senate floor, he condemned the disunionists as traitors and accused them of wishing to destroy not only the Union but political democracy as well. "I love the Constitution and swear that it and the Union shall be saved," he declared. ". . . Senators, my blood, my existence, I would give to save the Union." In the North his words were acclaimed; in the South he was hanged in effigy.

Following Fort Sumter and Lincoln's call for volunteers to suppress the rebellion, Johnson raced home to make a last desperate attempt to save Tennessee for the Union. Hostile demonstrators and threats against his life confronted him, and he began his speeches by slamming down a pistol on the podium for all to see. Although the mountain and valley people voted against secession, the richer and more populous western area took the state out of the Union. Now branded a traitor, Johnson returned to Washington, where he was the only Southern senator to spurn the Confederacy and remain loyal.

Johnson supported Lincoln's policies and pressed for the deliverance of east Tennessee, where Union sympathizers were being persecuted— among them his own wife and youngest child, who were turned out of their home.* Early in 1862, after General Ulysses S. Grant won control

---

*Two of Johnson's sons were serving with the Union army, and his son-in-law was fighting as a guerrilla in the Tennessee mountains.

of part of west Tennessee, Lincoln named Johnson military governor of the state with the rank of brigadier general. Virtual dictator of Tennessee, Johnson moved to rid the state of Confederate influence. He dismissed officeholders unwilling to swear allegiance to the United States, closed down anti-Union newspapers, and removed pro-Confederate preachers from their pulpits.

At Johnson's urging, Lincoln agreed to exempt Tennessee from the effect of the Emancipation Proclamation in an attempt to influence slaveholders to return to the Union, and it was the only rebel state to be totally exempt. The war swung back and forth, and in the fall of 1862, Nashville was besieged by Confederate troops. Johnson stubbornly rejected all suggestions that he evacuate the city. "I am no military man," he growled, "but anyone who talks of surrender I will shoot." Toward the end of the war, he rammed through an amendment to the state constitution abolishing slavery and established a pro-Union civil government.

Favorably impressed with Johnson's record, Lincoln supported him in 1864 for vice president on a National Union ticket to balance it with a Unionist Southern Democrat. The campaign was grueling, and at its end Johnson was exhausted and weak from a severe bout of typhoid. He arrived in Washington for the inauguration still feeling the effects of his illness. Eliza had remained in Greeneville, and the night before the inauguration, he imbibed a great deal of liquor while celebrating with friends.

Inauguration Day—March 4, 1865—was dark and rainy. Johnson stopped by the office of the outgoing vice president, Hannibal Hamlin, before the ceremony. Feeling unsteady, he asked for some whiskey and bolted several glasses before being escorted into the Senate chamber. The combination of poor ventilation, the heat generated by the crowd, and the whiskey quickly hit him. The result was a rambling, maudlin, almost incoherent harangue loaded with such statements as "I'm a-gonna for to tell you—here today; yes, I'm a-going for to tell you all that I am a plebeian! I glory in it; I am a plebeian!" Some of the spectators tittered. Lincoln's head drooped in humiliation. Hamlin finally nudged Johnson to stop and the ordeal was over.[12]

Fleeing in embarrassment, Johnson took refuge at the home of friends outside Washington and did not return to preside over the Senate until it was near adjournment. His absence gave rise to rumors that he was continuing his drunken binge, and some senators demanded his resignation. In fact, like many Americans of the day, Johnson drank but was not an alcoholic. Lincoln had made certain of that by having an agent check on the prospective vice-presidential nominee before putting him on the ticket. "I have known Andy Johnson for many years," the president told a worried cabinet member. "He made a bad slip the other day, but you need not be scared; Andy ain't a drunkard."[13]

Shortly before ten-thirty on the night of April 14, 1865, Vice President Johnson was awakened by heavy pounding on the door of his suite in the Kirkwood House, a second-rate hotel on Pennsylvania Avenue. Sleepily opening the door to a friend, he learned the dreadful news: President Lincoln had been shot at nearby Ford's Theater! Overwhelmed by shock, Johnson swayed, and the two men clung together for mutual support, neither able to speak. In that blinding instant, Andrew Johnson was whirled from obscurity into the principal role in a tumultuous drama.

More men arrived, bringing fresh news and rumors. The unconscious Lincoln was dying in a rooming house across the street from the theater; Secretary of State William H. Seward had been slashed in his bed and was not expected to live. Murder stalked the city and some awful conspiracy seemed afoot.* Following an all-night vigil, the mournful sound of church bells tolled the death of Lincoln at 7.30 A.M. Not long after, Johnson took the oath as president of the United States from Chief Justice Chase in a parlor at the Kirkwood. Lincoln's cabinet, including Seward, who had survived his wounds, remained in their places.

With Congress in recess until December 1865, Johnson inaugurated his own version of Reconstruction. Southerners, Radicals, and moder-

---

*John Wilkes Booth, Lincoln's assassin, had assigned George Atzerodt, a German-born carriage maker, to murder Johnson. But Atzerodt lost his nerve after renting a room at the Kirkwood directly above that of the vice president and went out and got drunk. He was later captured and was among the four conspirators hanged. On April 26, 1865, Booth was cornered by federal troops in a Virginia tobacco barn and killed.

ate Republicans were shocked by his leniency. Johnson demanded neither black suffrage nor any other change in the Southern political or social order. Despite his previous talk of punishing traitors, no mass treason trials occurred. Jefferson Davis spent two years in prison but was never put on trial and would die in bed at age eighty-one. Alexander H. Stephens, the Confederate vice president, spent a brief time in prison, later returned to Congress, and became governor of Georgia.

Rather than imposing rigorous penalties upon the South, Johnson's plan offered a pardon to all Southern whites who took an oath of allegiance, except Confederate leaders and wealthy planters.* Provisional governors were to be appointed and state conventions held to draft new constitutions, with the delegates elected solely by whites. Except for requirements that they abolish slavery and repudiate secession and the Confederate debt, these new state governments were granted a free hand. The question of black suffrage was ignored.

In enunciating these plans, Johnson had committed several egregious blunders from which he never recovered. Like a true Jacksonian, he was convinced that the chief executive had primary responsibility for reconstructing the Union, and Congress should have no role in it. But Congress, flexing its muscles now that the war was over, was not about to give him a free hand. He also failed to recognize that Northern public opinion was dead set against receiving the South back into the Union without some solid evidence that the Confederates had accepted defeat. Moreover, Johnson brushed aside the fact that even though he was a Democrat, he had come to power on what was basically a Republican ticket and owed, if not loyalty, at least some consideration to the views of those who had elected him.

Southerners, who had emerged from the war physically, economically, and psychologically devastated and feared severe punishment, were delighted by Johnson's lenient plan for Reconstruction. But the Radicals were outraged by the president's abandonment of the rights of the freedmen and were worried about the direction of his policy. With considerable justification, they felt he had deceived them. Navy Secretary Gideon Welles has noted that it was Johnson's usual habit to listen

*All but a handful later received individual pardons.

while others talked and, even if he disagreed, was "disinclined to controvert."[14] Thus, the Radicals may have mistaken his silence when they had urged him to grant suffrage to the blacks as acquiescence, when, in reality, Johnson opposed the idea. But most Northerners wished only unity and peace and, unconcerned about the Radicals' fixation on black rights, were willing to give Johnson's plan a fair trial.

Ideology and politics played the major role in Johnson's unexpected turnabout. First, he believed the Southern states had never been out of the Union because under the Constitution only individuals, not states, could commit treason; thus there was no need for reconstruction—only restoration. Black suffrage was regarded as a minor issue that should be left to the states, which, he contended, had the right to establish qualifications for voting, anyway. In the meantime, as he told Sir Frederick Bruce, the British minister, the freedmen needed to be "kept in order" while receiving the "care and civilizing influence of dependence on the white man."[15]

Second, as a self-proclaimed "plebeian," Johnson's anger was directed at the Southern aristocrats, not the entire South, and he sought to transfer political power in the region from the planters to Unionist yeoman farmers and mechanics. He assumed that when elections were held for legislators, governors, congressmen, and senators, they would replace the planters in power. Third, as a Southerner and a Democrat, Johnson was uncomfortable with the Northern prewar abolitionists and postwar Radicals who formed the backbone of the Republican party. He planned to use the power and prestige of the presidency to reshuffle the political deck and, by organizing a new party of Northern and Southern moderates, deal himself the winning hand in 1868—four more years in the White House.

The differences between Johnson and the Radicals were muted until December 1865, when Congress reconvened. In his first annual report, the president proclaimed that Reconstruction had been completed; every former Confederate state had met his qualifications for restoration to the Union. In reality, however, there were ominous signs of continued rebellion in the South, where efforts were being made by whites to forge a new class structure to replace the shattered world of slavery. Instead of transferring power to Unionist yeomen in the elections, as the president had expected, Southern voters defiantly, by and large, returned the old elite to power.

The newly established state governments, in response to the demands of the planters that the ex-slaves be forced back to the plantations, enacted Black Codes that denied the freed slaves their rights and human dignity. Freedmen were required to sign labor contracts with their former masters; those who were unemployed were declared vagrants and could be arrested, fined, and rented out to white landowners. In Florida, blacks who broke labor contracts could be whipped and sold for one year's labor. Restrictions were also placed upon the occupations open to blacks, and they were unable to own land. Open violence aimed at keeping blacks in line flared in some parts of the South.

These restrictions dealt a severe blow to the efforts of blacks to effect their own liberation. In certain areas of the South, such as the Sea Islands, the former slaves had, in the wake of the victorious Yankee armies, seized control of the plantations they had tilled, broken them up into individual plots, and tried to become self-sustaining farmers. These fragile efforts by the freedmen to achieve a secure political and economic base for themselves and their families were quashed by the new white-dominated regimes.

Years later, some Southerners, such as former Confederate treasury secretary Christopher G. Memminger, acknowledged that Southerners ought to have been more repentant and adopted "a different course as to the Negroes" in 1865. But they had not done so, he said, because Andrew Johnson "held up before us the hope of a 'white man's government.' "[16]

Unhappy with the outcome of "Presidential Reconstruction," the Radicals called for the end of the white-only governments and the establishment of new regimes from which "rebels" were excluded and in which black men could vote. Presidential reconstruction "is no reconstruction," said one New Yorker. Nor were the Radicals prepared to seat the newly elected Southern senators and representatives, who were largely Democrats eager to grasp control of Congress from the Republican party. Most Republicans, however, were moderates, not Radicals. Although they considered the president's plan flawed, they wished to work with him to modify it. Johnson would have been wise to accommodate the moderates, but relishing a fight, he ignored congressional and popular opinion. Radicals and moderates soon joined in support of a Joint Committee on Reconstruction to investigate conditions in the South.

Quick to equate opposition with evil intent, Johnson reacted with biting personal attacks on his critics. Speaking to a crowd that had come to the White House to serenade him on Washington's Birthday, he branded the Joint Committee a "cabal." Radical leaders such as Senator Charles Sumner of Massachusetts and Representative Thaddeus Stevens of Pennsylvania were called as much a threat to the Union as the secessionists. Johnson followed this performance by vetoing a bill extending the life of the Freedmen's Bureau and a civil rights bill designed to give the freed slaves citizenship and legal protection.

Passed by an overwhelming majority of both houses of Congress, the civil rights bill was described by one congressman as "one of the most important bills ever presented to the House for its action." While it left the new Southern governments in place, it voided the Black Codes and empowered the federal government to guarantee the principle of equality under the law. Johnson vetoed the bills on grounds that they threatened to centralize power in the federal government at the expense of the states. Moreover, he insisted that the blacks did not deserve citizenship. Shocked, the moderates voted with the Radicals in April 1866 to override the presidential veto.

A break between the president and the Republican majority in Congress was inevitable. Moderates now refused to accept Johnson's conservative states' rights interpretation of the Constitution and regarded him as a major obstacle to restoring loyalty in the Southern states. On the other hand, Johnson saw Congress—Radicals and moderates were all the same to him—as the enemy. He stubbornly ignored the advice of some of his cabinet to be more flexible, and more accommodating to the wishes of Congress. "I am right. I know I am right," he told his private secretary. "I am damned if I do not adhere to it."[17]

From this point, open warfare existed between Johnson and the Republican majority. Brushing the president's plan aside, Congress proceeded to adopt its own plan for Reconstruction. The key element was the Fourteenth Amendment, which would fix in the Constitution, beyond the reach of presidential vetoes and shifting electoral majorities, the legacy of the Civil War as understood by the Republicans. States were forbidden to deny *any* citizen "due process" or "equal protection" of the laws, although it stopped short of giving blacks the vote. Blinded by anger and a stubborn disregard for political reality, Johnson egged on the Southern states to reject the amendment. Such irresponsible actions convinced most Northerners that he was no longer a credible leader whom they could trust to reconstruct the Union.

Presidential credibility was also strained by the open violence in the South that paralleled the struggle between Congress and Johnson. Night riders such as the Ku Klux Klan were terrorizing blacks and their white supporters. Bloody race riots erupted in Memphis and New Orleans; rampaging whites engaged in pillage, arson, rape, and murder against blacks. The Radicals assailed Johnson for failing to use military force to curb the violence.

The embattled Johnson resorted to what had always worked for him in the past—a direct appeal to the people. Hoping to bring Northern public opinion to his side, he embarked by special train on a "swing around the circle." From Washington to upstate New York to Missouri and back to Washington, he delivered a series of fiery speeches urging voters to elect congressional candidates committed to his program.* It was a dismal failure. Johnson made wild charges that the Radicals were plotting to assassinate him. Hecklers greeted him at every stop, and the hot-tempered, impulsive president could not ignore their taunts. His speeches turned into shouting matches; his meetings into near riots.

"Hang Jeff Davis!" someone shouted.

"Hang Charles Sumner!" Johnson shouted back. "Hang Thad Stevens!"

Unused to the spectacle of a president on the stump, Americans were shocked, and Johnson's opponents pounced on his intemperate remarks. *The Nation* characterized them as "vulgar, egotistical and occasionally profane." Some writers accused him of being drunk, and James

---

*The "swing around the circle" was the first presidential whistle-stop campaign in American history.

Russell Lowell of the *North American Review* called the trip "an indecent orgy." Republicans opposed to the president won two-thirds majorities in both houses—a veto-proof Congress—and could thank Andrew Johnson for their success.

Traditionally, presidents have added to their prestige by foreign policy triumphs, and Secretary of State Seward, even though he never fully recovered from the wounds he suffered on the night of Lincoln's assassination, served Johnson well. While the United States had been occupied by the Civil War, Napoleon III of France had sent troops to Mexico and placed an Austrian archduke, Maximilian, on the Mexican throne. With Johnson's approval, Seward moved to reassert the Monroe Doctrine and sent fifty thousand soldiers to the Mexican border. Getting the message, the French pulled out, leaving Maximilian to the tender mercies of the Mexicans, who promptly shot him.

Seward's most ambitious coup was the purchase of Alaska from the Russians for $7.2 million after only three weeks of negotiation. The move was unpopular—Alaska was called Seward's Folly—but through the force of his personality, the secretary persuaded Senator Sumner, chairman of the Senate Foreign Relations Committee, to approve the deal. Johnson failed, however, to make the most of these accomplishments—and Reconstruction would not go away.

Life in the Johnson White House was gloomy. In fact, one aide described the moody, angry, and unsmiling Johnson as "the Grim Presence." Eliza Johnson was not well and spent most of her time in her bedroom, so her daughter, Martha, presided as official hostess over what little entertaining was done. Robert Johnson, one of the president's sons, was an alcoholic and was drunk most of the time. In desperation, Johnson appealed to Navy Secretary Welles to find a place for Robert on a vessel assigned to a long cruise. When it was time for Robert to join his ship, he disappeared on a spree. The president's ne'er-do-well brother, William, continually pestered him for money and a place on the government payroll.

Outraged by Johnson's intransigence and the refusal of Southerners to recognize the realities of emancipation, Congress seized control of Reconstruction. In March 1867, the Republicans overrode a presidential veto to enact a new Reconstruction Act, which overturned the existing state governments. The South was placed under military rule, many former Confederate officials were temporarily barred from voting or holding office, and "loyal" state governments were organized. The Southern states would be readmitted to the Union only after they had ratified the Fourteenth Amendment and given blacks the vote, decreed the Radicals.

The battles, agonies, and turmoils of the Johnson years did not end with the passage of the Reconstruction Act. Some Radicals proposed as early as October 1866 that the president be impeached, and for a year a House committee had been trying, without success, to gather evidence to support such an action. Now, Johnson furnished the Radicals with the excuse they had so long been seeking. In an effort to shield their policy from presidential interference, the Radicals had pushed through the Tenure of Office Act, which prohibited the president from removing from office certain officials, including cabinet members, without the Senate's consent. Johnson, who was planning to dismiss Secretary of War Edwin M. Stanton, an ally of the Radicals, bridled at this as an unconstitutional restriction upon his authority.

Passion, not sense, ruled the air as Johnson and Congress dueled over his right to fire Stanton. The fight grew so bitter that some Radicals even claimed the president was implicated in Lincoln's murder. Although threatened with impeachment—"Let them impeach and be damned!" Johnson replied—he sought to oust Stanton from the War Department. A game of musical chairs followed. Stanton refused the president's demand for his resignation; Johnson suspended him and appointed General Grant in his place. Initially, Grant seemed to side with Johnson but, already hearing the siren song of the presidency in 1868, later reconsidered. He handed the keys to the war secretary's office to the senile and besotted adjutant general Lorenzo Thomas, who, to complete the circle, returned them to Stanton. Johnson accused Grant of selling out to the Radicals in return for their support for the Republican presidential nomination.

Johnson was attempting "to govern after he has lost the means to govern," noted General William T. Sherman. "He is like a general fighting without an army." Still insisting upon his right to replace a cabinet member, he notified the Senate on February 21, 1868, that he had removed Stanton and appointed Thomas in his place. But the wily Stanton barricaded himself in the War Department under heavy guard and defied every effort to force him out. The Radicals quickly closed in. Three days later, the House, by a lopsided 126-to-47 majority, voted to impeach Andrew Johnson for his alleged breach of the Tenure of Office Act.

Was Johnson guilty? Should he have been removed?

Thirty-five senators certainly thought so, and he narrowly escaped being the first American president to be ousted from office. The verdict of history—confirmed by the Supreme Court—is that the Tenure of Office Act was unconstitutional. Moreover, it would have been wrong to remove a chief executive primarily for political reasons. But Johnson owed his one-vote margin of victory* not to his virtues but to the unwillingness of some moderates to elevate Ben Wade to the presidency. Others feared that if the president was convicted, it would permanently alter the constitutional balance of power between the legislative and executive branches.

Nevertheless, Johnson had exhibited political ineptitude on a colossal scale. He had thrown away the power and goodwill left him by his predecessor and the Union victory, disrupted the political life of the entire nation, and in spite of himself, assisted materially in blocking the reconciliation of North and South. As one historian notes, his administration "is an object lesson in how not to generate public trust."[18]

Johnson's acquittal gave new hope to the South and preserved it as a "white man's country." Although Radical Reconstruction lasted until federal troops were withdrawn from the South in 1877, it was undermined by continued Southern resistance inspired by Johnson. "The eyes of the rebels sparkle like those of the fiery serpent," observed one Southern Unionist soon after the news of the failure to convict Johnson was received in the South.[19] With good reason, Thaddeus Stevens, among others, was deeply despondent about the future of the freedmen.

Full of fire and fight, Johnson spent the rest of his life seeking vindication. Guilty of self-deception—the occupational disease of presidents—he tried to win the Democratic presidential nomination in

---

*Several others were said to be ready to switch their votes to Johnson if necessary. See Foner, *Reconstruction*, 336.

1868, but failed. Southern Democrats might cheer his name, but Northerners did not trust him. Once out of the White House, Johnson returned to Tennessee to run for Congress in 1869. Beaten, he tried and lost again in 1872. Three years later, the Tennessee legislature, once again in the hands of the Democrats, elected him to the U.S. Senate by a single vote after fifty-four ballots.

On March 5, 1875, Johnson took his seat in the Senate—the first and to this day the only former president to do so. There were only a few familiar faces as he looked about. "I miss my old friends," he said sadly. "Fessenden, Fowler, Trumbull, Grimes, Henderson, Ross, all are gone." Gone indeed. Johnson had named six of the seven Republican moderates who sacrificed their political careers to vote for his acquittal.

Johnson did not have long to enjoy his triumph. On July 31, 1875, while visiting his daughter and grandchildren at Carter Station, Tennessee, he died of a stroke at the age of sixty-six. The former president was buried as he requested, wrapped in an American flag and with his head resting on a well-thumbed copy of the U.S. Constitution. But Andrew Johnson, by undermining Reconstruction, left a legacy of racial oppression behind him that troubled America for generations to come.

CHAPTER VII

FRANKLIN PIERCE

Nathaniel Hawthorne put it best. Upon learning that his good friend Franklin Pierce had been elected president in 1852, the author of *The Scarlet Letter* wrote him: "Frank, I pity you— indeed I do, from the bottom of my heart."[1] In reality, Hawthorne should have extended his sympathies to the people of the United States because the nation's fourteenth president was one of our worst chief executives. Although Pierce was handsome, genial, and good-natured, he was overly fond of the bottle and well beyond his depth in the sectional quagmire of the 1850s, a pleasant mediocrity at a time that demanded political giants in the White House. Instead, the nation got Pierce and then James Buchanan—and eventually a fratricidal civil war.

Few presidents are ranked lower by their successors. "Pierce was the best-looking president the White House ever had—but as president he ranks with Buchanan and Calvin Coolidge," said Harry Truman.[2] And Theodore Roosevelt called him "a small politician of low capacity and mean surroundings, proud to act as the servile tool of men worse than himself but also stronger and abler."[3]

Frank Pierce, as intimates called him, came to office as the stars of America's "Silver Age"—its second flowering of political greatness— were fading from the scene. Andrew Jackson, the greatest of all the presidents between George Washington and Abraham Lincoln, survived numerous duels and pitched battles to die peacefully in bed. Henry Clay, the Great Compromiser, had staved off disunion one final time in 1850 before dying. "Godlike," spellbinding Daniel Webster and John C. Calhoun, the paladin of states' rights, were also gone. And John Quincy

Adams, stricken in his humble seat in the House of Representatives, had been carried from the Capitol to die.

In contrast to this galaxy, Pierce was, with the exception of Jimmy Carter, one of the most obscure men ever elected president of the United States. Although he had served in both the House and Senate and was a lackluster political general in the Mexican War, he had been out of national politics for a decade when he was nominated by the Democrats in 1852. Scarcely known outside his native New Hampshire backwater where he was the state's Democratic boss, he was the darkest of dark horses. He owed his nomination to the fact that he angered no one—the lowest common denominator at a convention that had gone on for forty-nine ballots.

Pierce was so lacking in national stature that when he stopped in New York City on the way to Washington for his inauguration, he strolled down crowded Broadway without anyone recognizing him.[4] Even his neighbors in Concord, New Hampshire, were completely taken aback by the news of his nomination. "Wall, wall, dew tell!" said one man. "Frank Pierce for President! Neow Frank's a good fellow, I admit, and I wish him well. He made a good State's attorney, thar's no doubt abut that, and he made a fair Jedge, that's no denying that, and nobody kaint complain of him as a Congressman, but when it comes to the hull Yewnited States, I dew say that in my jedgment Frank Pierce is a-goin' to be *spread durned thin.*"[5]

Pierce's ailing wife, Jane, who hated politics, fainted at the news of his nomination. She had not been told he was seeking the presidency, and he swore to her that he had not actively sought it. She had refused to live in Washington during his Senate term because the climate affected her health, and he had resigned back in 1842 at her insistence after his drinking got out of hand. The depth of Jane Pierce's antipathy to her husband's political ambitions was so open that Bennie, the couple's eleven-year-old son, wrote her from school: "Edward brought the news . . . that Father is a candidate for the Presidency. I hope he won't be elected for I should not like to be at Washington and I know you would not either."[6]

Cynical Democratic party managers chose Pierce for the presidency primarily because he was a blank slate. Thus, the Young Hickory from the Granite Hills, as they dubbed him, would appeal to both Northern and Southern voters, none of whom knew what he stood for—if anything. The candidate's only assets were a total loyalty to the Democratic party, family political connections, and above all, charm and a striking appearance.[7] "My God!" exclaimed Richard Henry Dana, author of *Two Years Before the Mast,* in horror at Pierce's election. "A third-rate county politician . . . President of the United States!"[8] And Georgia congressman Robert Toombs described the new president as "a man without claims or qualifications, surrounded by [a] dishonest and dirty set of political gamesters."[9]

"Vain, showy and pliant," in the words of Connecticut editor Gideon Welles,[10] Pierce was weak and congenitally incapable of handling the presidency. He had little knowledge of issues, policies, or principles, or interest in them. Stronger men, with their own agendas, ran his administration. Rather than confront those with whom he disagreed, he preferred to preserve the peace by seeming to endorse whatever policy was presented to him whether he concurred or not. Men who left Pierce believing he agreed with them only to see him adopt a different course naturally accused him of duplicity.

Understanding little of the great events occurring around him, and without intellectual depth, Pierce fled from the harsh realities of life into alcohol and mystical religion. Lacking deep convictions and strong will, he was all bright surface. Most of his four years in office were spent playing factional politics designed to ensure his reelection—and he failed at even that. With the exception of William Howard Taft, few presidents have so thoroughly squandered the goodwill offered them at the beginning of their terms in such short time. Pierce also has the dubious distinction of being the only elected president refused renomination by his own party.

On first glance, Pierce seemed a highly engaging figure. At forty-eight he was the youngest man to become president until then. He had chiseled features, a proud bearing, and a great sweep of curly, dark hair, all of which made him one of the handsomest men ever to hold the office. Always conscious of his appearance, Pierce dressed richly even when working in his White House office, sometimes wearing a dazzling dressing gown lined with cherry-colored silk. People liked him—until they realized that nothing was behind the backslapping and the casual invitations to lunch and dinner except a careless goodwill.

The tragedy of Pierce's presidency is that it was the last chance to prevent the breakup of the Union before the nation was engulfed by the Civil War. Swept into office by the largest Electoral College majority since James Monroe and backed by big majorities in Congress, Pierce had the best opportunity of any president of the period to resolve the disruptive slavery question. If the storm that climaxed in war is likened to a hurricane, he came to the White House within its eye. To many Americans, the Compromise of 1850 seemed to have settled the major differences between North and South. Indeed, when Charles Sumner of Massachusetts arrived in the Senate in 1851, he was told, "You have come upon the scene too late, sir. There is nothing left to settle except petty, sectional disturbances over slavery."[11]

In reality, the political system of the founding fathers was unravelling. The president was supposed to represent all the people, but the fight over slavery was destroying the basis for national consensus—and Pierce crossed the line to become an open supporter of the South. Had he been more imaginative, he might have made a Jacksonian appeal to the common man by supporting a homestead act to provide cheap land to small farmers, a bill to create land-grant colleges open to all, and tariff reduction. Franklin Pierce lacked the character, the broad vision, and the political skills to meet this challenge. The blame does not rest solely upon his diffident shoulders. It partially belongs to a volatile political situation that made it impossible to elect candidates in 1852 and again in 1856 who were qualified to deal with the crisis. Only nonentities who angered no one could attract enough votes to win.

Legend has it that in antebellum times there was an Alabama congressman who periodically amused himself and his colleagues by turning a somersault or two on the House floor while proclaiming, "America is a great country! America is a great country!" This was carrying exuberance a bit far, but the United States was indeed growing at a breathtaking pace when Pierce was elected to the presidency. Railroads, steamboats, the telegraph, the reaper, the thresher, and new factories and iron mills were changing the face of the nation while radical ideas and religious ferment had thrown social institutions into an upheaval.[12]

Much of the rest of the world, with the exception of Brazil and Cuba, had outlawed human slavery. But the United States remained half-slave, half-free, in Abraham Lincoln's words "a house divided against itself." Large segments of the population of the North and West, caught up in the spirit of change, opposed slavery, while Southerners insisted just as vehemently that not only must their "peculiar institution" be allowed to flourish where it existed, but to spread into the territories because cotton exhausted the soil. If slavery did not expand, it would die. Sectional rivalries for political and economic power rather than moral abhorrence of slavery were the driving forces of the conflict at this time.

In 1820, the question of the expansion of slavery had been temporarily put to rest by the Missouri Compromise, an effort by Congress to defuse the conflict triggered by the request of Missouri for admission to the Union as a slave state. The United States then contained twenty-two states, evenly divided between slave and free. If Missouri came into the Union as a slave state, this balance would be upset. Following bitter argument, a compromise was put together by Henry Clay that admitted Missouri as a slave state, balanced by Maine, formerly part of Massachusetts, as a free state. Furthermore, slavery was to be forever excluded from the lands of the Louisiana Purchase north of latitude 36 degrees, 30 minutes.

The Missouri Compromise worked for nearly thirty years, until the end of the Mexican War, when the United States acquired vast new territories in the Southwest and along the Pacific rim where, under Mexican law, slavery was illegal. Until then, slavery had merely asserted its right to continue unmolested where it existed and had not overstepped the bounds of the Missouri Compromise. Now, Southerners demanded the right to expand into the new areas won with their blood. Texas had slavery as an independent nation, so she entered the Union as a slave state. But what about California, New Mexico, and Utah? Once again, the dying Clay came to the rescue with a compromise plan.

The Compromise of 1850 had several parts: it admitted California as a free state to balance Texas, granted territorial status to New Mexico,* included a fugitive slave law requiring federal authorities to assist in the return of escaped slaves to their owners, and abolished the slave trade, but not slavery, in the District of Columbia. The Utah and New Mexico territories were to be admitted as states with or without slavery as their constitutions prescribed. This agreement seemed to settle the volatile issue of the extension of slavery because a majority of both the Whig and Democratic parties supported it. But extremists on both sides did their best to keep the issue alive.

The fatal flaw in the compromise was the Fugitive Slave Law. Northerners gagged on it, and in many states lawmen refused to take any part in catching slaves; in fact, runaways were assisted in escaping, and the Northern states were honeycombed with "underground railroad" stations that sheltered fugitives. Opponents condemned slavery as a stench to the whole nation and looked forward to the day, as Lincoln put it, when "the hateful institution, like a reptile poisoning itself, will perish by its own infamy." Efforts to seize fugitives provoked riots, and slaveholders regarded the refusal of the Yankees to comply with the law as proof positive of a dangerous conspiracy against the South's institutions and way of life.

No one did more to fan these flames to fever heat than Harriet Beecher Stowe, a pious New England lady living in the border city of Cincinnati. Horrified by the Fugitive Slave Law, she wrote a novel, *Uncle Tom's Cabin,* which appeared in 1852, and quickly became the shining grail of the antislavery movement. Wildly successful, the book sold three hundred thousand copies in its first year, and a stage version was an immediate hit. *Uncle Tom's Cabin* painted such a harrowing picture of slavery that it aroused a demand for the end of the institution rather than mere prohibition of its expansion. Resistance to the Fugitive Slave Law mounted, and slave owners pursuing runaways into free territory were often menaced by angry mobs and were glad to return home unscathed even if empty-handed.

Pierce, on the other hand, a conservative Northern Democrat sym-

---

*New Mexico then included what are now the states of New Mexico, Arizona, and Nevada.

pathetic to the South—a "doughface" in the political parlance of the time—viewed abolitionists as a lunatic fringe. During his years in the House and Senate he was a boon companion of slaveholders and had no moral objections to slavery or its extension. To his mind, blacks were unfit for freedom or participation in a democratic society. The Constitution, he insisted, protected slavery, and he thought those who agitated against it were a threat not only to private property but to the Union itself. Like many Americans, he believed slavery would eventually disappear, but until then the interests of the slave owner had to be protected. Even though more and more citizens of the Northern states were demanding that the new territories and states be closed to slavery, Pierce blindly insisted upon enforcement of the Fugitive Slave Law. It was a prescription for disaster.

Franklin Pierce—the name was pronounced "purse" by the family—was born with a silver political spoon in his mouth.[13] Benjamin Pierce, his father, was plowing a field in his native Chelmsford, Massachusetts, when on April 19, 1775, word reached him of the fighting at Lexington and the beginning of the American Revolution. Walking away from his plow and team, the eighteen-year-old Pierce shouldered a fowling piece and joined the colonial army. He fought in almost every major battle from Bunker Hill to Yorktown, survived the rigors of Valley Forge, and rose from private to captain. Following the war, he moved to Hillsborough County, on the New Hampshire frontier, where he prospered as a farmer. He married, was widowed, and in 1790, married again to Anna Kendrick, of nearby Amherst, New Hampshire.

One of six children to live to maturity, the future president was born fittingly enough in a log hut near Hillsborough on November 23, 1804. Not long afterward, the family moved out of these cramped quarters into an impressive and spacious house in Hillsborough Lower Village. By then, "Squire" Pierce had become a leading political figure in the Granite State. He was a brigadier general in the militia, a delegate to the state constitutional convention, and a member of the governor's council for a number of years. A staunch supporter of Thomas Jefferson and his Democratic-Republican party, he refused the offer of a colonel's commission in the new regular army raised by President John Adams, a Federalist. He served as sheriff of Hillsborough County for a number of years and was twice elected governor of New Hampshire.

The elder Pierce dominated his son's early life. Frank was an eager listener at the fireside to the tales of the glorious struggle for liberty related by the old soldier and was awed when his father wore his full regalia to review the militia. Of his mother, Frank recalled that "she was most affectionate and tender, strong in many points and weak in some. But always weak on the side of kindness and deep affection." He inherited her gaiety and fondness of fine clothes as well as two of her weaknesses—a tendency toward depression and alcoholism.

The high point of Pierce's childhood was the War of 1812. Unlike many New Englanders who were Federalists and opposed to the war, his father actively supported it. Two older brothers enlisted in the army as did a brother-in-law, and there was great excitement when letters arrived from them. Hillsborough was on the road to the Canadian border, and detachments of soldiers were always passing through the town. In the meantime, Frank attended the local schoolhouse, where he was said to be a quick and bright pupil. Further education came at various private academies in the surrounding area.

Like many unlettered men, Benjamin Pierce had faith in the benefits of education, and fifteen-year-old Franklin was earmarked for college. Under normal circumstances he would have gone to Dartmouth, but his father thought the school too much under the thumb of the Federalists and, instead, in 1820, enrolled him at Bowdoin College in Brunswick, Maine. In his sophomore year, young Pierce befriended Nathaniel Hawthorne, a shy, incoming freshman, and despite differing personalities, they became lifelong friends. Henry Wadsworth Longfellow, also a year behind Pierce, was another college mate.

Pierce was an indifferent student during his first two years at Bowdoin, more interested in having a good time than studying the Greek and Roman classics, algebra, geometry, and history. He ambled along, shamelessly cheating and borrowing work from others. In his junior year, however, shocked by standing last in his class, the youth began to study and struggled to make up lost ground. He also became chapel monitor, developed an interest in the works of John Locke, and was elected captain of the Bowdoin Cadets, a marching and drill club.

Pierce also became interested in religion, and he and his roommate, Zenas Caldwell, knelt nightly to pray. Pierce graduated in 1824, third in a class of fourteen, and was tapped to give a commencement speech, titled "The Influence of Circumstance on the Intellectual Character."

In view of the prominence of Frank Pierce's father in New Hampshire, a career in law and politics seemed natural for the young man. Over the next few years he read law with, among others, future Supreme Court justice Levi Woodbury and was admitted to the bar in September 1827, the same year the elder Pierce was first elected governor. Two years later, Frank began his climb up the political ladder by being elected to the state legislature, where he served four one-year terms, becoming Speaker at the age of twenty-six. In 1833, he took the next step upward and was elected without formal opposition to the House of Representatives, where he was a strong supporter of Andrew Jackson. Early on, he adopted a pro-slavery stand, calling abolitionists "reckless fanatics" and supported a gag rule that barred debate on petitions critical of slavery.

On November 10, 1834, just before his thirtieth birthday, Pierce married Jane Means Appleton, the twenty-eight-year-old daughter of the former president of Bowdoin. How they met is unknown. No couple could have been more ill-matched, for Jane was petite, shy, melancholic, and tubercular, while her husband was buoyant, gregarious, and at home at political meetings and taverns. With a host of aristocratic New England connections, Jane had a low opinion of Pierce's family as compared with her Federalist forebears. Yet they had a real affection for each other. Their first child having died in infancy and their second at four, they focused all their love and affection upon Bennie, their remaining son.

Elected to the U.S. Senate in 1836, Pierce was, at thirty-two, the body's youngest member. He was overshadowed by such giants as Clay, Webster, and Calhoun and, although he was an effective orator, had little opportunity to shine. For the most part, he was a dogged Democratic party wheelhorse and anti-abolitionist zealot. With his wife in New Hampshire, he lived the boisterous life of a bachelor—often drinking more than he could hold—a problem he fought for the rest of his life despite frequent efforts at temperance. Opposition newspapers called him "the hero of many a well fought *bottle*."

Following a Whig takeover of Congress and with the Democrats now in the minority, Pierce lost his interest in the Senate and, giving in to Jane's pleas, resigned in February 1842. He opened a law practice in Concord, New Hampshire, and over the next decade, because of his oratorical skills and personal magnetism, was remarkably successful with juries.* He was also the state Democratic boss, enforcing strict discipline to keep the party united in a period of political upheaval. In 1845, he accepted an appointment as U.S. district attorney for New Hampshire from President Polk, but the following year he turned down Polk's offer to make him attorney general in his cabinet.

With the coming of the Mexican War, Pierce sought to emulate the military renown of his father. Despite the objections of his wife, he enlisted as a private, but Polk quickly gave him a colonel's commission, and less than a month later, he was promoted to brigadier general, although his only military experience was in the militia. Late in June 1847, Pierce's New England brigade joined in the march on Mexico City led by General Winfield Scott, but his dreams of military glory proved elusive.

Just before the Battle of Contreras, Pierce's horse was startled by exploding shells, bucked, and threw him violently against the pommel of his saddle, injuring him in the groin. In excruciating pain, he fainted and tore his knee in falling from the horse. Not long after, Pierce injured the same knee while leading his men into battle at Churubusco and fainted again—amid charges of cowardice that followed him the rest of his life.

Mustered out of service, Pierce returned to New Hampshire to resume his leadership of the state Democratic party. He supported the Compromise of 1850 and received favorable notice in the South by dumping a Democratic candidate for governor because of his criticism of the Fugitive Slave Law. One of his rewards was Southern support

---

*His protégé was Albert Baker, whose sister, Mary Baker Eddy, was the founder of Christian Science.

for the vice presidency in 1852, but his wife vehemently objected and he reluctantly told his supporters he was not interested in the job.

The death of Levi Woodbury, New Hampshire's favorite-son candidate for the Democratic presidential nomination, pushed Pierce's name to the fore again—this time for the presidency. The convention, meeting in Baltimore in June, was likely to be bitterly divided among Lewis Cass of Michigan, James Buchanan of Pennsylvania, Senator Stephen A. Douglas of Illinois, and William L. Marcy of New York,* and Pierce's supporters saw him as a dark horse around whom the weary delegates could rally when the time came.

Frank Pierce, they reasoned, offered something for everyone. He supported the Compromise and had Southern support while he did not alarm Northerners. Moreover, he had all the touchstones for the presidency: he was born in a log cabin—although he had not lived in it long; was from a patriotic family; had a military record—even if it was questionable; and had served an apprenticeship in a state legislature and in Congress. Pierce only reluctantly agreed to have his name put in nomination if the proper moment occurred and insisted his wife not be told about the plan.

For four days, the six hundred delegates cast ballot after ballot. As predicted, no single candidate was able to win a two-thirds majority, nor were any of them willing to give way to another. Sweltering in the overpowering heat of a Baltimore summer, the delegates' tempers flared and they hurled curses and challenges to duels and fistfights at each other. On the thirty-fifth ballot, Pierce's backers put his name before the convention as a compromise candidate. Slowly, he gained support, and on the forty-ninth ballot, the North Carolina delegation switched to Pierce, starting a snowball effect that gave him the nomination. Senator William R. King of Alabama was the vice-presidential nominee.

The Whig convention, which also met in steamy Baltimore, was nearly as riotous as that of the Democrats. Hopelessly divided between

---

*Marcy is credited with the famous political observation "To the victors belong the spoils."

Northern and Southern wings, the delegates faced a choice between the incumbent president, Millard Fillmore,* who had succeeded to the presidency after the death of Zachary Taylor, and Winfield Scott, the hero of the Mexican War. Southern delegates favored Fillmore, who had signed the Compromise of 1850, while Scott, a Virginian but not a slaveholder, was the candidate of antislavery Northern Whigs. Scott finally won the nomination on the fifty-third ballot, paradoxically making him the candidate of the party that had opposed the war he had won.

As America's leading soldier, Scott had been in the public eye since the War of 1812, but Pierce was virtually unknown outside his native bailiwick, so the Democrats needed to quickly respond to Whig chants of "Who's Frank Pierce?" Nathaniel Hawthorne, the candidate's old friend, volunteered to supply an answer with a campaign biography designed to sell him to the electorate. Pierce, wrote Hawthorne, offered "patriotism, integrity, and courage" and had the "noble gift of natural authority." He is "deep, deep, deep." Hawthorne did his work so well that Pierce later rewarded him with the job of U.S. consul in Liverpool, where he had plenty of free time to write and to gather material for *The Marble Faun,* his only novel with a European background.

There was little to choose from between Pierce and Scott. Both the Whig and Democratic party platforms supported the Compromise along with strict enforcement of the Fugitive Slave Law—although some Southern Whigs doubted Scott's commitment—and pledged not to reopen the sectional conflict over slavery. With little of substance to debate, the rivals slung mud at each other. Scott was assailed as vain, pompous, anti-Catholic, and a man on horseback with imperial delusions. The Whigs portrayed Pierce as "the fainting general," a confirmed drunk, and a do-nothing in Congress. With the Whigs divided between pro- and anti-slavery forces and the Democrats more united than in any election since Jackson's day, Pierce won by a land-

---

*Millard Fillmore is remembered today—if at all—only because he supposedly installed the first bathtub with built-in plumbing in the White House. Unhappily, even that distinction eludes the nation's thirteenth president, because the tale was a hoax gleefully cooked up in 1917 by Henry Mencken. Nevertheless, it has a life of its own and still appears in some publications. For example, see Whitney, *The American Presidents,* page 109, published as late as 1989.

slide with the support of Southern Whigs who defected from Scott. Pierce carried all but four of the thirty-one states, although he had only a majority of about two hundred thousand in the popular vote. The election sounded the death knell of the shattered Whig party.

Even as Pierce was savoring his triumph, tragedy struck. On January 6, 1853, barely two months before the inauguration, the president-elect and his family were traveling by train from Boston to Concord. Suddenly, the car in which they were riding lurched violently, fell off the track, and toppled down an embankment. Pierce and his wife were only shaken up, but their son, Bennie, was killed before their horrified eyes. For weeks, the boy's parents tormented themselves over his death. Jane finally decided that God had gathered Bennie to his bosom so her husband would have no family distractions to take him away from his presidential responsibilities, while Pierce saw the death as retribution for his own sins. Burdened with guilt, a morose Franklin Pierce entered the White House under a cloud of depression and gloomy uncertainty rather than with the buoyancy and confidence that invites success.

Inauguration Day—March 4, 1853—was raw and blustery. In deference to the family tragedy, the ceremonies were restrained and Mrs. Pierce did not accompany her husband to Washington. Gusts of snowflakes fell on Pierce's shoulders as he affirmed rather than swore the required oath.* He also departed from tradition by speaking without text or notes. The new president tried to create harmony by offering something to both expansionist-minded radicals and the conservative supporters of the Compromise of 1850. Its provisions, including the Fugitive Slave Law, were constitutional, he said, and would be strictly enforced. To divert public attention from slavery, he rattled the saber of manifest destiny by proclaiming a spirited policy of territorial expansion that would plant the American flag in Cuba and the lands to the

---

*Vice President King, who was terminally ill with tuberculosis, was permitted by special act of Congress to take his oath in Havana. Rallying enough to return to the United States, he went home to Alabama a month after being sworn in, where he died without ever having assumed his office. He is the only nationally elected American public official to be sworn in on foreign soil.

south. "My administration will not be controlled by any timid forebodings of evil from expansion," he declared.[14]

There was no inaugural ball, but Pierce had to endure a long and exhausting reception at the White House. Finally, after seemingly endless hours of handshaking, the last of the public departed, leaving behind mud-stained rugs, broken plates and glasses, and silence. Pierce wished to retire for the night, but where would he sleep? No preparations had been made to receive him and with an aide he prowled the upstairs living quarters by candlelight looking for a room with a made bed, but none was ready. Finally, he gave up. "You had better turn in here," he told the aide as he pointed to one disheveled room, "and I will find a bed across the hall."[15]

Jane arrived soon after, accompanied by her aunt, Mrs. Abbey Kent Means, who became the official White House hostess because the first lady spent most of her time in her bedroom writing pathetic notes to her dead Bennie. The president, finding solace in a combination of drink and religious piety, conducted daily prayer services for his official family and the servants. The White House had an air of all-enveloping melancholy. "Everything in that mansion seems cold and cheerless," said a visitor. "I have seen hundreds of log cabins which seemed to contain more happiness."[16]

Upon taking up the reins of office, Pierce had a clear choice between two lines of policy. He could hold fast to the doctrine that the Compromise had settled the slavery issue and proclaim that he would tolerate no dissension on the matter. The alternative was to try to please everyone by being bland, conciliatory, and yielding. The first course would require courage. It would bring the president into conflict with both Northern and Southern extremists. The second was easier and offered the promise of party harmony. In his inaugural speech he had seemed to opt for the first course, but Pierce soon caved in. A man of keener perception might have seen that party unity cannot be won by smiles and giving away offices but only by a determined fight for principle. Something greater than party harmony was at stake—the safety of the nation—but Pierce was blind to it.[17]

Pierce's inexperience and ineptitude caused trouble even before he assumed office. He had offered the post of secretary of state to his friend John A. Dix of New York, an antislavery man, but when Southerners objected, rather than insisting upon his own choice, he backed down and withdrew the tendered appointment. Political leaders on all sides took due note of his weakness, and interpreted it to mean that the new president not only lacked the inner strength to command acceptance of his policies but could be intimidated.

Pierce's cabinet, as finally constituted, was an effort to please everyone. In consequence, he was saddled with an ill-assorted body of mostly able but highly incompatible men.[18] The key appointments went to William Marcy of New York, who was named secretary of state, and Jefferson Davis of Mississippi, who became secretary of war. No two men could have been further apart. Marcy was a passionate Unionist and opposed the extension of slavery, while the cold, unbending Davis was already talking of breaking up the Union if slavery was not free to expand.

Undoubtedly the president intended Marcy, the most politically experienced of his cabinet, to be his closest adviser. But the New Yorker was quickly shunted aside by Davis and his ally, Caleb Cushing, a tricky Massachusetts doughface of few moral convictions, who served as attorney general. It was a development pregnant with potential disaster, especially with such a vacillating chief executive as Pierce in the White House. Both men were efficient—Davis, a graduate of West Point, laid the basis for the army that crushed the rebellion he later led, and Cushing was also able—but they were too extreme to be given control over policy. Operating without any restraint from the president, Davis and Cushing directed the administration along a pro-Southern, pro-slavery course that alienated many Northern Democrats. Former senator Thomas Hart Benton later described Pierce's term as one where the president was powerless, "and in which nullifiers, disunionists, and renegades used his name . . . for their own audacious and criminal purposes."[19]

The Democrats had been out of power for four years, and thousands of job seekers besieged Pierce and his cabinet. "Washington is full of strangers," reported one observer. "It seems as if a resurrection had brought to life all our rotten fishy politicians."[20] Pierce stumbled into hot water by trying to create harmony by rewarding all party factions equally. Not enough jobs existed to buy off everyone, and some factions heatedly resented any recognition given their rivals. The bitter infighting spread to Congress, and increasingly, Pierce was seen as a man of willowy backbone and an inept administrator who had lost control of events. Even though the Democrats had overwhelming majorities in both houses, most of his legislative initiatives were ignored. The *New York Tribune* called him the weakest president in the nation's history.[21]

The bulk of Pierce's diplomatic appointments were also unfortunate. They included a band of romantic adventurers and headstrong expansionists whose actions brought embarrassment and ridicule on the administration. Cuba was the president's main object of desire. The annexation of the "Pearl of the Antilles" had long been urged by Southerners, and President Polk had in 1848 tried to purchase it from Spain for $100 million. The proud Spaniards flatly refused to sell the last vestige, save Puerto Rico, of their once extensive empire in the New World.

Initially, the administration encouraged futile schemes by several swashbuckling, pro-slavery filibusters to seize the island by force, but when these failed, Pierce shifted to a policy of acquiring Cuba through diplomatic means. He instructed Secretary of State Marcy to negotiate the purchase of the island, and Marcy, in turn, told Pierre Soule, the American minister in Madrid, to make overtures to the Spaniards. These attempts were thwarted, however, by the administration's own inept appointees.[22] Before sitting down with the Spaniards, Soule met in October 1854 with James Buchanan, the American minister to London, and James Y. Mason, the minister to Paris, in Ostend, Belgium, and then at Aix-la-Chapelle in the Rhineland to discuss the Cuban situation. Their recommendations were embodied in a remarkable diplomatic dispatch to Marcy subsequently known as the Ostend Manifesto in which they suggested that Spain be offered a price not to exceed $120 million for Cuba. If the Spaniards refused to sell the island, the United States would be "justified in wresting it from Spain."

A garbled version of the dispatch was leaked to the *New York Herald,*

and it created a sensation both in Europe and at home. Europeans has-
tened to criticize this blatant attempt to despoil Spain of its property,
with the *Times* of London sneering that the bumbling Yankees did not
even bother to hatch their mischief in secret. While Southerners
approved these machinations—in fact Buchanan received a leg up for
the Democratic presidential nomination in 1856—the dispatch created a firestorm of opposition in the North, where it was denounced as
a blatant attempt to extend slavery. An embarrassed Pierce was compelled to repudiate the Ostend Manifesto—and it ruined whatever
chance there was of acquiring Cuba.

Quite possibly Pierce might have drummed up enough public support
to annex Cuba despite the ineptitude of his administration had not
Congress, some months before, passed the Kansas-Nebraska Act, which
reopened the whole question of slavery in the Western territories. The
most disastrous event of the Pierce administration, it did more than any
other single occurrence to bring on the Civil War. Northern resistance
to the expansion of slavery was intensified, and Pierce's inability to sense
this is additional testimony—if needed—to his lack of political acumen.

The Kansas-Nebraska Act was the brainchild of Stephen Douglas, the
senior senator from Illinois. In contrast to the placid Pierce, the "Little
Giant" was five feet of brains, bounce, and swagger. Looking forward to
the 1856 presidential election, he wanted to make a dramatic stroke that
would reinvigorate the rudderless Democratic party. He found his
opportunity in the Pacific railroad. Ever since the Mexican War, most
Americans had favored the building of a nation-binding, transcontinental railway, but construction was delayed by a struggle among politicians and promoters over which route it should follow. Of the four
possible routes, two—the Central from Chicago to San Francisco and
the Southern from New Orleans to San Diego—had the most support.[23]

Congress, in March 1853, authorized surveys of these routes by U.S.
Army topographical engineers. Not surprisingly, since Jefferson Davis
headed the War Department, the Southern route was found to be the
shortest and to have the fewest physical obstacles to construction. Davis

saw such a route as strengthening the South and, although Southerners usually opposed federal projects for roads and canals, "internal improvements" as they were then called, he justified the transcontinental railroad as a military defense measure. When the survey made it clear that a Southern railway would have to pass through Mexican territory, he persuaded Pierce to buy the land for $10 million, making the Gadsden Purchase of the territory along the Mexican border the final contiguous addition to the territory of the United States.

The stage now seemed set for congressional approval of the Southern route, but Douglas launched a vigorous fight for the Central route. It would not only increase the wealth and power of Chicago, but it would line his pocket because he had speculated heavily in Western lands, including the site for the eastern terminus of the proposed railroad. But to gain approval of the Central route, the vast trans-Missouri West through which it was to run—the present states of Kansas, Nebraska, the Dakotas, and parts of Wyoming and Colorado—had to be organized into territories and opened to settlement. Bill after bill had been introduced only to be defeated by Southern opposition because the country lay north of the Missouri Compromise line that barred slavery.

In January 1854, Douglas introduced a bill to organize the Great Plains as the Nebraska Territory. As bait for Southern votes, states carved out of the area would be admitted to the Union as free or slave, depending upon the wishes of a majority of the settlers, or "popular sovereignty." This was the same language applied by the Compromise of 1850 to the Utah and New Mexico territories. It was not enough, however. Under the prodding of a group of influential Southern senators—known as the F Street Mess from their boardinghouse—Douglas was forced to sweeten his proposal, now called the Kansas-Nebraska Act, by agreeing to outright repeal of the Missouri Compromise. This will raise "a hell of a storm," he acknowledged.[24]

A fiery debate raged over the bill, but this time there was no Henry Clay to quench angry passions with a last-minute compromise. Resolutions, memorials, petitions, and letters opposing the bill poured in upon Congress. Douglas confessed that he could travel from Washington to Chicago by the light of the fires built to burn him in effigy. Northerners were bitterly opposed to ending an agreement of thirty-four years' standing that now had the force of moral authority in favor of allowing slavery to expand into virgin territory. They called it "a criminal betrayal of precious rights . . . part and parcel of an atrocious plot."[25] For their part, Southerners realized that Nebraska would probably become a free state, but thought they had a chance to win Kansas, which adjoined slaveholding Missouri. Paradoxically, the selection of the proper route for the Pacific railway, which had been the cause of the tumult, vanished amid the clamor over slavery.

Originally, President Pierce opposed repeal of the Missouri Compromise—and should have stuck to his guns. But under pressure from Davis, the docile chief executive surrendered after a highly unusual Sunday-morning meeting with several Southern senators. Once again, Pierce had blundered, this time by allowing administration policy to be made by a congressional caucus rather than the White House. Unwittingly, he had confirmed the widespread suspicion among Northerners that the secretary of war was the real power in his administration. Northern Democrats were dragooned into voting for the Kansas-Nebraska Act by the "whip and spur" of party discipline plus offers of patronage. In signing the bill, the obtuse Pierce hailed the measure as the first great accomplishment of his administration and expressed the opinion that the slavery question had been put to rest.[26]

In reality, Douglas and the administration had won the battle and lost the war. The Kansas-Nebraska Act stirred flames from the embers of sectional rivalry and reawakened the fear and anger of the struggle over slavery. As Senator Salmon P. Chase of Ohio walked down the Capitol steps amid the boom of cannon fired by the victorious Southerners, he turned to Charles Sumner and declared, "They celebrate a present victory, but the echoes they awaken shall never rest until slavery itself shall die."[27]

The Kansas-Nebraska Act resulted in the breakup of the old Whig-Democratic political system, and an antislavery party—the Republican party—was born. Many places claim to be the birthplace of the new party. But a mass meeting in a grove of oaks at Jackson, Michigan, on July 6, 1854, attended by antislavery zealots, disenchanted Northern Democrats and Whigs, as well as reformers of various stripes formally adopted Jefferson's old party label and a platform that demanded the exclusion of slavery from all the territories. Only a minority of Republicans had any humanitarian interest in the welfare of the slaves, however. Although opposed to slavery, they were also opposed to the idea of a free, multiracial society.

The disintegration of the old parties was also accompanied by the growth of nativism and restrictions on immigrants.[28] Many Whigs, faced with the collapse of their party and hating the Democrats, became anti-Catholic Know-Nothings. Among other measures, they demanded that immigrants be resident in the United States for twenty-one years before being allowed to apply for citizenship. Under attack from the Know-Nothings on the right and the Republicans on the left, the Democrats suffered a crushing defeat in the 1854 congressional elections, losing control of the House and dooming Pierce's legislative program.

"Bleeding Kansas" soon diverted the nation from the "Popish peril." Since the slavery question was to be settled by popular sovereignty, both pro- and anti-slavery forces scrambled to settle the territory. Slaveholders moved in from Missouri, and New England abolitionist societies financed antislavery settlers. Elections to organize a territorial legislature were marred by massive illegal voting by Missourians who crossed over into Kansas for the day. Pierce's open support of slavery made the situation worse. He upheld the legality of the fraudulently elected legislature, which expelled its free-soil members, passed a harsh legal code to protect slavery, and petitioned Congress for Kansas's admission as a slave state. Free-state men—branded by Pierce as "traitors" in another misguided moment—organized their own state government and sought to join the Union as a free state. With two state governments in existence, widespread fighting erupted, and some two hundred people were killed over the next two years in a nasty little guerrilla war.

Violence soon thrust its mailed fist onto the floor of the U.S. Senate. On May 19, 1856, Senator Sumner delivered a blistering speech that flailed away at the "harlot slavery" and the "murderous robbers of Missouri." Some of his choicest language was reserved for Senator Andrew P. Butler of South Carolina. Three days later, Butler's cousin, Representative Preston S. Brooks, also of South Carolina,* found Sumner at his desk in the Senate and avenged his uncle's honor by beating Sumner senseless with a stout cane while several Southern members looked on without interfering. Brooks was censured by the House and resigned—only to be reelected to Congress. He also received several suitably inscribed canes from admirers.

"Bleeding Kansas" wrecked Pierce's desperate efforts to be reelected in 1856. In the North he was treated with contempt; Southern Democrats, although they appreciated his efforts to help their cause, felt that his loss of support in the North made him unelectable. As president, his primary job had been to maintain the balance between the sectional rivals that existed when he came to the White House. Instead, by embracing the South, he had rekindled the animosities between the sections. He even failed in the comparatively simple task of protecting representative institutions in Kansas. Had Pierce restored order and mobilized moderate opinion behind a fairly elected territorial government, he might have at least partially restored public confidence in himself, but he failed in this task as in so many others.

Perhaps the most devastating of the numerous adverse judgments passed upon Pierce came from Benjamin B. French, his former secretary, who had broken with the president over the Kansas-Nebraska Act. "The Kansas outrages are all imputable to him," wrote French, "and if he is not called to answer for them here, in Hell they will roast him like a herring."[29] Brushing off Pierce, the Democrats turned instead to the flabby James Buchanan, who was nominated and elected. "There's nothing left . . . but to get drunk," said Pierce.[30]

And he followed his own advice.

The wife of Senator C. C. Clay of Alabama, who knew Franklin Pierce well, recalled that before he entered the White House, she had "seen him bound up the stairs with the elasticity of a schoolboy." Four years

---

*Brooks's previous claim to fame was a half-humorous proposal that congressmen be required to check their firearms in the cloakroom before appearing on the floor of the House.

later, she said, he left the presidency "a staid and grave man, on whom the stamp of care and illness was ineradicably impressed." And, Mrs. Clay might have added, he bore the stamp of abject failure as well.

Pierce's final years were bitter. Following the end of his term, he and his wife returned to Concord but avoided the harsh New England winters. They visited Madeira, took a prolonged tour of Europe, and spent a winter in the Caribbean. But Jane still grieved for her son and her health continued to deteriorate. She died in December 1863, and Pierce again began to drink heavily. In 1860, friends asked him to seek the Democratic presidential nomination, but he refused, suggesting Jefferson Davis instead.

Lincoln's election and the outbreak of war between North and South plunged the ex-president into despair. While he did not support secession, he claimed that Northern agitators and threats to the Southern way of life had impelled the South to leave the Union. This attitude made him even more unpopular, and he fell under suspicion as a secret Southern sympathizer. Even a substantial contribution to a fund for wounded Union soldiers did not stem the criticism. He died on October 8, 1869, so unpopular that the citizens of Concord did not see fit to raise a monument in his honor until fifty years later.

Nathaniel Hawthorne, against the advice of his editors, dedicated a book to Pierce during the Civil War and included a letter to his old friend that was full of praise. Ralph Waldo Emerson bought the book and cut out the dedication and letter before reading it.

CHAPTER VIII

JAMES BUCHANAN

With his head habitually tilted forward and to the side and with one eye closed, James Buchanan looked like nothing so much as a large, quizzical bird. Farsighted in one eye and nearsighted in the other—a perfect mix for a crafty politician on the lookout for opportunities either far or near—he compensated by cocking his head to the left and closing one eye when talking with someone. If the person was close by, he would shut his farsighted eye; if they were farther away, he closed the nearsighted one. The bird image was completed by a well-tailored black suit and spotless white collar and neckcloth.

Buchanan, who became America's fifteenth president in 1857, has four distinctions. He was the last American president born in the eighteenth century. He was the nation's only bachelor chief executive. At sixty-five, he was the oldest man to enter the White House until the seventy-year-old Ronald Reagan was inaugurated in 1981. And he had held down a government job of one sort or another for nearly forty years. So much for the upside on "Old Buck."

On the downside, "few presidents have entered office with more experience in public life, and few have so decisively failed" is the damning assessment of one authority on the era.[1] Although Buchanan had served as a Pennsylvania state legislator, congressman, and senator, minister to Russia and to Britain, and secretary of state before being elected to the presidency on his fourth try, this wide-ranging experience did not endow him with the vision, pragmatism, and political sensitivity required to preserve a nation from a bloody internecine struggle.

"Weak," "feeble," and "indecisive" are words usually used to describe

Buchanan. Along with Franklin Pierce, he unsuccessfully coped with rising sectional tensions and through his ineptness stoked the fires of discord. Although he was devoted to the Union, Buchanan's bumbling and one-sided pro-Southern policies helped bring on a civil war that consumed 620,000 lives. Moreover, his administration has been described by experts as the most corrupt before the Civil War.[2] "Poor, foolish Buchanan" is the way Samuel Eliot Morison describes him.[3]

Plodding caution and a passion for precision were Buchanan's stock-in-trade; an aura of red tape and musty precedents clung to him, and he was known—not always affectionately—as the Old Public Functionary. Flashes of genius never lighted up his mind, and he played politics as if it were a game of chess—cautiously, step-by-step, never chancing a dangerous gambit. A friend doubted that he ever uttered a genuine witticism in his entire life.[4] He was fussy and meticulous about trivial matters, keeping a daily record of his expenditures, including the pennies spent by his valet for pins and suspender buttons. Once, he refused to accept a check for $15,000 because it was short ten cents.

Buchanan was neither a dynamic nor a charismatic figure; his rise in politics was steady rather than spectacular. He did not win distinction as an orator, debater, or the author of important legislation. Instead, he was a conscientious committee member, party wheelhorse, and crafty "insider." Floating along with the political tides of the day, he switched from the moribund Federalists to the Jacksonian Democrats and was carried along by the current to ever higher prominence in national affairs. He was the living embodiment of the Peter Principle: people tend to rise to their level of incompetence—although he was no worse than most of his contemporaries.[5]

Buchanan was admirably qualified for diplomatic and judicial posts, and both he and the nation would have been far better off if he had accepted an offer by President John Tyler in 1844 of a seat on the Supreme Court, but he insisted on pursuing the presidency. As a diplomat in St. Petersburg and London, he served with some success. But he lacked the temperament for the presidency, especially in a time of great pressure. Where iron nerve, decisive action, and the ability to bend men to his will were needed, he could offer only wariness, legalisms, and a taste for shifty maneuvers. The key to his character, according to historian Allan Nevins, was an inability to make up his mind. "His deficiency in humor, his meager imagination, his secretive vein, his tortuous ways, were all connected to this trait."[6]

Nevertheless, Buchanan was a gregarious fellow. He was a prominent figure in Washington society, and most of his friends were Southerners and slave owners. For several years he shared rooms with his fellow bachelor Senator William R. King of Alabama, and they were so inseparable that they were known as "Buchanan & *his wife*."[7] Enemies whispered he was a closet homosexual, but no evidence was ever offered. Representative Barney Frank of Massachusetts, who is openly gay, described Buchanan as the nation's only homosexual chief executive in a 1997 television discussion.

Buchanan liked parties and balls, good food and wine, and the sparkle of pretty women. His orphaned niece, Harriet Lane, whom he had raised from childhood—which in our more suspicious day would probably inspire sly comments about a "Lolita complex" and "dirty old men"—served as his official hostess. Under her hand, the White House was transformed into a brighter and gayer place than it had been since Dolley Madison had reigned there nearly a half century before.* Not long after his inauguration, the new president chided his wine merchant for not providing champagne in large bottles. "Pints are very inconvenient in this house," he wrote, "as the article is not used in such small quantities."[8] Buchanan was also a regular visitor at the receptions and dinners given by Mrs. Rose O'Neal Greenhow,† a beautiful and vivacious widow who lived just across Lafayette Square from the White House. Some gossips wondered whether their relationship extended beyond being just good friends.

---

*Harriet Lane, then in her late twenties, was the first White House "media star." Women copied her low-cut dresses and elaborate headgear. Numerous babies, a paddle-wheel revenue cutter, a racehorse, and a flower were named for her. "Listen to the Mocking Bird"— one of Abraham Lincoln's favorite songs—was dedicated to her.

†Related to the Calverts of Maryland and the Lees of Virginia, Mrs. Greenhow was the aunt and namesake of Rose Cutts, the wife of Senator Stephen A. Douglas of Illinois. Mrs. Greenhow apparently used her contacts in the upper levels of government to indulge in a discreet form of influence peddling. She was arrested as a Confederate spy early in the Civil War and, after being imprisoned for some months, was sent to Richmond. She drowned in 1864 while trying to run the Union blockade. The Hay-Adams Hotel stands on the site of her house.

Buchanan was sensitive to slights, both real and fancied. Like Jimmy Carter after him, he trusted few people and insisted upon personally overseeing all the details of his office. Working in an old dressing gown and slippers and chewing on cigars until they frayed, he spent hours every night poring over papers and other matters that could profitably have been handled by others. The work aggravated his declining health and accentuated an ingrained stubbornness. When crossed, he could be petulant, and he sulked when he could not have his way.

Even some of his friends were irritated by his fussy manner. "Mr. Buchanan," wrote President James K. Polk in his diary, "is an able man, but in small matters without judgment and sometimes acts like an old maid." Still, Polk appointed him secretary of state, which caused Polk's mentor, Andrew Jackson, to register a strong protest.[9]

"But, General," replied the president, "you yourself appointed him minister to Russia."

"Yes, I did," said Jackson. "It was far as I could send him out of my sight, and where he could do the least harm. I would have sent him to the North Pole if we had kept a minister there!"

James Buchanan came into office with the intention of quieting the storm over slavery through compromise and believed that if he was successful, his presidency might rank with that of George Washington. "Should a kind Providence enable me to succeed in my efforts to restore harmony to the Union, I shall feel that I have not lived in vain," he assured a friend shortly after his election.[10] But the new president, a "doughface" or Northern Democrat who sympathized with the South on the slavery issue and whose cabinet was dominated by Southerners, was emotionally isolated from the antislavery fervor sweeping the country.

While Buchanan knew his rural Pennsylvania constituency and no American was more familiar with foreign affairs, he had traveled little in the United States. He did not comprehend the depth of feeling on both sides of the slavery question and thought both pro- and antislavery factions could be placated by concessions. He despised abolitionists, and seeing no injustice in the slave system could never understand the passion of its opponents. The slaves, he claimed, were "treated with kindness and humanity. . . . Both the philanthropy and the self-interest of the master have combined to produce this happy result."[11]

Buchanan's actions added fuel to the bitter North-South crisis. Upholding the Southern view that Congress could not prohibit slavery in the territories, he secretly influenced the Supreme Court's controversial Dred Scott decision by pressuring a Northern justice to vote with the Southern majority against the legality of the Missouri Compromise of 1820, which had limited the spread of slavery to the territories.* Giving way to pressure from the South, and despite campaign promises to do otherwise, Buchanan also endorsed the admission of Kansas into the Union as a slave state against the will of a majority of its settlers—an act that undermined the Democratic party in the North.

These blunders paved the way for a Republican victory in 1860, which brought about the war. Although a strong Unionist, once secession had occurred, Buchanan dithered because he believed there was nothing the federal government could do about it. True, as a lame-duck president he held a weak hand, but he undercut his position even further by his indecisiveness and the denial of his own authority to coerce a state to remain in the Union. One could not envision an Andrew Jackson, or even a Zachary Taylor, standing idly by in such a critical situation.

"I am the last president of the United States," Buchanan mournfully told visitors in an after-me-the-deluge mood as the country was falling to pieces about him.[12]

The son of a Scotch-Irish immigrant storekeeper also named James Buchanan, the future president was born in a one-room log cabin near Mercersburg, Pennsylvania, on April 23, 1791.[13] The elder Buchanan had come to America eight years before as an orphan from County Donegal. After working for a relative, he struck out on his own and opened a small trading post on the Pennsylvania frontier. In 1788, he

---

*Scott was a slave who had been taken from slaveholding Missouri into the Wisconsin Territory and Illinois in the 1830s by his master, an army doctor. He had eventually filed suit for his freedom on the grounds that his temporary residence in what was free territory under the Northwest Ordinance and the Missouri Compromise had automatically set him free. The Supreme Court rejected these arguments.

married Elizabeth Speer, a native of Lancaster County. She was twenty-one; he was twenty-seven. They had eleven children of whom eight—four boys and four girls—lived to maturity.

Young James, the oldest surviving child, was five when the family moved to Mercersburg, where his father prospered as a merchant and farmer. Until he was fourteen, the boy was the sole son and the adored favorite of his mother and sisters. Elizabeth Buchanan had no formal education but she had read much, especially Milton and Pope, and tried to imbue her children with a similar interest. As soon as James was old enough, he was put to work in the store keeping his father's books and accounts.

The boy both loved and feared his father. The "Squire," as the elder Buchanan was known, frequently assigned chores to his son that were beyond his years, carefully scrutinized his performance, and was far more ready with criticism than with praise. James learned fast but he rarely experienced the feeling of a task well done. Nothing was ever done well enough for his father. Throughout his life, he regretted that his father, who died in 1821, did not live to see him rise to the highest offices in the nation.

When young Buchanan turned sixteen, Dr. John King, pastor of the Presbyterian church in Mercersburg and a trustee of Dickinson College in nearby Carlisle, persuaded his father to send the boy to the school. His mother wanted him to study for the ministry, but the Squire thought that because of his growing business interests, it would be advantageous to have a lawyer in the family. Buchanan entered Dickinson in 1807 as a junior, and although he was a good student, out from under his father's hand for the first time in his life, he got into trouble.

Rowdy drinking bouts with his classmates and other escapades resulted in Buchanan's expulsion at the end of the first year. As a result of his father's influence and a promise to toe the line, the young man was readmitted. Keeping his promise, he graduated the following year at age eighteen—although he was denied the academic honors he had earned—and went to Lancaster to read law under the direction of a local attorney. Three years later, he opened his own practice.

In August 1814, Buchanan ran for the Pennsylvania State Assembly as a Federalist with the hope of attracting clients. News of the burning of Washington by the British arrived in Lancaster, and a local militia company volunteered to go to the defense of Baltimore, the next British target. Like most Federalists, Buchanan opposed "Mr. Madison's War," but realized that he would have to show his patriotism if he wished to be elected and marched off to Baltimore. The unit saw no action and Buchanan returned to Lancaster well in time to win the legislative seat.

After serving two terms, he left the legislature to build his law practice, winning case after case and gaining a reputation as an able attorney. Upon one occasion, he was retained by a man being sued for threatening the life of another. When the plaintiff took the stand, Buchanan asked him:

"Well, sir, suppose you were a man of nerve, a man not easily frightened by threat—put yourself in the position of a courageous man— would you have cared for the threat of my client?"

"I am a man," replied the plaintiff, "of as much courage as anybody, sir."

"Then you were not frightened when my client threatened you?"

"No, sir."

"Well, then," said Buchanan, "what did you bring this charge for? I move its dismissal."[14]

It was granted.

Buchanan fell in love in 1818, at the age of twenty-seven, with Ann Coleman, daughter of Robert Coleman, a wealthy iron-mill owner, and at twenty-two the belle of Lancaster. A willowy, black-haired girl with lustrous eyes, she was by turn affectionate and petulant, introspective and wild—and may have been emotionally unstable. Although the girl's parents suspected Buchanan of being a fortune hunter, Ann and James became engaged in the summer of 1819.

Somewhere along the way, however, the couple quarreled. Ann broke off the engagement and went to stay with relatives in Philadelphia. She died there not long afterward under mysterious circumstances, possibly a suicide. Rumors spread that she had become convinced that her father was right, that her fiancé was more interested in her money than in her. Buchanan was grief-stricken. "I have lost the only earthly object of my affections, without whom life now presents me a dreary blank," he wrote. "I feel that my happiness will be buried with her in the grave."[15] To add to his grief, Ann's parents denied his request to attend the funeral. Buchanan never again became engaged, although he carried on numerous flirtations.*

Before Ann's death, Buchanan had intended to continue to build his already lucrative law practice and to enjoy the life of a country gentleman, but with his future now unsettled, he again turned to politics. In 1820, he was elected to Congress, just as his father died after injuries suffered in a carriage accident. Buchanan ran as a Federalist, but after a cool appraisal of the political scene he became a supporter of Andrew Jackson.

There was talk of a place in the cabinet for Buchanan, but President Jackson did not trust him and, in 1831, sent him to Russia as U.S. minister. Buchanan's greatest accomplishment in St. Petersburg was to negotiate the first trade treaty between the United States and Russia. But the politically ambitious Buchanan did not wish to remain away from the United States too long and returned to be elected in 1834 to the Senate. He served eleven years and rose to the chairmanship of the Senate Foreign Relations Committee.

As a member of the conservative, pro-slavery wing of the Democratic party, Buchanan was a leader of successful Southern efforts to block the abolition of slavery in the District of Columbia. Because of abolitionist agitation, he claimed that efforts for a peaceful solution of the slavery question had been derailed. "Before this unfortunate agitation commenced, a large and very growing party existed in several of the slave states in favor of the gradual abolition of slavery," Buchanan declared. "Now, not a voice is heard there in support of such a measure."[16]

Buchanan sought the Democratic presidential nomination in 1844 and, when he lost, was influential in organizing support in pivotal Pennsylvania for James Polk, the eventual nominee and president. Buchanan was appointed secretary of state as a reward. Polk largely served as his own secretary of state, but Buchanan made the final

---

*In later years, Buchanan let it be known that he had placed under seal documents that were to be opened after his death that would explain the cause of the break with Ann Coleman. After he died, this material was discovered with a letter ordering that the documents be destroyed without being opened, and his wish prevailed.

arrangements for the annexation of Texas and negotiated the treaty with Britain establishing the northern boundary of the Oregon Territory as the forty-ninth parallel.

Worn-out by his exertions during the Mexican War, Polk chose not to run for a second term, and in 1848 Buchanan made himself available for the Democratic nomination. Rejected once again, he returned to Wheatland, the sprawling country estate he had recently purchased, to await developments. Several of his siblings had died and he had assumed the responsibility for supporting an army of orphaned and semi-orphaned nieces and nephews, and grandnieces and grandnephews who overran the place. When his friend Howell Cobb of Georgia complained about owning a thousand slaves who were an economic burden but could not be sold because Cobb would not separate families, Buchanan probably recognized a kindred soul.[17]

In 1853 Buchanan went abroad again, as U.S. minister to Britain, after having again lost the Democratic nomination, this time to Franklin Pierce. Not long after Buchanan's arrival in London, the State Department issued a circular instructing American officials abroad to wear only "the simple dress of an American citizen" when performing their duties and to avoid ribbons and gold lace. This put him in a quandary. British officials told him that if he did not wear court dress, he would not be admitted to official functions. Buchanan tried to think of a substitute. Perhaps a variation on a military uniform or a blue coat with gold American-eagle buttons?

Following much thought, Buchanan finally hit upon a solution: he would wear a plain black suit and carry a dress sword in his hand when he appeared at Court. That did the trick. "As I approached the Queen," he reported, "an arch but benevolent smile lit up her countenance—as much as to say, you are the first man who has ever appeared before me at Court in such a dress. I must confess that I never felt more proud of being an American."[18]

Buchanan was an effective minister, but his mission was clouded by the Ostend Manifesto, in which he joined his militantly pro-slavery colleagues in Paris and Madrid in urging the purchase of Cuba from Spain. If the Spaniards refused to sell, "we shall be justified in wresting" Cuba from its owners, declared the three diplomats. This irresponsible pronunciamento was cheered in the South, which looked to Cuba as fresh slave territory, and denounced in the North, where it aroused mistrust of Southern imperialism. President Pierce repudiated it, but the manifesto boosted Buchanan's popularity among Southerners as the 1856 presidential election loomed.

The Ostend Manifesto and Buchanan's absence from the country during the miniature civil war in Kansas over the extension of slavery served him well as the Democratic convention convened in Cincinnati. To Northern Democrats, both his chief rivals, President Pierce and Stephen Douglas, were tainted by their support of the pro-slavery cause in Kansas, while Buchanan was unconnected with "Bleeding Kansas" and at the same time fully acceptable to the South. He won the nomination by acclamation on the seventeenth ballot. John C. Breckinridge of Kentucky was the vice-presidential nominee.

In the November election, Buchanan faced the candidates of two new parties organized from the collapse of the old Whig party: John C. Fremont, the Western explorer, who was nominated by the antislavery Republicans, and former president Millard Fillmore, the candidate of the anti-Catholic, anti-immigrant, semisecret Native American or Know-Nothing party. Slavery and Kansas dominated the campaign with Southerners charging that if the "Black Republicans" won, they would breakup the Union. Wall Street, fearful of the effect of a Republican victory, made generous contributions to the Democrats. August Belmont, the Rothschilds' agent in America, alone gave $50,000. Naval construction contracts were offered in return for contributions, and a public-printing contractor kicked in $100,000. The Republicans were powerless against such largesse.

Buchanan polled less than half the popular vote but won in the Electoral College, 174 votes to 114 for Fremont, who went on to be one of the worst generals of the Civil War, and 8 for Fillmore. Ominously for the Democrats, while their candidate carried all the slave states except Maryland, which went for Fillmore, he won only four Northern states. The Republican party, in its first major test, had swept the Northeast and West and looked forward with eagerness to the election of 1860.

* * *

Pomp and glitter marked James Buchanan's inauguration on March 4, 1857. The president-elect came down to Washington from Lancaster in a special train along with his niece, Harriet Lane. Thirty thousand visitors poured into the capital, still a mixture of muddy streets and half-finished Greek temples, crowding hotel lobbies, boardinghouses, and saloons. Space was so short that some people paid fifty cents a night to sleep on a cot in a circus tent. Escorted by assorted state militias, brass bands, and fire companies, Buchanan rode to the Capitol in an open carriage with the outgoing President Pierce, where the eighty-year-old chief justice, Roger B. Taney, tottered forward to administer the oath.

No eloquence of phrase or glint of original thought brightened Buchanan's inaugural address. Seeking to place himself above party and sectional conflict, he began by announcing that he would not be a candidate for reelection—a blunder that made him a largely irrelevant lame duck at a time he needed all the power and support that he could summon to deal with the approaching crisis. The one striking passage in the speech referred to the bitter dispute over Kansas. Buchanan urged both sides to await a soon-expected Supreme Court ruling in the Dred Scott case, which would settle the matter. "To their decision," he declared, "I shall cheerfully submit, whatever this may be," and begged "all good citizens to do likewise."[19]

Harriet, resplendent in a flowing white dress and wearing a pearl necklace of many strands, presided over the Inaugural Ball, held in a sprawling temporary structure built in Judiciary Square. Gold stars twinkled against the white ceiling, and red, white, and blue bunting festooned the walls. "Such a jam, such heat," observed one guest. "The members of Congress got so overexcited with wine they had to be locked up in the upper rooms." Baron de Stoeckl, the Russian minister, told Madam Sartiges, wife of his French counterpart, that the situation in Washington reminded him of Paris just before the Revolution of 1830. There, at a ball given by King Louis Philippe, Talleyrand had whispered to the monarch, "Sire, we are dancing on a volcano."[20]

Two days later, Chief Justice Taney delivered the Supreme Court's decision in the Dred Scott case in a quavering voice. The brethren, as expected, ruled against Scott's plea for his freedom. Blacks, declared

Taney, "had no rights which a white man was bound to respect." Unexpectedly, however, the Court did not stop there, but went on to declare the congressional effort to restrict slavery in the territories illegal because it violated the right of slaveholders to their property without due process. Angry Northerners smelled a rat. Buchanan was accused of double-dealing by trying to make the country accept in advance a decision that he obviously knew would allow the extension of slavery into new areas.

In reality, the shifty Buchanan had been far more active in the Dred Scott case than was known at the time. A half century later, it was discovered that before the inauguration, Taney had informed the president-elect of the impending decision in clear violation of judicial ethics. Buchanan was told there was a seven-to-two majority against Scott, but only five justices—all Southerners—were ready to formally nullify Congress's efforts to impede the spread of slavery. Buchanan was asked to persuade a friend, Justice Robert C. Grier of Pennsylvania, to join them so the decision would not bear the stigma of a purely sectional ruling. In a breach of tradition and a clear violation of the doctrine of separation of powers, Buchanan influenced Grier, who "succumbed" as requested.

Buchanan's interference on behalf of the South was a blunder. Aside from the obvious impropriety of these contacts, he showed an appalling ignorance by assuming that this ruling would be acceptable to the North. Faith in the impartiality of the Supreme Court was destroyed, and the decision, seemingly on its face a Southern victory, created a massive backlash against the new president and the South. Buchanan's ineptness had angered the entire North, and the problem of extending slavery into the territories had been exacerbated.

Nevertheless, Buchanan continued to bumble about. With the Democrats holding a majority in both houses of Congress, he next tried to force through the admission of Kansas to the Union as a slave state. Pro-slavery forces had called a convention in Lecompton, Kansas, at which they had written a state constitution calling for Kansas to enter the Union with slavery, but it was under attack by antislavery settlers as a sham. Even so, Buchanan urged Congress to admit Kansas with the Lecompton constitution. Northern Democrats led by Stephen

Douglas, who supported popular sovereignty, in which the settlers determined whether a state was to be free or slave, heatedly objected to this as a swindle.[21]

Up for reelection as senator in 1858 and with Illinois voters firmly opposed to the spread of slavery, Douglas knew that if he supported the Lecompton constitution, he would not only doom his chance at the presidency in 1860 but lose his Senate seat. There was an angry confrontation over the issue at the White House. Buchanan warned Douglas against battling against the administration and reminded him that Andrew Jackson had destroyed politicians who had opposed him.

"Mr. President," snapped the Little Giant, "General Jackson is dead!"[22]

Buchanan persisted in trying to ram through the Lecompton constitution at the risk of splitting his party, while Douglas insisted that the document be resubmitted to the people of Kansas for a vote. The president angrily struck back. Postmasters and holders of patronage jobs loyal to Douglas were dismissed. "Contracts, commissions, and even hard cash" were dangled before wavering congressmen to swing their votes in favor of Lecompton.[23] A coalition of Douglas Democrats, Republicans, and Know-Nothings defeated the proposal. As Douglas had insisted, the pro-slavery constitution was put to a referendum in Kansas and rejected by an overwhelming majority. Kansas become a state in 1861, but by then the expansion of slavery was a moot point.

Buchanan defended himself by arguing that if he had not backed the Lecompton constitution, the Southern states would have either seceded from the Union or taken up arms. But these fears seem unjustified. In 1858, the South was guided not solely by fire-eaters spoiling for a fight but also by pragmatists who recognized that opposition to an honest vote in Kansas was not enough of a pretext for secession. With a pro-Southern Democrat in the White House, a Democratic majority in Congress as well as in the Supreme Court, and a tradition of North-South compromise during the period 1820 to 1854 as a precedent, the opportunity for a national consensus was present, but Buchanan lacked the political imagination to seize it.

Placing his personal hatred of Douglas before the welfare of the Democratic party, Buchanan engaged in a vindictive attempt to purge him in the 1858 election. As the party's leader, Buchanan should have preferred the reelection of a Democratic senator rather than a loss to a Republican, but he did not have the self-assurance to tolerate dissension or at least remain neutral. Douglas narrowly won reelection after a memorable series of debates with Abraham Lincoln, his Republican opponent, but Lincoln emerged as the man to reckon with in 1860.

For most Northern Democrats, the 1858 election was a debacle as Republicans were swept into governorships, the Senate, and the House. Buchanan was in a state of shock. The defeat was "so great that it is almost absurd," he acknowledged.[24] Even so, he was curiously detached from reality. Despite the dismaying outcome of the midterm elections, Buchanan made the amazing statement that "the prospects are daily brightening. From present appearances the party will ere long be thoroughly united."

With the exceptions of Thomas Jefferson and John Quincy Adams, no previous presidents matched Buchanan's experience in foreign affairs, and he planned a vigorous role for the United States on the international scene. In fact, he hoped to divert public attention from sectional rivalries by bold foreign triumphs. He intended to purchase Alaska from the Russians and Cuba from Spain, to win control of the interoceanic trade routes across Central America, to ensure American ascendancy over Mexico and in the Caribbean, and to span the nation with a transcontinental railroad.

Had there been no fight over slavery or no secession crisis, Buchanan, rather than Theodore Roosevelt, might be remembered as the most aggressive imperialist in American history. But his ambitious plans were upset by the congressional bickering accompanying the sectional conflict. Even ordinary appropriations bills needed to keep the government going had trouble passing. A financial panic and a nasty little guerrilla war with the Mormons in Utah added to a chaotic situation.

"Our present financial condition is without parallel in history," the president had boasted at his inaugural, and there was a fat surplus in the federal treasury. Within a few months, however, banks were failing, fear and terror gripped Wall Street, and mills and factories shut their doors. Crowds of hungry workmen flowed into the streets of the large

Northern cities chanting, "Bread or blood!" Frenzied railroad speculation, increased imports due to lower tariffs, and reduced demand for
food in Europe because of the end of the Crimean War were blamed for
the upheaval. Buchanan's reaction was typical of the day—the government sympathized with the people's suffering, but could do nothing to
alleviate their plight. The natural buoyancy and energies of the American people saw them through, but not before untold thousands had
suffered the misery of broken lives, hunger, and despair.[25]

Two ideas grew out of the panic that were to cast long shadows in
American politics. In the North, disaffected factory workers who felt
abandoned by the Democratic administration eagerly listened to
Republican claims that their plight was caused by low tariffs; when the
Republicans came to power, tariffs—and wages—would go up. In
the South, where the panic had scarcely touched the cotton economy,
the ruin of the North was looked upon as just retribution for the crime
of abolition and the corruption of its cities. "Cotton is King!" proclaimed Southerners. If the Yankees did not conform to Southern
wishes, the South would leave the Union—and flourish on its own.

Although Buchanan would later claim he had no power under the
Constitution to use force against the seceding Southern states, he had
no such scruples in putting down what he saw as a rebellion by the Mormons in the Utah Territory. Harried out of Ohio, Missouri, and Illinois,
the Mormons had been led in 1847 by Brigham Young to their new
Zion in Utah. Over the years, they grew in numbers, strength, and
wealth, a polygamous theocracy within a monogamous and democratic
country. Young had persuaded Congress to establish the Utah Territory
with himself as governor, but for the most part, Utah was ignored by
Washington as an ill-favored stepchild.

In 1855, however, President Pierce appointed three federal judges
for Utah—two renegade Mormons and a confirmed Mormon hater.
They complained to Washington that their rulings were disregarded by
the settlers, who obeyed only the laws handed down by Young and the
church hierarchy. Without waiting to verify these tales, Buchanan dismissed Young as governor and sent twenty-five hundred troops to
Utah to force submission to a new governor. Unhappily, the official letter informing the Mormon prophet that he was being replaced went

astray—Pierce had, in an economy move, closed down the Utah mail service. Knowing only that a large military force was on the way, Young mobilized an army of his own.

Two federal forts were burned, army wagon trains were attacked, and Mormon fanatics massacred some 120 California-bound immigrants. At last, Thomas L. Kane of Philadelphia, a friend of Buchanan's and a Mormon sympathizer, suggested he be sent to Salt Lake City to talk to Young. The president agreed. Following meetings with Kane, who told him more troops were on the way, Young accepted the inevitable, and matters were worked out. "I am happy to inform you that the governor and other civil officers of Utah are now performing their appropriate functions without resistance," Buchanan told Congress. ". . . Peace prevails throughout the Territory."[26]

It was more than could be said for the rest of the nation.

Night was falling on October 16, 1859, a Sunday, as a wild-eyed abolitionist fanatic and terrorist named John Brown seized the federal arsenal at Harpers Ferry in western Virginia with the intention of stirring a slave revolt. Several people were killed and Brown holed up in the arsenal's fire engine house with a handful of black and white supporters. Was this it, the irrepressible conflict at last? Shocked, Buchanan met hurriedly with Secretary of War John B. Floyd, who ordered a company of marines under Colonel Robert E. Lee to the scene. Within a few hours, Brown was captured, later tried, and hanged for treason against the state of Virginia.

Pikes that Brown had gathered for distribution to the liberated slaves were placed on view in Southern cities. White people fingered their necks and shuddered, for they knew full well for whom they were intended. Even Southern moderates were now being forced to choose between the Union and the protection of their way of life against a dangerous enemy. Throughout the Deep South, militia companies were organized, funds were appropriated for military supplies, and warnings issued that if a "Black Republican" was elected president in 1860, the South would secede. In the North, Brown was hailed as a martyr to the antislavery cause, who, in Ralph Waldo Emerson's words, made "the gallows glorious like the cross."

The events that led to the smashup of the Union followed rapidly, as if a great drum were beating out the march to war.[27] As a result of Buchanan's ineptness over Kansas, the Democratic convention that met in April 1860 in Charleston, at the very heart of aggressive slavery sentiment, split over a Southern demand for a platform calling for the protection of slavery in the territories. When it was voted down, the delegates of eight Southern states stormed out to meet at a separate convention. The rest of the delegates adjourned after fifty-seven fruitless ballots without choosing a presidential candidate. Reassembling in Baltimore, the Democrats gave their now worthless nomination to Stephen Douglas, while the rump convention nominated Vice President Breckinridge on a pro-slavery platform.*

With the Democrats hopelessly divided, Lincoln easily won the presidency, although only 39.8 percent of the voters cast ballots for him. President Buchanan voted for Breckinridge. Immediately after the election, calls for secession reached fever pitch in South Carolina and in the lower South, even though Lincoln implicitly denied any intention of molesting slavery where it currently existed. But the extremists were in the saddle and they charged that the election of Lincoln proved that the North intended to free the slaves. Fear, pride, and honor dictated that Southerners preserve their way of life by creating a new and independent republic.

Now frail at almost seventy and in deteriorating health, Buchanan despaired as the whirlwind of which he had warned swept across the land. Under the influence of a cabinet that included several scheming secessionists and a stool pigeon for the Republicans, he went about his duties with painful effort. Never known for swift or decisive action, he temporized with the hope that secession and civil war would be put off during the awkward four-month interregnum between the election and the day he would turn over his office to Lincoln. Unlike Andrew Jackson, who had met South Carolina's attempts at nullification in 1832 by asserting the supremacy of the federal government and the threat to use force, Buchanan did nothing. "Vacillating and obstinate by

*The remnant of the Whig and American parties organized the Constitutional Union party, upholding the Constitution and "the enforcement of the laws," and nominated John Bell of Tennessee.

turns, yet lacking firmness when the occasion demanded firmness, he floundered about in a sea of perplexity, throwing away chance after chance," in the words of one historian.[28]

In his annual address in December 1860, Buchanan had the opportunity to sound the Jacksonian trumpet; instead, he dithered. He blamed the abolitionists for pushing the nation toward fratricide, thereby further alienating Northerners who might have been prone to accept a compromise, while he begged Southerners to wait and see what Lincoln did before taking any precipitate action. Secession was unconstitutional, he argued, but the federal government had no means to prevent it or to suppress it once a state had left the Union. Events quickly overran Buchanan's appeals to reason.

The president was attending a ball shortly before Christmas when he heard a commotion outside and dispatched a young woman to find out what was happening. She found a South Carolina congressman in the hall gleefully waving a telegram over his head and shouting, "South Carolina has seceded! South Carolina has seceded!" Making her way back to the president through the excited throng, the woman passed on the news. Buchanan seemed to age on the spot. "Please—someone—won't someone call a carriage," he murmured weakly. "I must go."[29]

Six other states—Alabama, Florida, Georgia, Louisiana, Mississippi, and Texas—followed South Carolina out of the Union, and by February 9, 1861, they had organized the provisional government of the Confederate States of America in Montgomery, Alabama. Federal forts and arsenals as well as a subtreasury were seized by the new regime. Soon, said young Henry Adams, there would be nothing left to secede from. Rumors spread throughout the North that the secessionists surrounding Buchanan had conspired to send weapons to arsenals in the South and gold to the Southern mints, where they were captured, and had purposely scattered the navy to foreign stations. Only uncompleted and isolated Fort Sumter in Charleston harbor remained under control of the U.S. government, and it became the focal point of the crisis.

Emboldened by a new Unionist cabinet, Buchanan now showed a bit more initiative. But an attempt to reinforce Sumter's slender garrison failed when the unarmed steamer carrying the troops was driven off by batteries flying the palmetto flag of South Carolina. Now, the beleaguered president begged Congress to give him new powers and to create a legal solution to the situation. Bills for calling out the militia and augmenting Buchanan's military authority went nowhere as Lincoln and the Republicans did nothing to help him. Buchanan thought the best way to resolve the crisis was an amendment to the Constitution that would guarantee slavery in the states that wanted it, but Southerners were no longer interested.

Breathing a sigh of relief, the outgoing president turned the reins of government over to Lincoln on March 4, 1861, with the comment, "My dear sir, if you are as happy in entering the White House as I shall feel on returning to Wheatland, you are a happy man indeed."[30]

Buchanan returned home a scorned man. Although he supported Lincoln and the Union once Fort Sumter was fired upon, he spent his remaining years defending himself from accusations that his unwillingness to act against the South had helped bring on the war and that his cabinet had committed treason. The Senate considered a resolution censuring him for "sympathy with the conspirators and their treasonable project," which failed to pass by only a narrow margin. As the casualty lists lengthened, he stopped going into Lancaster because of the insults hurled his way, and there were threats against his life.

The old man's illusions died hard, however. Even as late as 1864, Buchanan still believed that "a frank and manly offer to the Confederates that they might return to the Union just as they were before . . . might be accepted." He never ceased to believe that the abolitionists were solely responsible for the war. He opposed the Emancipation Proclamation and believed giving the ex-slaves the vote was dangerous and unconstitutional. On January 1, 1868, James Buchanan died at seventy-six from the infirmities of old age. Shortly before his death, he told a friend, "I have no regret for any public act of my life, and history will vindicate my memory."[30]

Such faith was misplaced, however. History still bears him a grudge— and for good reason.

CHAPTER IX

WARREN GAMALIEL HARDING

With a whimsical delight in farce in any form, H. L. Mencken eagerly went over to Washington on the morning of March 4, 1921, to look in on the inauguration of Warren Gamaliel Harding. As the words of the twenty-ninth president's inaugural address trailed out on the frosty air like "a string of wet sponges," Mencken shifted uneasily on a folding chair. He readily confessed to having voted for Harding after a night spent, as he put it, on his knees in prayerful meditation, but now he was having second thoughts. Later, hunching over his battered old Corona, Mencken tapped out a column assessing the new president: "No other such a complete and dreadful nitwit is to be found in the pages of American history."[1]

Over the years, others eagerly confirmed the Sage of Baltimore's judgment. William G. McAdoo, treasury secretary in the cabinet of the outgoing president, Woodrow Wilson, said Harding's speeches "leave the impression of an army of pompous phrases moving over the landscape in search of an idea."[2] The poet e. e. cummings observed that Harding was "the only man, woman or child / who wrote a simple declarative sentence / with seven grammatical errors."[3] Harding "was not a bad man," opined Alice Longworth. "He was just a slob."[4]

Harding certainly had a wonderful way with words. "We must prosper America first" was choice Gamalielese. And so was "I would like the government to do all it can to mitigate." When he wasn't mitigating, Harding was alliterating. "Progression," he once said, "is not proclamation nor palaver, nor play or prejudice. It is not of personal pronouns, nor perennial pronouncement. It is not the perturbation of a people passion-wrought, nor a promise proposed."*[5] Whew!

Harding is a prime example of incompetence, sloth, and feeble good nature in the White House. Yet he was probably no dimmer than such other presidential nonentities as Franklin Pierce or Calvin Coolidge. Harding ranks so low because his name is forever linked with an era of unbridled graft and corruption, and it immediately conjures up visions of Teapot Dome and the "Ohio Gang." Sporadic attempts have been made to rescue his reputation but have been unable to make much headway.† Harding also gave "in the closet" new meaning: he supposedly had assignations with his mistress in a small closet conveniently near the Oval Office.

There is no evidence that Harding stole so much as a nickel, but his friends, associates, and some of his cabinet made back-alley deals with predatory businessmen to plunder the nation. Years before Harding became president, his father had an inkling of the chain of disasters that lay in the offing: "Warren, it's a good thing you wasn't born a girl because you'd be in a family way all the time. You can't say no." Harding brought with him to Washington as jolly a gang of small-town sports and backroom fixers as were to be found in any county courthouse in Ohio. One observer said the rollicking refrain of "Hail, Hail, the Gang's All Here!" could almost be heard resounding across the city on inauguration night. In no time, they were trying to pry the dome off the U.S. Capitol.

Harding's interior secretary became the first cabinet member to go to jail; his attorney general only narrowly escaped similar infamy, and his navy secretary was forced to resign due to a combination of sheer stupidity and criminal negligence. Fraud in the Veterans Bureau, graft in the Office of the Alien Property Custodian, and conspiracy in the Jus-

---

*Harding is also the author of the phrase "the founding fathers." He first used it in a speech to the Sons and Daughters of the American Revolution on Washington's Birthday, 1918.

†The most recent is Robert H. Ferrell, *The Strange Deaths of President Harding* (Columbia, Mo.: University of Missouri, 1996).

tice Department were all part of Harding's dubious legacy. Such high officials would not again face indictment and jail until the presidencies of Richard M. Nixon and Ronald Reagan. Unlike Nixon, named by a federal grand jury as an unindicted coconspirator in the Watergate scandal, Harding did not encourage or condone violations of public trust. He drifted lazily over this bubbling morass of corruption like a hot-air balloon in Macy's Thanksgiving Day Parade.

Few Americans had heard of the handsome, easygoing Ohio senator and small-town editor until he emerged from a smoke-filled Chicago hotel room during the Republican convention of 1920 with the party's presidential nomination in his pocket. Nevertheless, he was elected with 61 percent of the votes—the largest percentage that had been won by a presidential candidate. Women, voting in a national election for the first time in 1920, went overwhelmingly for the handsome, white-haired senator. Perhaps they needed more experience. It was, says a biographer, as if "a clothing store model, after years of faithful service in displaying choice garments in the front window, should suddenly find itself manager of the store."[6]

Harding's smashing victory was no accident, however. He was exactly what the American people wanted. Harding had a gut feeling for the hopes and fears of ordinary Americans in an age of kaleidoscopic change. Only a few years before, Theodore Roosevelt and Wilson had ridden the crest of a crusade for reform. Progressive politicians and muckraking journalists had exposed the symbiotic relationship between the trusts and the political machines and had created an urgent demand for change. Unhappily, reform was swallowed up by World War I, and the postwar years brought widespread disillusion with great moral crusades—whether for reform at home or for international order abroad. "If I am convinced of anything," said Mencken, "it is that Doing Good is in bad taste."

Weary of sacrifice and moralistic appeals to idealism, fearful of rad-icalism and frightened by racial strife, the American people wanted to shape their own affairs without interference from the government. Harding's campaign slogan was "Back to Normalcy"—he had meant to say *normality* during a campaign speech, but fluffed it—but *normalcy* struck a responsive chord among the voters.* "There might be no such word in the dictionary," observed Frederick Lewis Allen, the chronicler of the twenties, "but normalcy is what [Americans] wanted."[7]

Warren Harding was the epitome of a predominately rural and small-town America that was already fading before the implacable onslaught of urbanization, standardization, and Henry Ford's Tin Lizzie. Born on November 2, 1865, on the family farm near Blooming Grove in north-central Ohio, he was the oldest of six children of George T. Harding, a country schoolteacher turned homeopathic physician, and his wife, Phoebe, who practiced as a midwife. The boy grew up amid gossip that haunted him all the way to the White House, that the Hardings had African-American blood. At school, Warren and the other Harding children were taunted as "niggers."

Following a meager three years of schooling at a backwoods academy, Harding taught for a year in a one-room schoolhouse for $30 a month. It was, he said later, the hardest job he ever had. Once the term was over, he strapped his effects on a mule and rode into the bustling town of Marion, Ohio. Spiritually, he never left. Harding studied law briefly and, when it proved beyond his limited capabilities, tried selling insurance, also without much success. Then, he turned to journalism as a $1-a-week reporter on a county weekly. He succeeded so well that within a few years he was the owner and editor of a struggling small daily, the *Marion Star.*

Harding was soon pursued by Florence "Flossie" Kling De Wolfe, the divorced daughter of Amos Kling, the town's leading banker. Flossie was five years older than "Wurr'n," as she called him, had a voice that shattered glass, cold blue eyes, and a domineering manner. Harding lazily tried to avoid her advances, but he was no match for her, and in 1891, at the age of twenty-six, found himself married. Old Mr. Kling opposed the union, once accosting his future son-in-law in the street and calling him a "nigger."

---

*"America's present need is not heroics but helping, not nostrums but normalcy, not revolution but restoration, not agitation but adjustment, not surgery but serenity," Harding declared in a speech in Boston on May 20, 1920.

The marriage was childless and not happy. Flossie was ambitious and penny-pinching and did not have a high opinion of her husband's business skills. She is largely credited with making the *Star* a financial success and pushing the diffident Harding much further along than his own ambitions and abilities would have taken him. "Mrs. Harding in those days ran the show," recalled Norman Thomas, later the perennial Socialist candidate for president and one of her newsboys.[8] As for Harding, he called his wife Duchess and sought refuge from her shrill demands in the camaraderie of his frowsy poker-playing pals and in the sporting houses down by the railroad tracks.

Harding bore a striking resemblance to Sinclair Lewis's fictional real estate salesman, George F. Babbitt. Like Babbitt, he was a natural backslapper and all-around good fellow. He played cornet in the town band and was active in the Kiwanis, the Rotarians, the Masons, and the Shriners, as well as the Moose, the Elks, and the Odd Fellows. He enjoyed cracking off-color jokes with men like himself. "What d'ya know?" they greeted each other, straw boaters kicked back on their heads and thumbs in the armholes of their vests. "What d'ya know?" Sociability led him into politics, the chief diversion of the Ohio hinterland. Harding was a meandering orator, but his apparent sincerity, combined with a resonant voice and a gassy pomposity, made him a welcome speaker at crossroads Republican rallies.

It was at one of these festivities in Richwood, Ohio, in 1899, that Harding met Harry M. Daugherty, who was to be a major influence on his life. Harding had just delivered a speech to the faithful and had lined up at an outdoor privy to relieve himself when Daugherty, next in line, mused upon what a handsome and genial-looking fellow Harding was. He was then thirty-four, a tad under six feet tall, with massive if slightly stooped shoulders, and a bronzed complexion. A swatch of pale hair swept across his forehead. "Gee, what a great-looking president that man would make!" Daugherty said to himself—or so he later claimed.[9] After Harding became president, Daugherty sanitized the tale to say they were waiting to have their shoes shined when vouchsafed this vision.

Harry Daugherty was five years older than Harding and had a similar small-town background. He had won a few minor state offices, but by the time he met Harding was primarily a lobbyist at the state capital in Columbus for an assortment of utilities and business interests. Mark Sullivan, a leading journalist of the day who knew Daugherty well, wrote: "Always he knew what wire to pull; always he kept a web of wires running from his office out to all sorts of men who occupied places of leverage; always he knew how to get results."[10]

Ohio had provided the United States with six presidents—Harding was to be the seventh—but the state's politics were a cesspool. Political control was divided between the battling forces of Mark A. Hanna, a Cleveland industrialist and gray eminence behind President William McKinley, and Senator "Fire Alarm Joe" Foraker,* later exposed as being on the payroll of Standard Oil. In 1899, Harding was elected to the first of two terms in the state senate, where he made himself useful to the Foraker faction. As a reward for his loyalty, he was elected lieutenant governor. Like most Ohio politicos of the day, Harding regarded graft as part of the system, and the columns of the *Star* were for sale. He accepted stock in a local brewery in return for puffing it in the paper and is said to have taken $10,000 from a farm-implement company for similar services.[11]

Harding's roving eye also settled upon Carrie Fulton Phillips, a tall, attractive woman ten years younger than him and wife of James Phillips, a successful dry-goods merchant and a close friend. For several years, neither Flossie nor Jim Phillips was aware of the torrid affair conducted by their spouses, even though the two couples often socialized and traveled together to Europe and Bermuda. Eventually, Carrie left her husband and demanded that Harding divorce his wife and marry her. When he refused, she decamped to Europe.

Meantime, Harding's political star was rising. In 1910 and again in 1912 he won the Republican nomination for governor, only to be beaten both times by his fellow publisher, James M. Cox—who after three terms as governor of Ohio was to lose the presidency to Harding in 1920. Two years after his last defeat for the governorship, with progressivism on the wane and the Democrats badly hurt by a business slump resulting from the outbreak of World War I, Harding was easily elected to the U.S. Senate.

---

*So named because of his arm-flourishing, spread-eagle oratorical style.

With his silver mane and high-octane smile, Harding looked like a senator. In fact, someone suggested that he was probably the only member who would appear at home in a Roman toga. But his six years of service in the Senate were undistinguished even by the terms of that rather undistinguished body. There was no Harding Act or even a Harding Amendment to attract public attention. He introduced little legislation and most of it was petty, designed to provide some advantage for a constituent or campaign contributor.

Harding was comfortable in the clubby atmosphere of the Senate. Nothing taxed his intelligence or his energies. The pay was good—$5,000 a year plus allowances. Along with the $20,000 or so coming in from the *Star,* he was well-off. For amusement, he played middling golf at the exclusive Chevy Chase Club—the members were obviously unaware of his questionable racial background—and sneaked off to burlesque shows. Most of his colleagues considered him a swell fellow. Flossie had taken to the Washington social scene, where she was befriended by one of the leading hostesses, Evalyn Walsh McLean, the wife of the hard-tippling publisher of the *Washington Post* and owner of the Hope Diamond. Harding now supposedly enjoyed the favors of a young blonde named Nan Britton, thirty years his junior, and in 1919, she claimed to have given birth to a daughter fathered by Harding. He had also resumed his affair with Carrie Phillips, who had returned to the United States after the outbreak of World War I.

"Had his career stopped with the Senate, he would have been only an obscure and forgotten name preserved like thousands of others in old Congressional Directories," Mark Sullivan observed.[12] Harding's record was so lackluster that political observers looking over the Republican presidential possibilities for 1920 did not even bother to include him in their calculations—except for Harry Daugherty.

Daugherty had never forgotten his first impression of Harding, but his task was to persuade the senator that he had a chance to win the nomination. In recent years, historians have debated whether Harding was really as reluctant a presidential candidate as Daugherty was led to believe. Andrew Sinclair, a Harding biographer, traces Harding's White House ambitions at least from his election to the Senate in 1914 and maintains that his repeated denials of interest in the presidency were a smoke screen. On the other hand, Francis Russell, another biographer, contends that unpublished letters between Harding and Carrie Phillips make it clear that he had no such early ambitions.

No matter where the truth may lie, Daugherty threw himself into his holy work with evangelical fervor. When a worried Harding asked, "Am I a big enough man for the race?" Daugherty had a ready answer: "Don't make me laugh! The day of greatness in the presidential chair is over. . . . Greatness in the presidential chair is largely an illusion."[13]

Daugherty had a simple strategy. He expected the front-runners for the nomination—Major General Leonard Wood, former army chief of staff, and Governor Frank O. Lowdon of Illinois—to tear each other to pieces while Harding angered no one and remained quietly in reserve. As early as February 1920, Daugherty confidently predicted how his candidate would win the nomination: "I don't expect Senator Harding to be nominated on the first, second, or third ballots, but I think we can afford to take chances that, about eleven minutes after two on Friday morning at the convention, when fifteen or twenty men, somewhat weary, are sitting around a table, some of them will say, 'Who will we nominate?' At that decisive time, the friends of Harding can suggest him and can afford to abide by the result."[14]

Later, Daugherty embellished his prediction to say that the choice of the Republican standard-bearer would be made by "fifteen men in a smoke-filled room." He not only added a vivid phrase to American political folklore, but turned out to be an amazingly accurate prophet.

Sweltering in a Chicago summer, the convention quickly became a maelstrom of conflicting ambitions. Just as Daugherty had predicted, Wood and Lowdon deadlocked through the fourth ballot. Harding, however, had only 65½ votes on the first ballot and slipped on the succeeding tallies. Tempers flared, nerves rubbed raw, and fights broke out on the floor and in the gallery. Finally, the convention recessed on Friday night so a solution to the impasse could be worked out off the floor before the party tore itself to pieces. The moment Harry Daugherty had forecast was now at hand.

A group of the party's Old Guard gathered in Suite 404–6 on the thirteenth floor of the Blackstone Hotel, quarters of Will H. Hays, the Republican national chairman. Party leaders and influential senators wandered in and out as the liquor flowed and cigar smoke coiled about. Wood and Lowdon had knocked each other out—that much was agreed upon. But who was to take their place? The names of all the various other possibilities were trotted out: Herbert Hoover, who had brilliantly directed the postwar effort to feed Europe's starving masses; the conservative Governor Calvin Coolidge of Massachusetts; Senator Hiram Johnson of California . . . and Warren Harding.

One by one, all were ruled out and only Harding's name remained. The consensus was that he was the best of the second-raters. He had no political enemies, was from a pivotal state, had voted for Prohibition and women's suffrage, and could be relied upon to take advice rather than give orders. About two o'clock in the morning—close enough to the time prophesied by Daugherty to fit the legend—a stunned Harding was summoned to the "smoke-filled room" and told it was likely that he would be nominated when the convention met later that morning. Was there any reason he could not be president?

"Gentlemen, I should like to be alone a little while," Harding is reputed to have replied. He was ushered into an adjoining room where he spent about ten minutes—thinking perhaps of the whispering campaign that he had African-American blood, or his affair with Carrie Phillips, or about Nan Britton and their child, or even of his own adequacies. No matter. When he reappeared, Harding said, "Gentlemen, there is no reason in the sight of God that I cannot be president of the United States."[15]

When the convention reconvened, there was no massive, sudden shift to Harding's standard, but his share of the votes mounted steadily, and he was nominated on the ninth ballot with 692⅕ votes. Nan Britton watched from a seat high up in the gallery procured for her by her lover. "We drew to a pair of deuces and filled," observed Harding.

As a result of Daugherty's talk about the "smoke-filled room," a legend was created that Harding's nomination was the handiwork of a cabal of corrupt insiders who foisted him onto the convention. Big oil controlled the convention, according to the Kansas editor William Allen White. "I have never seen a convention—and I have watched most of them since McKinley's first nomination—so completely dominated by sinister predatory economic forces as was this."[16] Wood, it was reported, had been offered the nomination if he would promise the oil interests three seats in his cabinet. The ramrod-honest soldier fired his campaign manager for even considering the proposal—and lost his chance to be president.

Nevertheless, even though the convention was dominated by business interests "who knew what they wanted out of government and were willing to pay for whatever privileges they got," according to White,[17] Harding was not forced upon the delegates by a conspiracy. In reality, he was the candidate who best suited the mood of the convention—and the nation. He would be a caretaker president, modest and unassuming, and would not browbeat business or Congress like the intellectually arrogant Wilson.

The election was anticlimactic. Harding and the vice-presidential candidate, Calvin Coolidge, waged a front-porch campaign. While James Cox and his running mate, Franklin D. Roosevelt, Theodore Roosevelt's distant cousin and assistant secretary of the navy under Wilson, tried to make the campaign a referendum on the Wilsonian dream of American participation in the League of Nations, Harding remained in Marion and mouthed canned platitudes and was peddled to the country like a patent medicine. "Keep Warren at home. . . . Don't let him make any speeches," advised Senator Boies Penrose, the Republican boss of Pennsylvania. "If he goes out on tour, somebody's sure to ask him questions, and Warren's just the sort of damned fool that will try to answer them."[18]

Singer Al Jolson stumped for Harding with a campaign song he had written: "We need another Lincoln / To do this country's thinkin' / Mis-ter Harding / You're the man for us." Taking no chances on a last-minute scandal, the Republican National Committee gave Carrie Phillips $20,000 plus a monthly stipend and put her on a slow boat to Japan.*

Superficial similarities between Harding and Harry S Truman abound. In fact, wiseacres called Truman a "white Harding" when he was sud-

---

*Carrie Phillips saved Harding's letters to her, but they remain under seal in the Library of Congress until 2014.

denly elevated to the White House by Franklin Roosevelt's death in 1945. Both men were products of the rural Middle West, were poorly educated, and had come up through corrupt political machines. Both liked nothing so much as a friendly round of bourbon and ribald stories with their cronies. And both became president because they were acceptable to all factions of their parties—or in other words were the lowest common political denominator. There, the resemblance ends. Harry Truman had a flinty integrity and a boundless capacity to expand his limited horizons.

Harding's problem was that he clung to a vision of a small-town America that had never existed, a utopia of the mid-Victorian dream. He lacked understanding of the forces at work in the United States in the postwar era: a mix of social change and moral crisis; economic opportunity and massive economic dislocation. Harding's remedy was to return to a mystical time that never was rather than to use the federal government to further long-range, large-scale solutions to the problems facing the American people. Under Harding, the country was cast adrift without moral leadership while the president was content to sit back and watch.

Recognizing that he was no "brain," Harding announced that he would appoint a cabinet of the "best minds" in the country. Charles Evans Hughes, onetime governor of New York and the unsuccessful Republican presidential candidate in 1916, was named secretary of state. Herbert Hoover was appointed secretary of commerce. Andrew W. Mellon, whose fortune rested on control of Gulf Oil and Alcoa and who was among the richest men in America, was chosen as treasury secretary. These appointments were well received, but they were followed by others that inspired jokes about Harding's concept of the best minds.

With Prohibition just getting under way and with several wartime fraud cases pending, the post of attorney general offered an opportunity for either exercising the utmost integrity or amassing unprecedented loot. Harding gave the job to Daugherty. "It won't be long before Harry Daugherty is selling the sunshine off the Capitol steps," observed a cynic. To the consternation of conservationists and the delight of the oil barons, Harding appointed Senator Albert B. Fall of New Mexico as secretary of the interior. With his drooping mustache, snakelike eyes, and wide-brimmed black hat, Fall looked like the crooked sheriff in a western movie. The appointment of Edwin N. Denby, a dim ex-congressman, as secretary of the navy was another tragic blunder. Will Hays, at just over five feet tall, so short that he had trouble putting his elbows on the cabinet table, was named postmaster general and doled out patronage in the trusted Ohio manner: he demanded almost a day's work for a full day's pay from nearly qualified jobholders. Henry Mencken summed up Harding's cabinet as "three highly intelligent men of self-interest, six jackasses and one common crook."[19]

Nor did Harding forget his old Ohio pals. Dr. Charles E. Sawyer, a Marion homeopath and a favorite of Flossie's, was appointed a brigadier general and presidential physician. Donald R. Crissinger, a boyhood friend whose financial experience consisted of a few months in a small-town bank, was named governor of the Federal Reserve System, the country's ranking bank official. Another old crony, Ed Scobey, who had never risen above sheriff of Pickaway County, was appointed director of the Mint. The post of superintendent of prisons was removed from civil service and went to Heber H. Votaw, Harding's brother-in-law. To head the newly formed Veterans Bureau, the president chose Colonel Charles H. Forbes, a smooth-talking confidence man whom he had met on a senatorial junket to Hawaii.

Daugherty brought with him a curious character named Jess Smith. Big-bellied and loose-limbed, he followed Daugherty about like a friendly puppy. Smith had no official duties in the Department of Justice, but he had an office near that of the attorney general. No one seemed to know what he did there. The two old friends shared bachelor quarters in the fashionable Wardman Park Hotel and were often seen at a small townhouse at 1625 K Street not far from the White House.

There, Howard Mannington, a slick Ohio lobbyist and Daugherty's longtime friend, operated a combination speakeasy, gambling hell, and brothel where the Ohio Gang could arrange and celebrate its secret deals. Open for business day and night, the "little green house of K Street" was the place to secure protection for bootleggers, permits for withdrawal of alcohol from federal stockpiles, judgeships and appointments to office, and to purchase paroles, pardons, and privileges. Charlie Forbes claimed he had once seen Mannington studying a Justice Department file of federal judgeships that had been sent over to be auctioned off to the highest bidder. "Gee, how the money rolls in!" Jess Smith hummed to himself—and with good reason, for he was the Ohio Gang's bagman.[20]

Harding did not attend the parties on K Street. Instead, he invited the boys over to the White House for a poker session a couple of nights a week. The regulars included Daugherty, Fall, Forbes, and "Doc" Sawyer. Sometimes Andy Mellon and Harry F. Sinclair, an oil tycoon and friend of Fall's, also took a hand. Prohibition was the law of the land, but not in the White House. Alice Longworth, certainly no prude, once went to the president's second floor study while an official reception was going on down below. "No rumor could have exceeded the reality," she reported. "The study was filled with cronies . . . the air heavy with tobacco smoke, trays with bottles containing every imaginable brand of whiskey stood about, cards and poker chips to hand—a general atmosphere of waistcoat unbuttoned, feet on the desk, and the spittoon alongside."[21]

Ike Hoover, who served as a White House usher through ten administrations, said no president spent more time at his desk than Harding. Perhaps he needed more time than some. Harding was anxious to be worthy of his office, but nothing in his career as small-town, semi-educated journalist and political glad-hander had prepared him for the presidency, and as was to be expected, he was overwhelmed by it. He paced the long corridors of the old mansion—half grand hotel, half museum—restlessly, day and night. Once, a knotty tax matter was dropped on his desk and he threw up his hands in desperation and told a secretary:

"John, I can't make a damn thing out of this tax problem. I listen to one side and they seem right and then—God!—I talk to the other side and they seem just as right, and here I am where I started. I know somewhere there is a book that will give me the truth, but hell, I couldn't read the book. I know somewhere there is an economist who knows the truth, and I don't know where to find him, and haven't the sense to know and trust him when I find him. God, what a job!"[22]

Foreign affairs were also a puzzlement to Harding. When a *New York Tribune* correspondent dropped by the Oval Office after a trip to Europe, the president called in Judson Welliver, his secretary, and told the newsman, "I don't know anything about this European stuff. You and Jud get together and he can tell me later; he handles these matters for me."[23]

To be fair, the Harding years were not without some accomplishment. With presidential approval, Secretary of State Hughes organized the Washington Arms Limitation Conference of 1921–22, which ended the threat of a costly naval race between the United States, Britain, and Japan and reduced tensions in East Asia for a decade.* Harding also established the Bureau of the Budget, and Charles G. Dawes, its first director, brought sound budgetary practices to the federal government for the first time. And it fell to Harding to bring a formal end to World War I because the Republican Senate had rejected the Treaty of Versailles, negotiated by Wilson. He was summoned off a New Jersey golf course on July 2, 1921, to sign the joint congressional resolution at a friend's home. Harding glanced over the document as a dog sniffed his shoes, signed it, and returned to the links.

While doing nothing to resist nativist pressures to curb foreign immigration into the United States, Harding, perhaps haunted by his own shadows, raised the hopes of blacks by being the first president since the Civil War to speak out for civil rights on Southern soil. Blacks had migrated to the North in search of jobs during the war, and racial tension was still running high following bloody race riots in 1919.

"I want to see the time come when black men will regard themselves as full participants in the benefits and duties of American citizens," Harding told a rigidly segregated audience in Birmingham, Alabama. "We cannot go on, as we have gone on for more than half a century, with one great section of our population . . . set off from real contribution to solving national issues, because of a division on race lines." There were yelps of approval from blacks while whites sat in stunned silence. But black hopes were soon dashed as the president took no steps to back up his words.[24]

---

*Sixty-six battleships and battle cruisers were sent to the breakers by this proposal— "more than all the admirals of the world had sunk in a cycle of centuries," wryly noted a British observer.

In the meantime, the administration was honeycombed with corruption. Albert Fall was the first to pick the pockets of his countrymen. With the conversion of the world's navies from coal to oil, the government had established several large petroleum preserves, to provide emergency fuel for the U.S. Navy, at Elk Hills, California, and Teapot Dome, Wyoming, among others. From the beginning, the oil companies tried to get at these reserves, but each attempt was blocked—until Fall appeared on the scene.

As soon as he was firmly in charge at Interior, Fall launched a vigorous campaign designed to rustle the reserves away from the Navy Department. He convinced Harding that it would be more efficient to have them administered by his agency than by the navy. Next, he turned his attentions to Edwin Denby, the none-too-swift navy secretary. Denby, who seems to have had little interest in his department except to administer it with the least possible annoyance to himself, readily acquiesced in the transfer.

The Harding administration had been in office less than three months when on May 31, 1921, the president signed, no questions asked, an executive order placed before him by Fall that turned over stewardship of the reserves to Interior. Two months later, Fall turned over drilling rights to Elk Hills to the Pan-American Petroleum and Transport Company, headed by Edward Doheny, an old friend. In exchange, Doheny sent Fall a little black bag containing $100,000. "We will be in bad luck," Doheny gleefully told an associate, "if we do not get one hundred million dollars profit." Not long afterward, Fall turned drilling rights to the Teapot Dome reserve over to Harry Sinclair and received $233,000 in Liberty bonds and $70,000 cash.*[25]

While Fall was siphoning off the navy's petroleum reserves, there were lightning flashes of other scandals on the horizon. The only one to break while Harding was alive centered about Charlie Forbes, who looted the Veterans Bureau. Forbes's betrayal was particularly bitter to Harding because he had come to the White House determined to do something for the human debris cast up by Wilson's "war to end all

---

*Elk Hills was sold to the Occidental Petroleum Corporation for $3.65 billion in 1997. (New York Times, October 7, 1997.)

wars." Thousands of wounded and disabled veterans had been shunted to poorhouses, insane asylums, and other inadequate charitable institutions, and some received no care at all. No existing government agency was equipped to deal with problems of such magnitude, so Harding, a generous man if nothing else, created the Veterans Bureau from a half dozen or so overlapping agencies.

The fast-talking Forbes had no trouble convincing Harding that he was building hospitals at a rapid rate—Congress had approved $36 million for this purpose—and the men who had served the nation were receiving the care they deserved. In reality, Forbes solicited "loans" from a construction firm bidding for contracts to build hospitals and was looting government warehouses of medical supplies and equipment, which he sold to private contractors. Forbes disposed of supplies worth upward of $7 million for $600,000 while disabled veterans lacked bandages, bedding, and drugs.[26]

Early in 1923, Doc Sawyer, whose toes had been stepped upon by Forbes, took these facts to Harry Daugherty. Undoubtedly angered by Forbes's failure to share the loot, Daugherty told Harding what Forbes was up to. Forbes was immediately summoned to the White House. A White House visitor who had an appointment with Harding during this period reported that he was directed to the Red Room by mistake. As he approached the room, he heard a voice that sounded as if it were choking with anger. Entering, he was astonished to see Harding with a tight grip on the throat of a man cringing against the wall.

"You yellow rat!" the red-faced president was shouting. "You double-crossing bastard! If you ever—"

The visitor said something in shocked surprise, and Harding whirled about. He immediately loosened his grip on the other man, who staggered out, his face discolored and distorted with fear. The president curtly told his visitor, "I am sorry. You have an appointment. Come into the other room."

On his way out of the White House, the visitor asked a doorman for the name of the man who had left just after he came in.

"That was Colonel Forbes of the Veterans Bureau, sir."[27]

Forbes fled to Europe from where he submitted his resignation. Harding seemed satisfied to have kept the lid on the scandal and did nothing more, but a Senate investigating committee began looking into Forbes's stewardship of the Veterans Bureau. The inquiry took a surprising turn when Charles Cramer, the agency's general counsel, who had shared in the loot, locked himself in his bathroom and put a bullet into his head.

Under Harry Daugherty, the Justice Department was known as the "Department of Easy Virtue." The genial attorney general was regarded as the center of a web of graft that extended throughout the administration. Almost immediately after taking office, it was charged that he had received payoffs to quash war frauds and profiteering cases. The word in Washington was that such cases could be settled out of court if the "proper" approach was made to the attorney general—through Jess Smith.

The most notorious case to which Daugherty was linked concerned the Alien Property Bureau, which held property seized from German interests during the war. Smith received $224,000 in exchange for "expediting" a dubious $7-million claim through the bureau. He deposited $50,000 in a joint account he held with Daugherty in a bank operated by the attorney general's brother in their hometown, Washington Court House, Ohio.[28]

Rumors of illegality in the Justice Department became so widespread that as early as 1922 there were demands for Daugherty's ouster. "I wouldn't have given thirty cents for the office of attorney general," he told newsmen, "but I won't surrender it for a million dollars." Cynics said it was probably worth that much to him. The following year, Congress took up a resolution calling for his impeachment, a move that spurred Daugherty to take defensive action. William J. Burns, an erratic private detective brought in by the attorney general to head the Bureau of Investigation—not yet the FBI—and Gaston B. Means, his shady chief operative, were assigned to investigate the investigators. Burglaries and telephone taps became commonplace in Washington, and efforts were made to trip up Daugherty's chief inquisitor, Senator Burton K. Wheeler of Montana, on a morals charge.

Even though the legal bloodhounds were baying at his heels, Daugherty maintained his equilibrium, but the strain began to tell on Jess

Smith. He was suspicious and jumpy, and on a visit home to Washington Court House, he urged Roxy Stinson, his ex-wife, to help him destroy some bank records, canceled checks, and other papers. "I don't think I have long to live," he told a friend. Upon his return to the capital, Smith was alone for several days in the apartment he shared with Daugherty—the attorney general was staying at the White House temporarily—except for Daugherty's secretary, Warren E. Martin.

Early on the morning of May 30, 1923, Martin found Smith lying on the floor with his head in a metal wastebasket and a pistol in his right hand. A bullet had entered his left temple and come out the right side. Martin summoned William Burns, who took over the case rather than let the Washington police in on the investigation. No autopsy was performed and the death was written off as a suicide. But Roxy Stinson insisted that Jess Smith had been right-handed—and it would have been extremely awkward for a right-handed man to shoot himself in the left side of the head. Such a thing "don't hardly ever happen," said one Washington police official.[29]

Just when Harding realized—if he ever did—that his administration was plagued by corruption is unknown. By the summer of 1923, enough evidence had piled up to have aroused questions in the mind of any prudent man. The blatant graft of Charlie Forbes, the Cramer and Smith suicides, the rumors about Harry Daugherty's activities, and the rumblings from Fall's handling of the oil reserves were too much to be ignored. Tired and depressed, Harding resorted to a remedy that had never failed him in the past. He would go off on a speaking tour—or as he put it, he would "go out into the country and 'bloviate.' "

On June 20, the presidential party left for Alaska. Harding stopped to speak along the way, and it was noted that the farther he got from Washington, the more the crowds grew in size and enthusiasm. But the shadow of scandal still fell across his path. In Kansas City, Albert Fall's wife was said to have been smuggled past the reporters covering the president for a private meeting. What she and Harding supposedly discussed—if the meeting took place—was never revealed, but Harding was said to have emerged from the interview with an agitated look.

The next day, he told William Allen White, "My God, this is a hell of a job! I have no trouble with my enemies. I can take care of my enemies all right. But my damn friends, my God-damn friends . . . they're the ones that keep me walking the floor nights!"[30]

In Alaska—he was the first president to visit there—Harding heard complaints from conservationists about the way Fall had run the Interior Department. Just before leaving, the president received a long, coded message from Washington that plainly upset him. For a day or two, he appeared near collapse. During the sea voyage back to the United States, Harding called Herbert Hoover to his cabin and told the commerce secretary that a great scandal was brewing within the administration. Should it be aired or covered up? Hoover replied that the scandal should be exposed to "at least get credit for integrity on our side." To fight off the nightmare that haunted him, Harding played bridge day and night on the return trip home, while the others played in shifts. The atmosphere was so strained that Hoover could never bring himself to play bridge again.[31]

Harding reached San Francisco worn-out in body and mind. He was only fifty-seven, but looked and acted like an old man. He was resting in his suite in the Palace Hotel on the evening of August 2, 1923—Doc Sawyer said he was suffering from a touch of food poisoning—while Flossie read from a friendly article in the *Saturday Evening Post*. "That's good," he said. "Go on; read some more." Not long after, his face suddenly twitched, his mouth opened, and his head fell lifelessly to the side. Harding had a history of heart trouble, and the doctors concluded he had died of a stroke. But Gaston Means soon spread a more lurid tale: the president had been poisoned by his wife, possibly with the collusion of Sawyer, to spare him from public disgrace. Flossie had refused permission for an autopsy, so the charge could not be disproved.

A national outpouring of genuine grief greeted Harding's unexpected passing. The American people were still largely unaware of the scandals brewing behind the facade of his administration, and his popularity was high. As the funeral train moved across the nation to Washington, the tracks were lined with mourners singing Harding's favorite hymns and paying their last respects. The Kiwanis Club magazine published the following tribute to its departed brother:

> Oh, Son of God—to God returned—
> Peace to thee with a rest well earned,
> Thy gentle face and quiet calm
> Remains to us a golden balm.

When the cortege finally reached the White House, Flossie had the coffin opened and sat for hours beside it as Harding's body lay in state in the East Room. Putting her face close to that of her late husband, she whispered, "No one can hurt you now, Wurr'n."[32]

For Republican leaders, Harding's death was a godsend. It allowed the party to pass off culpability for Teapot Dome, and all the other scandals soon to be public, onto the dead man and his associates, forever burying Harding's reputation in muck. Albert Fall took the Fifth Amendment when hauled before the Senate committee investigating his activities. He was eventually convicted of conspiracy to defraud the government by transferring the oil reserves to Doheny and Sinclair in exchange for $400,000 in bribes, and sentenced to a year in jail—the first cabinet member to meet such a fate. The oil tycoons, who had done the bribing, escaped punishment.

There was talk of impeaching Edwin Denby, the blundering navy secretary who had turned the petroleum reserves over to Fall without asking any questions. The charges were dropped after Senator Thomas Walsh of Montana, who was heading the inquiry, said, "Stupidity is not a ground for impeachment, so far as I can learn." Charlie Forbes eventually returned from Europe to be tried for bribery and conspiracy. He was fined $10,000 and sentenced to two years in Leavenworth. He had gotten away with some $2 million in graft.

Harry Daugherty tried to hold on to his job as attorney general but was finally ousted by Calvin Coolidge, Harding's successor, when he refused to supply Senate investigators with documents bearing on such issues as bootlegging, oil deals, and the sale of prosecutorial favors.

These papers were vital to national security, he claimed, and the senators responsible for the inquiry "were received in the inner Soviet circles as comrades." Daugherty deserves credit not only for imagination, but for being ahead of his time.

Indicted on charges of defrauding the government in the alien-property case, he refused to take the stand, implying that he was protecting the late president's memory. This created the widespread impression that somehow Harding had been involved in the scandals. The jury could not agree on Daugherty's innocence or guilt. Tried again, Daugherty got off with another hung jury. He had saved himself, but at the cost of Harding's reputation.

Nan Britton sought money from the Harding family for her illegitimate daughter, but she was rebuffed and published her memoirs, *The President's Daughter.* It was "dedicated with understanding and love to all unwed mothers, and to their innocent children" and was a best-seller. Of her first visit to the White House, she claimed that Harding had taken her "to the one place where, he said, we might share kisses in safety. This was a small closet . . . [where] . . . we repaired . . . many times in the course of my visits to the White House, and in the darkness of a space no more than five feet square the President of the United States and his adoring sweetheart made love."[33]

Sometime after Warren Harding's death, a committee to select a design for a memorial at Marion met to consider a proposal from John Russell Pope, a distinguished architect. Arriving late, one member took a glance at the model and threw up his hands.

"My God, gentlemen! You aren't going to take *this*?"

"Why not?" demanded the chairman.

"Stick a handle on here, and what have you got? A teapot!"[34]

CHAPTER X

RICHARD MILHOUS NIXON

Richard Milhous Nixon began his career as a barker at the Slippery Gulch Rodeo in Prescott, Arizona. Nixon, then a teenager, ran a legal wheel of fortune where hams and sides of bacon were a come-on for backroom poker and crap games. This seems altogether fitting because, for nearly a half century, Nixon was the consummate pitchman of American politics. Throughout his career, he favored such oratorical sleight of hand as "I'm glad you asked that question" and "Now what I am going to do is unprecedented in the history of American politics."[1]

With practiced ease, Nixon gave his pitch a soft sell for young people, changed it subtly for the citizens of calendar-pretty New England towns, and then altered it again for a hard sell that brought the Republican faithful at Midwestern rallies to their feet with cheers.* A skilled debater and amateur actor—he could make his own tears flow by swallowing an imagined lump in his throat—he possessed a mellow baritone voice. Nixon knew all the slick tricks of the practiced orator. Like a master pitchman, he scoffed at the "easy way," which in his view was always the way of the weak, the liberal, or the ill informed. And he easily handled hecklers with a pitchman's skill: "Now let me talk and you might learn something."

Nixon, the nation's thirty-seventh president, was said to be one of the best-prepared men ever to enter the White House. He had been elected

---

*The writer, as a political correspondent for the *Baltimore Sun,* observed this process at close range during the 1968 presidential campaign.

to the House and to the Senate and served two terms as vice president under Dwight D. Eisenhower. He had read the lives of Caesar, Genghis Khan, Napoleon, Gladstone, and Disraeli. He had pumped Alice Longworth for information about the way her father, Theodore Roosevelt, had handled the presidency. He had even learned to play golf. But the avid study of great men's lives—and even indulgence in their hobbies—is no guarantee of presidential greatness.

Nixon is America's worst president not only because he is the one chief executive to resign to escape impeachment, but he blatantly violated the Constitution. Had he not been pardoned by his handpicked successor, Gerald R. Ford, he might have been convicted of a felony for his part in the crimes collectively known as Watergate. Nixon is different from the rest of those on my list, however. Although far more intelligent and able than any of the others, he had a cynical contempt for the American people and democratic institutions that was unique.

"I am not a crook!" he said, but he was a crook. Nixon was "the most dishonest individual I ever met," wrote Barry Goldwater, the Republican presidential candidate in 1964 and a onetime friend. "He lied to his wife, his family, his friends . . . his own political party, the American people, and the world."[2] The Internal Revenue Service ruled that Nixon owed $432,787 in back taxes plus another $33,000 in interest and penalties when he left office. He had made a deductible gift of what were supposedly his vice-presidential papers to the National Archives, but they turned out to be of little worth. The appraiser who set such a large value on these papers was convicted of fraud.

Moreover, there were highly questionable government expenditures on Nixon's homes in Florida and California, reports that he had paid only $800 in income taxes on a $200,000 income, and had tried to deduct $5,000 for a dance he gave for one of his daughters as "expenses incurred in the performance of official functions as President of the United States." The evidence of crookedness was circumstantial, but as Henry David Thoreau said, "Some circumstantial evidence is very strong, as when you find a trout in the milk."

But Nixon's crimes go far beyond his sleazy attempts to enrich himself at the expense of the taxpayers. The Ohio Gang, which nearly stole the dome off the Capitol during the Harding era, and the corrupt squadrons surrounding Ulysses S. Grant were mere money-grubbers. Nixon was out for bigger game. He tried to make off with the Constitution itself.

The psychological toll of Watergate upon the American people was heavy. Coming on top of Vietnam and the assassinations of John and Robert Kennedy and Martin Luther King Jr., it legitimized paranoia and conspiracy and increased cynicism about the federal government. National security and secrecy were used not as tools for the defense of the nation but as convenient covers for hiding wickedness and bungling from public scrutiny. The "credibility gap" between what the government said and what many Americans believed became a yawning breach that swallowed up whatever faith they had in their government and their leaders.

From his resignation until his death twenty years later, Nixon and his most loyal supporters steadfastly refused to acknowledge any responsibility for Watergate. Even in accepting Ford's pardon, the nation's most famous unindicted coconspirator declined to confess to any crimes. Mistakes? Indecision? Poor judgment? Yes. Crimes? No. Nixon partisans claimed that Lyndon B. Johnson and John F. Kennedy also bugged the Oval Office—in itself not a crime—and used the FBI and IRS to harass political opponents. The "you're another" argument doesn't take us far, however. Nixon and his loyalists never understood what Watergate was really about: the accountability of a president to the people in a democratic system. While his predecessors sinned, they were not caught red-handed trying to subvert the Constitution.

Unfortunately, as a result of Ford's pardon, the American people never received a full accounting of Nixon's misdeeds. But the Appellate Division of the State Supreme Court of New York, in words like drumbeats, implacably laid out the charges against Nixon in upholding his disbarment as a lawyer:*

"Mr. Nixon improperly obstructed an investigation by the Federal Bureau of Investigation into the unlawful entry into the headquarters of the Democratic National Committee in Washington on June 17, 1972.

*Nixon tried to avoid disbarment by resigning from the New York Bar without admitting any misconduct, but the court ruled that he could not circumvent disbarment procedures through such means after a grievance had been brought by the Bar Association.

"He improperly approved the surreptitious payment of money to E. Howard Hunt, who was indicted in connection with the break-in.

"He improperly concealed and encouraged others to conceal evidence relating to the unlawful activities of members of his staff and the Committee to Re-Elect the President."[3]

And in the Oval Office tapes, Nixon recorded his own unworthiness for the presidency. Americans heard the leader of the free world talking as if he were a Mafia don organizing the rackets in Brooklyn. "I don't give a shit what happens," he told White House aides at one point. "I want you all to stonewall it [the Watergate inquiry], let them plead the Fifth Amendment; cover-up or anything else if it will save it, save the plan." They also heard him order his aides "to get the Jews" and suggest, two weeks after the Watergate break-in, that the offices of the Republican National Committee be burgled and vandalized, with the blame pinned on the Democrats.

In only the narrowest sense, however, did Nixon's presidency founder on the bungled "third-rate burglary" of the DNC office in the Watergate building. He was, in reality, the victim of his own character. Nixon's ambitions, his insecurities, his rage, his aloofness, his intense resentments, his penchant for secrecy, his lack of humor—these were the things that forced him from the presidency. As the Greek philosopher Heraclitus observed many centuries ago, "A man's character is his fate."

Perversely, in spite of a spectacular rise from near-poverty to the White House, Nixon saw himself as an outsider and harbored a visceral resentment toward those he felt had slighted him, while he masked his hatred in a sanctimonious Uriah Heepish humility. He saw life as simultaneously a series of "crises" that had to be overcome and a battle between "have-nots" such as himself and "those who have everything [and] are sitting on their fat butts."[4] No matter how far he went in life, he never lost this angry Main Street voice—a voice audible on today's call-in radio shows.

This struggle was first observed while he was at Whittier College, where social life was dominated by a group called the Franklins, who, Nixon felt, looked down upon the "have-nots." He organized a competing group, which he called the Orthogonians, or Square Shooters, composed of athletes and students working their way through college.* The Franklin-Orthogonian battle was a recurring theme in his life: Jerry Voorhis and Helen Gahagan Douglas, his first political opponents, were Franklins. So was the elegant diplomat Alger Hiss. And John Kennedy was figuratively a Franklin.

Nixon kept a permanent mental ledger of the slights and injustices that he fancied had been his lot and saw plots and conspiracies everywhere: in the despised press, in the wealthy Eastern establishment that then dominated the Republican party, and in the upper reaches of the Washington bureaucracy—especially the Central Intelligence Agency, which he believed had helped Kennedy narrowly defeat him in the 1960 presidential race.

Yet Nixon was more than Watergate. It is already conventional wisdom that history will treat him kinder than his contemporaries, for he had a solid record of accomplishment in both domestic and foreign affairs. Although he rose to power as a fervent crusader against Communism, his efforts to build bridges to China and the Soviet Union and continue the nuclear disarmament process were acts of imaginative statesmanship. No social troglodyte, he was the most liberal Republican president of the twentieth century except for Theodore Roosevelt.[5] While he tried to trim what he considered the excesses of Johnson's Great Society programs, his administration was, in domestic policy, much more in line with the ideas of the New Deal than with those of Ronald Reagan or Newt Gingrich. Despite his "Southern strategy," he forced more school integration than any other president since the Supreme Court had outlawed educational segregation in 1954.[6]

Nixon's contradictions were Shakespearean in dimension. Despite Bob Dole's mordant crack upon seeing former presidents Ford, Jimmy Carter, and Nixon together—"Hear No Evil, See No Evil, and Evil"—Nixon had some saving graces. In contrast to some recent presidents, he was a devoted husband and family man. He was capable of repeated kindnesses. Shy and ill at ease with strangers, he was acclaimed by a sizable segment of the electorate. Long lines of Americans—many of

---

*The symbol of the Orthogonians was the boar—and although Nixon may not have known it, the boar was also the mark of King Richard III, with whom Nixon's detractors are fond of comparing him.

whom had not even been born when he entered politics—paid their respects at his funeral.

The only man other than Franklin D. Roosevelt to be nominated by a major party on five national tickets—winning four times—he was derided as a man from whom you would not buy a used car. He had many associates but few real friends. He was a perpetual campaigner but was so insecure that he shrank from the accustomed rituals of American politics. He disliked shaking hands, had no small talk, and instructed traveling companions to speak only when spoken to. Even his body language when he spoke—arms outstretched in the victory sign or sweeping about him like a matador's cape—seemed "a little out of sync with what he was saying, as if a sound track were running a little ahead or behind its film."[7]

A hundred Nixons torment our memories. Tricky Dick with his aura of second-rate villainy . . . Hiss's relentless pursuer . . . the scourge of the Democrats . . . the man who debated Nikita Khrushchev in a kitchen and made peace with the Chinese Communists . . . the lugubrious hero of the "Checkers" soap opera . . . And at the end, the elder statesman dispensing political wisdom. Ray Price, a longtime aide, has said that Nixon was like Winston Churchill's description of Russia: a mystery wrapped in an enigma enclosed in a paradox. Harry Truman saw no mystery, however. "Nixon," he declared, "is a shifty-eyed, goddamn liar, and people know it."

Nixon's career was a triumph of will. Essentially an introvert, he worked hard at creating a false image of himself. Unlike many politicians, John Kennedy among them, who try to convince the voters they are cleverer or more courageous or better qualified than they really are, Nixon pretended to be less than he was—less intellectual, less introverted, less cerebral. He tried to portray himself as an average middle-class American: sentimentally patriotic, conventionally religious, and openly gregarious. Nixon was none of these, and the concentrated effort to maintain such a pose must have been psychologically draining.

That effort also showed a basic contempt for the ordinary Americans Nixon was trying to influence. He thought they were incapable of understanding the subtleties of his policies and unlikely to vote for him merely because he was intelligent and hardworking. In politicians, he reasoned, people want artistry more than industry. Nixon thought he could win the votes of the common folk only if he lowered himself to their level, rather than try to raise them up to his as did Adlai E. Stevenson, the Democratic presidential nominee of 1952 and 1956. "You've got to be a little evil to understand those people out there," Nixon told Hugh Sidey of *Time*.

Following his narrow loss of the presidency to Kennedy in 1960 and his infamous "last press conference" after the loss of the California governorship two years later, Nixon's enemies gleefully thought he had been buried at the crossroads with a stake through his heart. But he rose once again to win the presidential elections of 1968 and 1972. He seemed to have more lives than Lazarus. These victories reflected the success of his calculated effort to identify with ordinary Americans. Angry with the turmoil and violence resulting from the civil rights and anti-Vietnam protests of the sixties, these "forgotten Americans" turned to the candidate who offered stability, law and order, and "peace with honor"—Richard M. Nixon.

But now that the American people were ready to trust him, Nixon was incapable of trusting America and its institutions. The resentments that had smoldered and grown on the long road to the White House fed the animus that produced the "Enemies List"; the use of the CIA, the FBI, the IRS, and the White House "plumbers" to harass and strike out at opponents and critics; intimidation of the press; "dirty tricks"; and the invocation of national security and the police state to cloak criminal action.

In August 1971, John Dean 3d, the White House counsel, circulated a memo to the staff with Nixon's approval that showed the malignancy that was to destroy his presidency. "How can we maximize the fact of our incumbency in dealing with persons known to be active in their opposition to our Administration?" he asked. "Stated a bit more bluntly—how can we use the available federal machinery to screw our political enemies?"[8]

Richard Nixon's father, Francis Anthony Nixon, drifted to southern California in the early years of the century.[9] Working at odd jobs, he was seeking a warmer climate after his toes were frostbitten while he was a motorman on an open trolley in Columbus, Ohio. In the sober Quaker community of Whittier, he met Hannah Milhous, the daughter of an orchardist of some substance, and in 1908, after only a four-month courtship, they were married. The Milhous family thought he was below her. The young couple moved to a lemon grove near the town of Yorba Linda, where Frank built a small clapboard house. Hard-working and churchgoing, the Nixons were typical of the people their son would call "the silent majority." The second of their five sons was born January 9, 1913, and named for Richard the Lionhearted.

Frank had adopted the Quaker faith of his wife, but he was combative, profane, and a rough disciplinarian. Richard was sometimes frightened of his father and avoided the beatings his brothers received by repressing an already introverted personality. Hannah was just the opposite: soft-spoken, tightly controlled, never allowing anger to get the better of her. She had, said her son, "a passionate concern for peace," and he called her a "saint." In 1916, she broke with her staunch Republican convictions to vote for Woodrow Wilson because "he kept us out of war." Later, Nixon made it evident that he wished she had shown him more open affection, but that was not her way. Hannah insisted he be called Richard, not Dick, taught him to read before he entered school, and made certain that he said his prayers daily and went four times to Quaker meeting on Sunday. She hoped he would be a Quaker missionary.

Tom Wicker, who has written much about Nixon, suggests that his goal of building a global "structure of peace" was a form of atonement to his mother for the abandonment of her ideals in favor of the politician's dissembling and reliance on naked power. "The most powerful of the forces that drove him," says Wicker, "may have been the wish to go in spirit to Hannah Nixon—despite all the un-Quakerish grapplings and betrayals of his political life—and say: 'Mother, I have made peace. Now I am worthy of you.' "[10]

The family lemon grove failed, and when the boy was nine, the Nixons moved to Whittier. Frank bought a gas station and added a general store, and the whole family worked there, sixteen hours a day, seven days a week. "We were poor," Nixon was to recall. "We had very little. We all used hand-me-down clothes. I wore my brother's shoes and my brothers below me wore mine. . . . We certainly had to learn the value of money." But he was able to put it in perspective. "We had a pretty good time with it all."[11]

Richard was a shy but bright boy, gifted at reciting poetry, but he was not popular with the other children. His cousin, the novelist Jessamyn West, said he "wasn't a little boy that you wanted to pick up and hug."[12] The resentments that festered in childhood were still there years later. "What starts the process, really, are laughs and slights and snubs when you are a kid," Nixon told an aide.[13] From his father, he inherited a passionate interest in politics and devoured the political news in the papers. When the Teapot Dome scandal broke, Richard heard his father denounce the crooked politicians and corrupt lawyers and avidly read the newspapers for more details. "When I get big," the boy told his mother, "I'll be a lawyer they can't bribe."[14]

When Richard was fourteen, his oldest brother, Harold, was stricken with tuberculosis and was taken by Hannah to Prescott, Arizona, in a frantic and futile search for a cure. There, she made ends meet by taking in other tuberculosis patients and performing the most menial sickroom tasks. One by one, all her patients, including Harold, died. While visiting his mother and brother over two summers, Richard worked as a barker at the Slippery Gulch Rodeo, and his concession made more money than any other. Harold was his closest friend, the one person in whom he could confide, and biographer Stephen Ambrose theorizes that Harold's death brought an end to the boy's only warm, trusting relationship with a contemporary.[15]

Nixon won a scholarship to Harvard after high school, but it included only tuition; in the midst of the Great Depression, there was no money for room and board and other expenses. Besides, he was needed in the store. He settled for Whittier College, a local Quaker school, and later said he was never disappointed. At Whittier, he was a big man on a small campus. Although he rose at 4 A.M. every day to buy fruits and vegetables for the store and to arrange them, he was an ambitious student politician, an accomplished actor, a champion debater, played the piano well, and went out for football with a suicidal intensity even though he was laughably awkward.

The law school of Duke University, where Nixon had won a scholarship, was his next training ground in persistence, success, and frustration. A loner, he lived frugally, studied endlessly, and was known to classmates as Gloomy Gus. Nixon graduated third in his class and hoped for a job with a top Eastern law firm or the FBI, but was rejected by both. Returning to Whittier, he settled down to practice small-town law, but wills and land-sale contracts bored him; he was merely awaiting the proper moment to get into politics.

One day, a friend suggested that Nixon visit the Whittier Little Theater and check out a "gorgeous redhead" who had just joined the company. Thelma Catherine Ryan—called Pat because she was born on St. Patrick's Day—was the daughter of a Nevada miner turned California farmer. Orphaned in her teens, she had worked as a secretary in New York, saved her money, and come back to California to attend college and take a job as a teacher of typing, shorthand, and related subjects at the Whittier High School. She also worked as a $7-a-day extra in Hollywood.*

For Nixon, who had few female friends, it was love at first sight. He immediately auditioned for the upcoming play and won a role opposite the pretty young teacher. On their first date, he proposed, but Pat turned him down. "I thought he was nuts, or something," she said later. But Nixon was a persistent suitor. Over the next two years, he pursued Pat, even driving her to Los Angeles, where she had dates with other men, then waiting around to take her home again. They married in June 1940. Nixon made a few speeches for Wendell Willkie, the Republican presidential nominee that year, and was active in the Young Republicans, but war came and his political ambitions had to be put on hold for five years.

Breaking with his Quaker upbringing, Nixon sought a commission in the navy. While waiting for it to come through, he worked for eight months in Washington as an attorney in the tire-rationing section of the Office of Price Administration—a period that soured him on the bureaucracy. He went into the service in mid-1942 as a lieutenant junior grade—his mother cried when she first saw him in uniform.

---

*Pat Ryan had a one-line speaking role in *Becky Sharp*, the first Hollywood all-Technicolor movie, but it was cut.

Nixon spent most of the war in the Solomons as the operations officer of an air transport unit that included a commissary known as Nixon's Hamburger Stand. He was efficient and liked by his officers and men, but made no close friends.

Nixon also learned to play poker in the navy, not just to pass time but to win big money. Never a plunger, he cautiously analyzed the possibilities of each hand before anteing up and threw in his cards if they were not good ones. Eventually his winnings totaled some $7,000, the equivalent of two years' pay. Lieutenant Commander Nixon was awaiting demobilization when he was approached by a group of Republican bankers and businessmen who were seeking a candidate to oppose Jerry Voorhis, the five-term liberal Democratic congressman from California's Twelfth District. Nixon leaped at the opportunity.

In 1946, Nixon established the rock-'em, sock-'em campaigning style and ethical shortcuts that were his stock-in-trade for the next thirty years. While presenting himself as a firm believer in middle-class values, he tied the leftish Voorhis to the Communists. "Of course, I knew Jerry Voorhis wasn't a Communist, but I had to win," Nixon later explained. *"The important thing is to win."*[16] He was swept into office with 60 percent of the vote, part of a nationwide surge that gave the Republicans control of Congress for the first time in twenty years.

In the Eightieth Congress, Nixon was assigned to the Education and Labor Committee, where he became friendly with another congressional freshman, John F. Kennedy, a Massachusetts Democrat. The committee's major effort was the writing of the Taft-Hartley Act, which was assailed by the unions as the "slave labor bill." Long before they became rivals for the presidency, the two men debated the merits of Taft-Hartley before a public meeting in McKeesport, Pennsylvania. "I was for the bill. Kennedy was against it," Nixon recalled. "I had the better of the argument because most of those present, as employers, were on my side."

But it was Nixon's assignment to the controversial House Un-American Activities Committee that thrust him into the national spot-

*Italics mine.

light. The wartime alliance between the United States and the Soviet Union had collapsed, and the committee was in the forefront of the hunt for alleged Communists and fellow travelers in government, the movies, and other areas of American life. With his dogged pursuit of Alger Hiss, a well-connected former State Department official identified as a secret Communist agent, Nixon made headlines, despite bitter criticism from President Truman and the Eastern press.

Hiss's conviction on a perjury charge—the statute of limitations had run out on espionage—ensured Nixon's reelection in 1948 despite Truman's upset victory over Thomas E. Dewey. It was also a watershed for Nixon because it ratified the conspiracy theory of history that he unconsciously shared with those he opposed. And it made him, at thirty-five, a national figure. Two years later, Nixon set his sights on the Senate, where his opponent was Helen Gahagan Douglas, a onetime movie actress and ultraliberal congresswoman.* The campaign unfolded against a background of Communist expansion in Europe and Asia, the theft of atomic secrets by a Soviet spy ring, war in Korea, and wild charges by Senator Joseph R. McCarthy of Wisconsin that Communists in government were responsible for all these calamities.

Turning Mrs. Douglas's Hollywood "parlor pink" reputation against her, Nixon implied that she was a Communist by distributing a "pink sheet" noting that while in the House, the "Pink Lady" had voted 354 times with Representative Vito Marcantonio, who toed the Communist line. Many were votes on which Republicans as well as Democrats were recorded the same way. Infuriated Democrats charged that the wolfishly ambitious Nixon was reckless with the truth and relied on innuendo and deceit and tricky statistics. Nevertheless, Nixon won by almost seven hundred thousand votes, the largest plurality in any Senate race that year.

After less than two years in the Senate, Nixon was nominated in 1952 for vice president—on a ticket with Dwight Eisenhower—because of his reputation as an elbow-in-the-eye, knee-in-the-groin anti-Communist

*Mrs. Douglas was hardly the favorite of all Democrats. John Kennedy contributed $1,000 to Nixon's campaign, saying, "It won't break my heart if you can turn the Senate's loss into Hollywood's gain."

crusader. Eisenhower kept to the high road while Nixon was point man in flailing away at the Truman administration for botching the Korean War and the hunt for subversives and corruption in government. Nixon talked of "twenty years of treason" under the Democrats and charged that the Truman regime "is going to go down in history as the scandal-a-day administration."

Suddenly, Nixon faced a scandal of his own. The liberal *New York Post* reported with lip-smacking relish that some wealthy California businessmen had set up a secret $18,000 fund for Nixon's personal use. In view of Eisenhower's emphasis on morality, the Democrats demanded that Nixon be dropped from the ticket, and even some Republican newspapers called for his resignation. In reality, the fund was no secret and was earmarked exclusively for political expenses, but the damage had been done. Was Nixon on or off the ticket? From Eisenhower, who wanted his running mate "as clean as a hound's tooth," there was only silence.

Fifty-five million Americans—the largest television audience until then—watched on the evening of September 23, 1952, as Nixon fought to save his political career. He began by assuring his audience that the fund had been merely for political purposes and not for his personal use. He listed his modest assets and emphasized that Pat did not have a mink coat—a pointed dig at the mink-coat scandals of the Truman administration—"but she does have a respectable Republican cloth coat."

And then the pitchman's masterstroke: "One thing I should tell you . . . we did get something—a gift. . . . It was a little cocker spaniel dog—black-and-white spotted," Nixon continued, projecting sincerity into the camera. "And our little girl—Tricia, the six-year-old—named it Checkers. And you know, the kids love that dog and I just want to say this right now: that regardless of what they say about it, we are going to keep it."

A tearful Nixon left the studio convinced the speech had been a flop, but much to his surprise, viewers inundated the Republican National Committee with telephone calls, telegrams, and letters of support. Mamie Eisenhower, the general's wife, dabbed at her eyes with a hankie as she watched the screen. "You're my boy!" Eisenhower said, beaming at Nixon the next day. The Eisenhower-Nixon ticket won the election by a landslide. Six years after entering politics, Richard Nixon had become vice president of the United States—and now had his eye on the White House.

Nixon once described the vice presidency as "a hollow shell—the most ill-conceived, poorly defined position in the American political system"—but he used the office well.[17] While never close to Eisenhower,* who worried whether Nixon had the character and strength to be president and unsuccessfully tried to dump him in 1956, he was given a more prominent role than previous vice presidents. He traveled abroad for the White House, debated Khrushchev on television on the merits of democracy and Communism—and won—and faced an attack by a leftist mob in Caracas without flinching. In the 1954 off-year elections, and again in 1956, his attacks on the Democrats aroused their anger, but he handled the crises resulting from Eisenhower's several illnesses with skill and restraint. There was talk of a "new Nixon" as he launched his drive for the presidency in 1960.

That election is usually told in terms of John Kennedy's triumphant coming to power, but it is also the story of how Richard Nixon clumsily squandered his chance to govern. Nixon had the initial advantages of Eisenhower's support and of considerable policy experience, while Kennedy was looked upon as a playboy. But Nixon failed to make good use of his assets. First, he never played the Eisenhower card. Jealous of the president's popularity and, aware that he did not enjoy Eisenhower's full confidence, he wanted to win on his own. Second, going against Eisenhower's advice, he consented to a series of televised debates with Kennedy that, unless he scored a knockout, could only enhance his opponent's reputation without providing himself any benefit.

Having blundered by agreeing to the debates, Nixon, who was noto-

---

*The writer was present as a "pool" reporter during the first visit made by then President-elect Nixon in 1968 to his outgoing predecessor, Lyndon Johnson, in the Oval Office. Nixon, who had a passion for wood fires, asked early on if the fireplace was in working order. This struck me as odd because he must have been a frequent visitor to the White House during his eight years as vice president and could have observed whether Eisenhower used the fireplace or asked him that question. Finally, it dawned on me that either he had never felt close enough to Eisenhower to do so or feared the president might regard him as too eager to take his place if he asked about the fireplace.

riously unphotogenic, compounded the error by wearing no makeup for the first encounter. Although some people thought he won—especially those who heard the debate on radio—his baleful, blue-jowled visage turned off a large segment of the audience that saw it on television. Nixon did not realize anything had gone wrong until his mother, concerned about his appearance, telephoned from California to ask if he was "feeling all right." Even worse, most Americans were exposed for the first time to a sustained dose of the Kennedy charisma, and for many it was love at first sight.

The outcome of the November balloting was so close—only 112,881 votes separated Kennedy and Nixon, one-tenth of one percent of the total—that it may well have been the second stolen presidential election in American history. There was strong evidence of fraud in Illinois and Texas, both won by Kennedy by only the narrowest of margins, but to everyone's surprise, Nixon refused to press a claim. "No one steals the presidency of the United States," he said. It was probably Nixon's finest hour. But he was forever embittered by the experience. Never again would he be caught short, never again would he give an opponent an even break, never again would he trust the normal operations of politics to function as intended.

Nixon returned to California where in 1962, in an effort to keep his name before the public, he challenged the incumbent governor, Edmund G. Brown, and was badly beaten. He had been away from the state too long and had made too many enemies. Blaming his defeat on biased media coverage, he angrily told reporters they "won't have Nixon to kick around anymore" as he stalked out of his "last press conference." Nixon moved to New York, where he practiced law with considerable success. Barring a miracle, said *Time,* Nixon's political career was over.

But powerful forces soon drew him back into the arena. In 1968, the world known to most Americans seemed to be spinning out of control. Communist guerrillas shot their way into the U.S. embassy in Saigon, and the long-running war in Vietnam appeared more unwinnable than ever. Anger over the war forced Lyndon Johnson, successor to the assassinated Kennedy, to withdraw from the presidential race. Robert F. Kennedy, the emerging Democratic front-runner, was shot and killed.

Riots following the murder of Dr. Martin Luther King Jr. turned the cities into bloody battlegrounds. Inflation was heating up. The country had not seen such turmoil since the Civil War, and many Americans yearned for a leader who promised safety and stability.

Nixon carefully avoided controversy during the three-way campaign against Hubert Humphrey, Johnson's vice president, and former Alabama governor George C. Wallace, the populist third-party candidate, preferring instead to benefit from the raucous disarray among the Democrats. He claimed to have formulated a plan to bring "peace with honor" to war-ravaged Vietnam, but refused to disclose its details for fear of jeopardizing the peace negotiations then stalemated in Paris—or so he said in his best pitchman's manner. On domestic matters, he celebrated law and order, denounced Great Society programs, and attacked the liberal decisions of the Supreme Court. Reflecting a "Southern strategy" designed to corral the white-backlash vote in the emerging Sun Belt, Nixon chose Governor Spiro T. Agnew of Maryland as his vice-presidential running mate because of his slashing attacks on black street rioters.

Once again, observers claimed to see a "new Nixon," a man who had tempered his harsher positions in the ashes of defeat, who was less strident, less accusatory than the "old Nixon." Nixon's television spots were particularly artful, showing the candidate at his best before carefully controlled audiences. And he avoided a debate with his opponents. In one of the great political comebacks of American history, he defeated Humphrey, albeit by only a slightly larger margin than his loss to Kennedy eight years before. Obviously, a large segment of the American people still considered him "tricky" and unappealing. Nevertheless, at the age of fifty-six, after twenty-two years of political struggle, Nixon had finally become president of the United States, the office that had tantalized him for so long.

In claiming victory, he recalled a sign held up by a teenage girl that he had seen during a campaign whistle-stop in Ohio: "Bring Us Together." Even as he denounced black rioters and white antiwar demonstrators, Nixon said it would be "the great objective of this administration . . . to bring the American people together." But the homogenized America that he represented no longer existed. The nation was increasingly divided along cultural and generational fault lines; Americans reacted to events in ways and had goals unenvisioned by Nixon and his supporters. In the end, Richard Nixon did bring Americans together, but hardly in the way he intended.

Not long after he entered the White House, President Nixon was discussing some of his predecessors with William Safire, a senior speechwriter. "You think of Truman—a fighter," Nixon mused. "Eisenhower—a good man. Kennedy—charisma. Johnson—work. Me—what?"

"Competence," said Safire. Then, seeing Nixon's disappointment, he quickly added, "Sorry about that."

"Hell!" exclaimed Nixon. "If all we do is manage things ten percent better, we'll never be remembered for anything."[18]

Nixon desperately wanted to be remembered—and for the same things for which Woodrow Wilson was remembered. He wished to emulate Wilson by creating a worldwide "structure of peace" with the United States at the center. Uninterested in domestic affairs, Nixon devoted himself almost entirely to that goal. Foreign policy was concentrated in his own hands and those of his national security adviser, Dr. Henry A. Kissinger, a former Harvard professor of international relations, while Secretary of State William Rogers and Melvin Laird, the defense secretary, were cavalierly bypassed.

To run the domestic side of affairs, Nixon relied upon a staff of mostly young, hard-core loyalists instead of his rather undistinguished cabinet. H. R. Haldeman, a former southern-California advertising man, who was closest to the president, was chief of staff. He was, as he said, proud to be known as Richard Nixon's "son of a bitch." John Ehrlichman, a Seattle lawyer and onetime advance man, was named White House counsel. Together, Haldeman and Ehrlichman, known as the Berlin Wall because of their surliness and Germanic-sounding names, controlled access to Nixon. Only the tough-talking attorney general, John Mitchell, a New York law partner with whom Nixon had found an affinity, saw him frequently. Unhappily, these apparatchiks not only had contempt for the democratic process but were also totally ignorant of the intricacies of policymaking.

Nixon worked hard, usually twelve hours a day, largely alone. In the

White House he shed the sham personality he had created for campaign purposes and became the loner he really was. He didn't want to hear about the details of government, nor did he read newspapers or magazines, depending instead on a summary prepared by the staff. He had no television in the Oval Office or in his sanctuary in the Executive Office Building where he holed up with his closest friends—his yellow pads. He conducted most of his business through a flood of memos. Unable to delegate authority because of his conspiratorial cast of mind, he obsessed over trivial details such as which red wines should be served at formal dinners, his dental appointments, and the design of his phone service. There was no one to question his ideas or to help him poke fun at himself. Insulated from criticism and surrounded by flatterers, he became increasingly contemptuous of Congress and the bureaucracy and impatient with obstacles.

Nixon was determined not to be driven from office by Vietnam as Lyndon Johnson had been. His highest priority was extricating the United States from the Vietnamese quagmire before the 1972 election without overtly abandoning South Vietnam, America's ally. In furthering this goal, he resorted to a deviousness remarkable even for Washington, in which he was assisted by Kissinger. Ruthless, charming when it served his purposes, cleverer than most of the men he dealt with—and not averse to letting them know it—Kissinger looked like a Bronx butcher and operated with the cynicism of a Renaissance cardinal. Like Nixon, he loved intrigue and was a born conspirator.

Insisting that he would not condone a policy of surrender, Nixon initiated policies designed to limit opposition to the war without actually ending the fighting until he was ready. He announced a policy of "Vietnamization" in which American combat troops were slowly withdrawn from Vietnam, thus reducing draft calls and with them protests from young people. But the killing went on because Nixon insisted on the withdrawal of all Communist forces from the South before making peace, while the North Vietnamese and their Viet Cong allies refused to abandon their commitment to the unification of the country.

In April 1970, to get the stalled negotiations moving, Nixon ordered a strike at Communist supply bases in neighboring Cambodia. This "incursion" made military sense but it relit the embers of revolt. Campuses across the country exploded into violent rebellion, which lasted for days, and several people were killed. Nixon and Kissinger, while startled by the intensity of the protests, sold this flagrant escalation of the war to the public as a peace crusade. The pitchman was running true to form: Three years later, Americans learned that Nixon had secretly been bombing Cambodia since 1969 while avowing Cambodian neutrality.

Nixon rallied his supporters while denouncing opponents as "thugs and hoodlums" and blaming critics in Congress and the press for prolonging the war. Vice President Agnew, now Nixon's Nixon, trotted out the acid rhetoric that had made him a hero to conservatives. He attacked those opposed to administration policy as "nattering nabobs of negativism" and an "effete corps of impudent snobs."*

Increasingly frustrated and suspicious, Nixon ordered stepped-up surveillance of the antiwar movement and administration foes. A sense of siege pervaded the White House, fueled by leaks to the press and constant antiwar demonstrations. Political enemies were targeted for tax audits and their telephones tapped. Distrusting even his own closest advisers, Nixon had the Oval Office bugged, in part so that his aides could not later claim to have disagreed with his decisions.

Late in his first term, the president was sitting around with several aides talking about some antiwar Democratic senators. He was seething with anger. "One day we will get them—we'll get them on the ground where we want them," Nixon declared. "And we'll stick our heels in, step on them hard and twist—right, Chuck, right?"

Charles E. Colson gave his assent.

"Henry knows what I mean," Nixon continued. "Get them on the floor and step on them, crush them, show no mercy."

Kissinger supposedly smiled and nodded.[19]

The approach of the 1972 presidential election finally did what years of military frustration and escalating public protests had failed to do: it forced Nixon and Kissinger to abandon their insistence on the removal of North Vietnamese troops from the South as a condition to a full American withdrawal. On October 26, only days before the elec-

---

*Agnew's alliterative attacks were largely written by Patrick Buchanan and William Safire.

tion, Kissinger announced that "peace is at hand." Although the negotiations again broke down, the announcement was, along with the president's tradition-shattering visits to China and the Soviet Union,
sufficient to propel him to a landslide victory over the hapless Democratic candidate, Senator George S. McGovern. Nixon won with 60.7
percent of the vote—one of the largest margins in history.

Safely reelected, Nixon now felt free to launch a furious twelve-day
bombing campaign against North Vietnam in mid-December, known
as the "Christmas blitz." The American people were told the assault
was aimed at forcing the North Vietnamese to end the fighting, and
Nixon claimed it accomplished its end. But this was mere pitchman's
patter. The real obstruction to peace was the Saigon regime's insistence
that the United States guarantee its survival after American troops
went home. Thus, the bombing was, in reality, intended to convince
South Vietnamese officialdom that Washington would protect them at
all costs.

The Paris Accords were little different from what Nixon and
Kissinger could have gotten four years before. In the meantime,
another 20,553 Americans had been killed, and the social fabric of the
nation was in tatters.* For this, Kissinger was awarded the Nobel Peace
Prize along with his North Vietnamese opposite number. The two most
important components of the agreement were an immediate cease-
fire and the release of several hundred American prisoners of war.
Beyond that, everything was murky. There was no withdrawal of North
Vietnamese forces from the South or abandonment of the Communist
commitment to a reunified Vietnam. What Nixon and Kissinger trum-
peted as "peace with honor" was in reality little more than a formula for
allowing the United States to get out and to provide a "decent interval"
before the Saigon regime was overrun.

Nixon should have been jubilant as his second term began. American troops had all but been withdrawn from Vietnam. The cities were
comparatively peaceful after a decade of turmoil. Most hopeful of all
was the prospect of real peace throughout the world. His initiatives
toward China and the Soviet Union and efforts to end the nuclear arms

---

*This was more than a third of the some 58,000 U.S. troops who died during the war.

race were universally acclaimed. Kissinger's shuttle diplomacy in the Middle East would ultimately lead to peace between Israel and Egypt. Yet a long shadow lay over these triumphs—the shadow of Watergate.

Six months before, on the night of June 17, 1972, five men wearing rubber gloves and carrying bugging equipment had been arrested in the headquarters of the Democratic National Committee in the Watergate complex. No one seemed to know what they were doing there. Nixon was visiting Key Biscayne in Florida when, the following day, he learned of the arrests. "It sounded preposterous" and he dismissed the affair as "some sort of prank." Bob Haldeman was instructed to "get it confused as possible."[20]

And so began the cover-up.

More than a quarter century later, several questions about the Watergate affair still remain unresolved:

•Why was the office of the DNC burglarized?

•Who actually ordered it?

•Why didn't Nixon, once the cover-up began to unravel, admit that some of his people had, in mistaken zeal, tried to bug the DNC—then apologize and get on with the presidential campaign?

•Why didn't he just destroy the tapes of the Oval Office conversations in which the cover-up was organized—the "smoking gun" that was instrumental in driving him from the White House?

It all began with the anger of Nixon and Kissinger at the steady leakage of policy initiatives to the media. Wiretaps had been placed on the telephones of White House aides and journalists, and other efforts were made to ferret out leakers. The publication in 1971 by the *New York Times* of the Pentagon Papers, a highly classified history of the American involvement in Vietnam, was the last straw. John Ehrlichman organized a special investigative unit—the "plumbers"—to plug these leaks, and G. Gordon Liddy and E. Howard Hunt were hired to supervise the operation.

Had a computer search been made for the two most absurdly dangerous men in Washington, it would have come up with Liddy and Hunt. Both had histories of flamboyance—and trouble. Hunt, a one-time CIA officer and writer of paperback thrillers, had a reputation for off-the-wall "cowboy" antics. Liddy's major claim to fame was that as an agent for the Bureau of Narcotics, he had devised a plan to stem the flow of drugs from Mexico that created miles-long tie-ups for tourists at border crossing points.

Liddy and Hunt hired James W. McCord, a former CIA security man, and four Cuban exiles known to Hunt from the agency's Bay of Pigs fiasco. Their first task was the burglary of the office of the Los Angeles psychiatrist treating Daniel Ellsberg, the National Security Council staffer suspected of divulging the Pentagon Papers, with the hope of finding information that would discredit Ellsberg. The CIA provided the plumbers with spy paraphernalia for the break-in.

In early 1972, Liddy and Hunt were transferred to the staff of the Committee to Re-Elect the President, or CREEP, and produced an elaborate plan—known as Gemstone—to spy on opponents and disrupt their activities. Checks totaling $89,000 in illegal corporate contributions to the Nixon campaign were laundered through a Mexican bank and earmarked for the project. This was supplemented with another $25,000 check direct from CREEP funds.

George McGovern was Gemstone's first target, but an attempt to bug his office failed. The team then turned its attention to the Watergate office of Lawrence F. O'Brien, the Democratic National Committee (DNC) chairman. Nixon always claimed to know nothing of the break-ins. He and some of his supporters claim they were the work of the CIA or the Joint Chiefs of Staff, which they said were eager to undercut the architect of détente with China and the Soviet Union.

Nevertheless, Nixon was obsessed with Larry O'Brien, whom he regarded as the architect of his defeat by Kennedy in 1960. He also feared that O'Brien might have evidence concerning secret contributions to the Nixon campaign said to have been made by the reclusive billionaire Howard Hughes. No one ever assumed ultimate responsibility for actually ordering the break-in, but the evidence indicates the order was given by John Mitchell, who had resigned as attorney general to head CREEP, in response to unrelenting pressure from the president to discover whatever O'Brien knew.

Following two botched attempts, the burglars got into the DNC office on May 27, 1972, and placed taps on O'Brien's phone and that of an assistant. The bug on O'Brien's line failed to work, and McCord and the four Cubans returned to the Watergate to fix it. A security guard spotted a garage door taped open and called the police. The burglars were arrested at gunpoint. They had bugging equipment and $3,200 in consecutively numbered $100 bills in their possession. Hunt and Liddy, who had been monitoring the operation from a nearby motel, fled in panic into the night.

The basic pattern of lies and deception was quickly put in place. Worried that the trail might lead to Mitchell and the White House aides who had organized the plumbers, the president involved himself in the cover-up from the very beginning. He sought a way to channel hush money to the burglars to ensure their silence and attempted to obstruct an FBI investigation of the break-in. Nixon was concerned that the FBI might stumble over the trail of the secret funds that had been laundered in Mexico and funneled to the burglars by CREEP. Meeting with Haldeman and Ehrlichman on June 23, 1972, Nixon agreed to use the CIA to persuade the FBI to call off its Mexican inquiries on grounds that national security was involved. The CIA, however, refused to do so and also rejected a White House proposal that it post bail and pay the legal and family expenses of the burglars.

The president apparently felt he could not come clean on the break-in and apologize, even if he wanted to, because it would lift the curtain on what John Mitchell called the "White House horrors"—all the other crimes committed by the plumbers and the dirty-tricks division of CREEP. In an effort to deal with any public outcry, Nixon directed John Dean 3d, the White House counsel, to launch an inquiry into the affair. Dean's real job was to keep the lid on until after the November election.

Meanwhile, as a result of leaks, two young *Washington Post* reporters, Carl Bernstein and Bob Woodward, dredged up enough material to keep the story on the front page. Yet a Gallup Poll shortly before the election reported that 48 percent of the American people had never heard of the Watergate break-in, and the affair had no effect on Nixon's landslide victory over McGovern.

Within a few months of the election, however, the cover-up began to unravel. The key figure was Chief Judge John J. Sirica of the U.S. District Court in Washington. Gordon Liddy's swaggering soldier-of-fortune decision to protect the higher-ups by assuming full responsibility for the break-in, plus the stonewalling of Hunt, McCord, and the four Cubans, angered him. Once they had pleaded guilty, Judge Sirica made it plain that he intended to impose harsh sentences upon them to get at the truth.

Buckling under Sirica's judicial blackmail, McCord wrote the judge a letter in which he said that "political pressures" had been brought to bear upon the defendants to plead guilty, that perjury had been committed, and more exalted figures than Liddy were behind the affair. The Senate had also established a Watergate investigating committee headed by Sam Ervin, a crusty North Carolina Democrat and onetime judge. Interviewed by Senate investigators, McCord implicated Dean and Jeb Magruder, the deputy director of CREEP, in the affair.

A wave of fear swept through the White House, and it was everyone for himself. Nixon's aides obtained lawyers, went to the prosecutors, testified before the grand jury, were interviewed by Senate investigators, and leaked to the press. Like a striptease, the various elements of the cover-up were gradually peeled away. Nixon also began throwing aides overboard in an effort to save himself. Haldeman, Ehrlichman, and Dean were fired. Attorney General Richard Kleindienst and FBI director Patrick L. Gray resigned. But the scandal continued to grow. Six separate probes were under way, and Boston attorney Archibald Cox was named special prosecutor. And on May 17, 1973, the Senate Watergate Committee began its hearings.

Over the next thirty-seven days, the ornate old Senate Caucus Room, where the Teapot Dome hearings had been held, was the scene of a combination morality play, mystery story, soap opera, and psychodrama. If Richard Nixon was the unseen villain of the piece, Senator Ervin was the hero. A slow drawl, white hair, quivering pink jowls, and eyebrows that seemed permanently atwitch, along with his eloquence in defense of the Constitution, made him an instant cult figure.

The hearings began with the small fry—the diligent but lowly members of CREEP—and built up to the star performers. John Dean appeared on June 25, and over four days he spun a tale that placed the president at the center of the gravest crimes. Hunched over his micro-phone, he outlined the progress of the cover-up in startling detail. But the central questions of Watergate seemed unlikely to be resolved: What did the president know, and when did he know it? Dean had incriminated Nixon, but no one supported his testimony.

And then, on July 16, Alexander Butterfield, who was in charge of White House security, revealed that there was an Oval Office taping sys-tem. Every word spoken there had been recorded, making it possible to verify Dean's charges. With the noose tightening inexorably about his neck, Nixon attempted to head off the demands of special prosecutor Archibald Cox for the tapes by firing him. Attorney General Elliot Richardson resigned rather than do the firing. This "Saturday Night Massacre" convinced doubters that Nixon had something to hide and created a firestorm of protest.

Meantime, Spiro Agnew was forced from office after it was discovered he had taken bribes and kickbacks from highway contractors while he was county executive of Baltimore County and governor of Maryland. Some of the graft was delivered even after he became vice president. Gerald Ford, the veteran Republican leader of the House, was chosen by Nixon as vice president—a move that heightened the possibility of Nixon's ouster. Agnew, he had joked, was his "insurance policy." Not even his worst enemy would vote to impeach him to put Agnew in the White House."*

The sleazy Agnew sideshow did not deflect interest from the main ring for long, however. House Democratic leaders ordered an inquiry into the possibility of impeaching the president, and a new special prosecutor, Texas lawyer Leon Jaworski, was named. Several top presi-dential aides, including Haldeman, Ehrlichman, Mitchell, and Klein-dienst, pleaded guilty to assorted charges or were convicted of various Watergate-related crimes. Nixon himself was named in a secret grand jury report as an "unindicted coconspirator."

On July 24, 1974, the Supreme Court rejected the president's argu-

---

*Following Ford's pardon of Nixon, there were charges of a "corrupt bargain" in which Ford agreed to pardon Nixon if he was ousted in return for being appointed. Barring the dis-covery of an Oval Office tape to that effect, such charges are likely to remain in the realm of conjecture.

ment of national security and executive privilege and directed him to turn the Oval Office tapes over to Jaworski. Three days later, the House Judiciary Committee voted articles of impeachment on grounds that Nixon had acted "in a manner contrary to his trust as President and subversive of constitutional government." Under duress, Nixon released the tape of the June 23, 1972, meeting—the "smoking gun"—in which he had instructed Haldeman and Ehrlichman to use the CIA to block the investigation.

"I should have destroyed the tapes," Nixon later told a television interviewer. Kissinger, Nelson Rockefeller, and John Connally urged him to do so. But he claimed that he had not done so because he was not well: "I just couldn't make tough decisions like that." The lawyers also told him he would be destroying evidence—or so he said. In reality, the tapes owed their survival to Nixon's obsession with his place in history. They represented personal immortality; to destroy them would have been akin to an act of self-mutilation.

Following these thunderbolts, Nixon resigned on August 9, 1974. True to character, he could not exit without a typically Nixonian farewell. Resorting to sleight of hand once again, he claimed his resignation had been prompted not by the threat of impeachment, but because he no longer had "a strong enough political base in Congress" to maintain himself in office. As he departed the White House for exile in California, Nixon spoke briefly to his aides:

"Always give your best. Never get discouraged. Never be petty. Always remember others may hate you, but those who hate you don't win unless you hate them, and then you destroy yourself."

It was good advice. Too bad Richard Milhous Nixon hadn't taken it to heart, himself.

EPILOGUE

THOMAS JEFFERSON AND JOHN F. KENNEDY

THE TWO MOST OVERRATED PRESIDENTS

Thomas Jefferson and John F. Kennedy occupy a special niche in American presidential history. Both enjoy reputations far more impressive than they deserve based upon their accomplishments in office. Jefferson is usually listed among the great presidents, while Kennedy, although ranking lower, is still more highly regarded than he should be. But unlike most of our presidents, their reputations are not based upon their records in the White House, but are colored by events, sentiments, and feelings that have little to do with their presidencies. Having transcended history, Jefferson and Kennedy are beyond the bounds of the usual standards of judgment.

Jefferson is the favorite of most Americans among the Founding Fathers because of his championship of the cause of liberty, love of gadgetry, and insatiable curiosity. One need only see the worshiping throngs of tourists as they troop through the Palladian shrine at Monticello—built with the sweat of black slaves while Jefferson prattled about liberty*—to gauge the truth of this phenomenon. Kennedy well described the fascination of later generations with Jefferson in a talk to a group of Nobel laureates on April 29, 1962: "I think this is the most extraordinary collection of talent, of human knowledge, that has ever been gathered together at the White House, with the possible exception of when Thomas Jefferson dined alone."

---

*Not only did Jefferson own several hundred slaves and never freed any in his lifetime, he purchased at least eight more slaves while in the presidency.

239

Perhaps the greatest difficulty in analyzing Jefferson's presidency is the tendency to be blinded by the brilliance of the man. The Sage of Monticello was a statesman, philosopher, diplomat, scientist, farmer, architect, inventor, rationalist theologian, founder of the University of Virginia, author of the Declaration of Independence,* and apostle of freedom. Moreover, he was the organizer of the political party that was the forerunner of today's Democrats. Over the years, Jefferson has in the words of Joseph J. Ellis become "a kind of free-floating icon who hovers over the American political scene like one of those dirigibles cruising above a crowded football stadium, flashing words of inspiration to both teams."[1]

Jefferson is undeniably a great American, but he has difficulty qualifying as a great president. The Louisiana Purchase, the crowning achievement of his administration, came about inadvertently rather than through any astute diplomacy on his part, and to approve it he subverted his own long-held views of the Constitution. In fact, the practical necessities of politics—particularly foreign affairs—forced Jefferson to abandon almost every policy that he had espoused while challenging the conservative doctrines of Alexander Hamilton and John Adams, leaders of the opposition Federalist party. And even his greatest admirers all but avert their eyes from his second term because of its calamities.

In Kennedy's case, the tragic way in which he died influences us more than anything he accomplished in life. To many Americans, he is a martyred Sir Lancelot who, before being cut down in his prime, enabled us to briefly embrace the legend of Camelot. No president elected since

---

*It should be pointed out that the Declaration of Independence did not achieve its spare elegance until Congress heavily edited Jefferson's draft. Take the majestic words that are the core of the American creed. Jefferson's version read:

We hold these truths to be sacred & undeniable; that all men are created equal & independent, that from that equal creation they derive rights inherent & inalienable, among which are the preservation of life, & liberty, & the pursuit of happiness.

The revised version has much more punch:

We hold these truths to be self-evident, that all men are created equal, that they are endowed by the Creator with certain inalienable Rights, that among these are Life, Liberty and the pursuit of Happiness.

Kennedy's assassination has combined his rhetoric, wit, charm, youth, and star quality. Forgotten is his role as a cold warrior who blundered into unnecessary crises, led the country into the quagmire of Vietnam, and was initially cool toward the civil rights struggle. Womanizing and other blemishes on his character are shrugged off. To millions all over the world, he continues to embody an almost mythical view of the ideal American president. Kennedy's most enduring contribution to national life may well have been to raise the curtain on an age of political imagery—hardly a gift to be welcomed with gratitude.

Although a century and a half separate Kennedy and Jefferson and they are polar opposites in personality and outlook, they have a certain unity. Writing of some eighteenth-century aristocratic reformers, Sir Isaiah Berlin saw a common thread that also applies to these two American presidents. "Their minds see large and generous horizons, and above all, reveal a unique intellectual gaiety," the British philosopher declared. "At the same time they are intellectually on the side of everything that is new, progressive, rebellious, young and untried, of that which is about to come into being."[2]

The inflation of Jefferson's reputation as president is based upon two misconceptions: First, that the ouster of the Federalists from power and his elevation to the presidency—which he called the "Revolution of 1800"—meant the victory of egalitarian political democracy over the decaying forces of privilege and aristocracy. Second, that by clever diplomacy, Jefferson managed to purchase the vast Louisiana territory from France—an achievement that practically doubled the size of the United States.[3]

The cold truth is that Jefferson's election hardly qualifies as a revolution. While he claimed that the struggle was between those who cherished the people and those who distrusted them, essentially it was a clash between two kinds of property, not two philosophies. Hamilton believed in a strong national government with sufficient revenue to carry out its business, while Jefferson supported a minimum of government. Hamilton's system of funding the national debt, with its banks and taxes, subsidized the mercantile and investing classes, while Jefferson was supported by the landed interests who believed they bore most of the burden of Hamilton's system. In the final analysis, Hamilton was the better prophet, and Jefferson's hope for a nation of yeoman farmers and artisans proved a dream.

Whatever revolutionary intent Jefferson may have had was undermined by his narrow margin of victory. In fact, his presidency was almost stillborn. In 1800, the Constitution made no distinction between ballots cast for presidential and vice-presidential candidates, and Jefferson and his running mate, Aaron Burr, won the same number of votes in the Electoral College, throwing the final selection into the House of Representatives. Hamilton, viewing Jefferson as the lesser of two evils, urged Federalist congressmen to vote for him—but not before receiving assurances from Jefferson's supporters that the Virginian would prove less radical than he appeared. Burr became vice president.

In office, Jefferson and his Swiss-born treasury secretary, Albert Gallatin, found to their dismay that Hamilton had done his work well and Hamiltonism had become the foundation upon which the American economy was built. Unable to liquidate this system, they were reduced to abolishing the hated excise taxes that financed it while slashing government spending, especially for the armed forces. But the key element of Hamilton's system, the Bank of the United States, remained intact if somewhat weakened. Jefferson found himself in a position much like that of modern politicians who, after attaining office, find themselves unable to launch large-scale social reforms out of fear of disrupting the economic order. "We are all Federalists now," Jefferson might well have muttered to himself. In fact, some of his more radical supporters accused him of "out-Federalizing the Federalists."

The Louisiana Purchase also forced Jefferson to abandon or modify long-held principles. He had sought to buy merely New Orleans and a small amount of territory to the east of the mouth of the Mississippi from France, but much to his surprise, Napoleon made him an offer he couldn't refuse—half a continent at a bargain $15 million. But the offer came with strings attached. No one was quite sure of the boundaries of Louisiana. Did it include what later became Texas? Was Florida part of it? The $15-million purchase price would increase the public debt by 20 percent—no small matter to a president whose concern with retiring the federal debt amounted to a fetish. Did the French even have the right to sell Louisiana, which had not yet been transferred to them by Spain? Most important, Jefferson had for years preached the doctrine of strict construction of the Constitution and dutiful obeisance to its niceties. Nothing in that document gave him the right to buy a partially inhabited wilderness as large as the Union itself.

With considerable anguish, Jefferson turned over the problem in his mind. The only alternative seemed to be a constitutional amendment. But that would take months or years, while his agents in Paris were urging haste before the French changed their minds. The only sensible solution was to accept the purchase and hope that it could be legalized later on. Privately, Jefferson admitted that it was "an act beyond the Constitution," but he compromised with his conscience. The Louisiana Purchase is the great triumph of his presidency, but the result would probably have been the same if Aaron Burr or John Adams had been president—and without all the agonizing.

Jefferson's second term ran aground on the shoals of the Napoleonic Wars. Britain and France tried to subjugate each other by cutting off their overseas commerce, and the United States, as the only neutral with a significant carrying trade, was caught between them. Having failed to provide the nation with an adequate defense because of his cheeseparing economies, Jefferson was forced to either endure humiliation at the hands of the British and French or to seek a substitute for war in the form of economic coercion.

The resulting Embargo Act of 1807 was the greatest failure of Jefferson's presidency. The embargo, which essentially closed American ports to trade, practically wrecked the nation's economy and plunged it into its first depression while having absolutely no effect upon its targets. Moreover, the embargo required the federal government to use coercive measures to enforce it, including restrictions on civil liberties, thereby contradicting the Jeffersonian principle of limited government. Nevertheless, Jefferson foolishly clung to the illusion that economic sanctions would eventually win respect for the United States. But even he finally confessed that the embargo was three times as costly as war. Had only a small portion of the revenue lost by the embargo been used to build frigates, the British certainly would not have provoked the United States to the point of war in 1812. It was "a policy of criminal folly," wrote Theodore Roosevelt in his *Naval War of 1812*.*[4]

Jefferson's record in the presidency is further blemished by his handling of the Burr Conspiracy. Having killed Hamilton in a duel and with his term as vice president over, Burr went west to launch a fabulously ambitious scheme: either to seize Mexico or to pinch off from it a sizable share of the American Southwest and set up his own regime. To this day his actual intent is unclear. As long as Burr seemed interested in depriving Spain of part of its empire, Jefferson met with him several times and winked at his machinations. But Burr's activities became too embarrassing and he was eventually arrested on charges of plotting against the United States. Jefferson was so eager to get him convicted of treason—possibly to cover his own tracks—that he condoned the violation of basic constitutional guarantees. To the chagrin of the president, Chief Justice John Marshall, his distant cousin and the high priest of Federalist defiance to Jeffersonism, found Burr innocent.[5]

Jefferson's presidency came to a hollow end. Having announced in December 1807 that he would follow George Washington's precedent and retire at the end of his second term, he abandoned most essential decisions to Gallatin and James Madison, the secretary of state, and his last year in office was a period of drift. Some critics bitterly compared him to Pontius Pilate, washing his hands of the disastrous effects of the embargo.[6] "Never did a prisoner released from his chains feel such relief as I shall on shaking off the shackles of power," Jefferson declared upon turning his office over to Madison.

In the end, Thomas Jefferson delivered the final benediction upon his presidency. It had been so painful that he chose not to even mention it in the epitaph he composed for his tombstone.

John Kennedy understood better than any other politician of his time that in the television age image is power. From the outset, he communicated a glittering image of himself and his presidency through his

---

*Roosevelt called Jefferson "perhaps the most incapable Executive that ever filled the presidential chair" (p. 405).

lofty, inspiring speeches, his youth and personal elegance, and his stylish and glamorous wife. Amid the grayness of American politics, he seemed a dashing cavalier, laughing and tossing a sword into the air. This image, so painstakingly crafted, with its aura of hope and unfulfilled promise, may be his greatest achievement. Kennedy's death left a permanent mark on the national psyche. In later times, when Americans looked back and wondered where the bright promise of their country had unraveled, many put their finger on November 22, 1963.

How realistic was this image? Kennedy believed that only a president could evaluate his own performance. "Only the President himself can know what his real pressures and real alternatives are," he declared.[7] Perhaps. But one can compare the promises made by a president with his actual performance. Like Thomas Jefferson, Kennedy came to power with the promise of change—to revitalize a floundering America by offering the most ambitious program for domestic reform since the New Deal. But like the Virginian, he was forced to operate within constraints, in his case imposed by his narrow victory over Richard Nixon.

Kennedy did have some accomplishments. His legacy included the Peace Corps, an idea originally advanced by Hubert H. Humphrey, one of Kennedy's rivals for the Democratic nomination; the lofty Alliance for Progress, which proved unable to bring about reform in Latin America; and a space program that put Americans on the moon by the end of the decade.

But he failed to deliver on his vow to "get America moving again." He proposed to provide medical assistance to the elderly, end racial discrimination, modernize education and transportation, rebuild the cities, and eliminate poverty. Primarily as a result of his lack of clout with conservative members of his own party and his reluctance to fight for his programs, most of these initiatives were in limbo when he died. Moreover, he showed wavering leadership in advancing civil rights until events beyond his control forced him to take an active role.

Largely stymied at home, Kennedy decided to prove his manhood in foreign affairs. Projecting an image of toughness and impatience, he welcomed confrontation with the Soviet Union and personalized diplomacy as a struggle of wills. Kennedy was a confirmed cold warrior, and one of his top priorities was military expansion. He had been elected with the promise to close a supposed "missile gap" with the Soviets. Once in office, he found the United States well ahead of the Russians—but pressed ahead with a massive and costly buildup that spurred the Soviet Union to build up its own missile arsenal, heightening international tensions.

Kennedy's belief in democratic self-determination was clouded by a childish delight in paramilitary operations, counterinsurgency, and secret wars that made a mockery of his glib rhetoric. The first test came in Cuba, where the Central Intelligence Agency had been plotting to oust Fidel Castro, the island's Communist leader. CIA-trained Cuban exiles invaded the island on April 17, 1961, but at the last minute Kennedy, worried about the "noise" generated by the operation, withdrew the air support upon which it depended, and a fiasco resulted. If Kennedy considered Castro a threat to national security, critics said, he should have sent in the Marines instead of mounting a risky paramilitary operation held together with hope and baling wire.

This misguided effort to topple Castro triggered a grim chain of events. The Soviets lost no time in showing their contempt for Kennedy. At a summit meeting at Vienna, Khrushchev "just beat the hell out of me," the president later acknowledged. "I think he did it because of the Bay of Pigs."[8] The Communists followed it up by building a wall dividing the Eastern sector of Berlin from the Western sector and later installed missiles in Cuba as a deterrent to a possible U.S. attack. Risking nuclear war, Kennedy decreed that the missiles would not be allowed to remain. Two weeks of eyeball-to-eyeball confrontation followed before the Russians, who lacked the capacity to carry out their threats, blinked. They agreed to withdraw the missiles in exchange for an American pledge not to invade the island plus the removal of U.S. missiles in Turkey pointed at the Soviet Union. But Kennedy-inspired plots against Castro's life continued—and may well have played a role in his own murder.

On the other side of the world, Kennedy embarked on a bold campaign to blunt what he saw as a Communist plot to take over Vietnam and the rest of Southeast Asia. The president and his can-do aides viewed what was in actuality a long-running civil war through the prism of the Cold War and mistakenly transformed South Vietnam into the "cornerstone of the Free World." And when the South Vietnamese were unable—or unwilling—to carry on the struggle, the Americans shouldered the burden. Vietnam became an American colony. Under President Eisenhower there were about 650 U.S. military advisers in Vietnam; at the time of Kennedy's assassination in Dallas, the number of American troops had reached 17,000 and was growing.

Nevertheless, some claim that had the president lived, he would have begun a withdrawal. But this seems entirely out of character. Kennedy was too much the dedicated cold warrior, too concerned about winning the game, to have pulled out without victory. In an interview with Walter Cronkite a little more than two months before his death, he flatly stated, "I don't agree with those who say we should withdraw. That would be a great mistake."[9]

Kennedy loyalists argue that by late 1963, he was showing signs of a new moral awareness that revealed itself in his willingness to reach a nuclear test ban agreement with the Russians. Personal and political greatness lay ahead during a second term, they say. But could the cover-up of the dark side of his personal life have remained in place for another four years? Would—or could—the journalists whom Kennedy made his coconspirators in hushing up stories about his reckless behavior and sexual liaisons have remained silent?

Some analysts say a president's private life is irrelevant to his qualities as chief executive, but they are mistaken. Character is what you are, and the quality of the inner man is relevant to the public man. Kennedy knew this, but he did not believe it applied to him. He had the recklessness of a man who had always been indulged because of his money, his good looks, his charm. He was like Tom and Daisy Buchanan in F. Scott Fitzgerald's novel *The Great Gatsby*: "They smashed up things and creatures and then retreated back into their money or their vast carelessness . . . and let other people clean up the mess they had made."

A brutal assassination cannot be condoned, but Kennedy's ghastly death may have spared the nation from being torn apart by public disclosure of his extracurricular activities. In the mid-1960s, the moral climate of America was still high enough that the spectacle of the president of the United States bedding down inside and outside the White House with women not his wife, and having questionable relations with mobsters, would probably have dwarfed Watergate. In those days, most Americans still thought that the power and prestige of the presidency were precious and should come before all self-indulgence.

My, how times have changed.

NOTES

CHAPTER I

1. Quoted in Dallek, *Hail to the Chief,* 195.
2. Smith, *The Power Game,* 337–39.
3. Burns, *The Crosswinds of Freedom,* 530.
4. Quoted in DeGregorio, *The Complete Book of Presidents,* 630.
5. *Wall Street Journal,* March 15, 1979.
6. *Baltimore Sun,* January 7, 1979.
7. Kaufman, *The Presidency of James Earl Carter, Jr.,* 9–10.
8. Hertzberg, *Character Above All,* 180.
9. Stroud, *How Jimmy Won,* 133.
10. Lasky, *Jimmy Carter,* 23–24.
11. Boller, *Presidential Anecdotes,* 340.
12. In the best book on Carter's background, Glad, *Jimmy Carter.*
13. Carter, *Why Not the Best?* 7–8.
14. Ibid., 14.
15. *The Lucky Bag,* 1947.
16. Carter, *Why Not the Best?* 58.
17. Ibid., 64.
18. DeGregorio, *Complete Book of Presidents,* 620.
19. Jordan's memo is in Stroud, *How Jimmy Won.*
20. Boller, *Presidential Anecdotes,* 341.
21. The most complete account of Carter's presidency is Kaufman, *Presidency of James Earl Carter, Jr.*
22. Kaufman, ibid., 30.
23. Burns, *Crosswinds of Freedom,* 558–60.
24. Dallek, *Hail to the Chief,* 35.
25. Donovan, *Roosevelt to Reagan,* 235.
26. For the Iranian affair, see Sick, *All Fall Down,* chapter 5.

CHAPTER II

1. Russell, *The President Makers,* 87.
2. Anderson, *William Howard Taft,* 4.
3. Boller, *Presidential Anecdotes,* 215.
4. Coletta, *The Presidency of William Howard Taft,* 2.
5. Burton, *William Howard Taft,* 11.
6. Butt, *Taft and Roosevelt,* 21.
7. *The Autobiography of William Allen White,* 425–26.
8. Manners, *TR and Will,* 47.
9. Roosevelt, *Autobiography,* 364–65.
10. Quoted in Miller, *Theodore Roosevelt,* 485.

11. Ibid., 486.
12. Longworth, *Crowded Hours*, 145.
13. Manners, *TR and Will*, 53.
14. Sullivan, *Our Times*, vol. 4, pp. 331–32.
15. For Taft's early life, see Pringle, *The Life and Times of William Howard Taft*, vol. I.
16. Manners, *TR and Will*, 32.
17. Russell, *President Makers*, 91.
18. Coletta, *Presidency of William Howard Taft*, 4.
19. Manners, *TR and Will*, 17.
20. Russell, *President Makers*, 110–11.
21. See Coletta, *Presidency of William Howard Taft*, chapter 3, for the fight over the Payne-Aldrich Tariff.
22. Ibid., chapter 4, for the Ballinger-Pinchot affair.
23. Butt, *Taft and Roosevelt*, 418.
24. Russell, *Presidency Makers*, 118.
25. Butt, *Taft and Roosevelt*, 839.
26. Russell, *President Makers*, 123.
27. Ibid., 122.
28. Boller, *Presidential Anecdotes*, 216.
29. Manners, *TR and Will*, 305.
30. Burton, *William Howard Taft*, 129.

CHAPTER III

1 Josephson, *The Politicos*, 433.
2. Ibid., 438.
3. Morris, *The Rise of Theodore Roosevelt*, 426.
4. Miller, *Theodore Roosevelt*, 205.
5. Garraty, *The New Commonwealth*, 297.
6. Boller, *Presidential Anecdotes*, 184.
7. For political change see Garraty, *New Commonwealth*, chapter 6. Also Wiebe, *The Search for Order*.
8. For Blaine's career, see Hofstadter, *The American Political Tradition*, 171–74, and Josephson, *Politicos*. He is a central figure in the latter book.
9. For Harrison's biography see Sievers, *Benjamin Harrison*, vols. 1 and 2.
10. Morgan, *From Hayes to McKinley*, 328.
11. Garraty, *New Commonwealth*, 296–97.
12. Ibid., 297–98.
13. Josephson, *Politicos*, 430–33.
14. Miller, *Stealing From America*, 254.
15. Josephson, *Politicos*, 439.
16. For Reed, see Tuchman, *The Proud Tower*, chapter 11.
17. Morgan, *From Hayes to McKinley*, 329.
18. Josephson, *Politicos*, 437.
19. Morgan, *From Hayes to McKinley*, 395.

20. Ibid., 338.
21. Stoddard, *As I Knew Them*, 178.
22. Socolofsky and Specter, *The Presidency of Benjamin Harrison*, 81.

CHAPTER IV

1. McCoy, *Calvin Coolidge*, 159.
2. Manchester, *Disturber of the Peace*, 217.
3. Parrish, *Anxious Decades*, 93.
4. Lathem, *Meet Calvin Coolidge*, 52.
5. *Memoirs of Herbert Hoover*, vol. 2, p. 55.
6. Burner, *Herbert Hoover*, 247.
7. Longworth, *Crowded Hours*, 337.
8. McCoy, *Calvin Coolidge*, 6.
9. Boller, *Presidential Anecdotes*, 234.
10. Ibid.
11. Parrish, *Anxious Decades*, 50.
12. McCoy, *Calvin Coolidge*, 161.
13. Lathem, *Meet Calvin Coolidge*, 59.
14. Ibid., 80.
15. Hoover, *Forty-two Years in the White House*, 251.
16. DeGregorio, *The Complete Book of Presidents*, 460.
17. *Time*, January 5, 1981.
18. McCoy, *Calvin Coolidge*, 8.
19. Ibid., 31.
20. Lathem, *Meet Calvin Coolidge*, 64.
21. McCoy, *Calvin Coolidge*, 50.
22. Boller, *Presidential Anecdotes*, 245.
23. The fullest account of the Boston police strike is in Russell, *A City in Terror.*
24. The story of Coolidge's presidency is related in McCoy, *Calvin Coolidge*, and Goodfellow, *Calvin Coolidge.*
25. McCoy, *Calvin Coolidge*, 157.
26. Ables, *In the Time of Silent Cal*, 43.
27. For the Democratic Convention of 1924 and its aftermath, see Murray, *The 103rd Ballot.*
28. Coolidge, *Autobiography*, 190.
29. Goodfellow, *Calvin Coolidge*, 372.
30. White, *A Puritan in Babylon*, 366 n.
31. Lathem, *Meet Calvin Coolidge*, 58.
32. Ibid., 171.
33. Boller, *Presidential Anecdotes*, 235.

CHAPTER V

1. Edmund Wilson, *Patriotic Gore*, 169.
2. Woodrow Wilson, *A History of the American People*, vol. 5, p. 112.

3. See Morgan, ed., *The Gilded Age.*
4. White, *The Republican Era,* 8–9.
5. Nevins, *The Emergence of Modern America,* 181–82.
6. For Grant's biography, see McFeely, *Grant,* and Carpenter, *Ulysses S. Grant.*
7. Wecter, *The Hero in America,* 320.
8. Boller, *Presidential Anecdotes,* 159.
9. Wecter, *The Hero in America,* 327.
10. Welles, *Diary,* vol. 3, pp. 184–85.
11. For a modern account, see Foner, *Reconstruction.*
12. Adams, *The Education of Henry Adams,* 260–62.
13. Rugoff, *America's Gilded Age,* 29.
14. Boller, *Presidential Anecdotes,* 160.
15. For the accomplishments of Grant's administration, see Hesseltine, *Ulysses S. Grant, Politician.*
16. The Gold Corner conspiracy is covered in Ackerman, *The Gold Ring.*
17. For the Santo Domingo affair, see Nevins, *Hamilton Fish: The Inner History of the Grant Administration.*
18. Rugoff, *America's Gilded Age,* 26–27.
19. For the Crédit Mobilier story, see Hesseltine, *Ulysses S. Grant.*
20. Adams, *Education of Henry Adams,* 261.
21. The scandals of the Grant era are covered in Hesseltine, *Ulysses S. Grant.*

CHAPTER VI

1. The description of the roll call is based on Thomas, *The First President Johnson,* 597–603, and Trefousse, *Andrew Johnson,* 325–27.
2. See Castel, *The Presidency of Andrew Johnson,* 218–30.
3. Foner, *Reconstruction,* 176–77.
4. Castel, *Presidency of Andrew Johnson,* 30.
5. Ibid., 8.
6. Bailey, *Presidential Greatness,* 204.
7. Trefousse, *Andrew Johnson,* 196.
8. Ibid., 197–98.
9. The fullest and most accurate account of Johnson's background is in Trefousse, *Andrew Johnson.* Thomas, *The First President Johnson,* is marred by numerous errors.
10. Castel, *Presidency of Andrew Johnson,* 6.
11. Trefousse, *Andrew Johnson,* 119.
12. Thomas, *First President Johnson,* 294–97, and Castel, *Presidency of Andrew Johnson,* 9–10.
13. Trefousse, *Andrew Johnson,* 191.
14. Castel, *Presidency of Andrew Johnson,* 27.
15. Foner, *Reconstruction,* 191.
16. Ibid., 192.
17. Castel, *Presidency of Andrew Johnson,* 72.

18. Thomas, *First President Johnson*, 489–98.
19. Dallek, *Hail to the Chief*, 180.

CHAPTER VII

1. Rossiter, *The American Presidency*, 101.
2. Ferrell, ed., *Off the Record*, 266.
3. Kenin and Wintle, eds., *Dictionary of Biographical Quotations*, 600.
4. Nichols, *Franklin Pierce*, 232.
5. Boller, *Presidential Anecdotes*, 113.
6. Nichols, *Franklin Pierce*, 205.
7. Gara, *The Presidency of Franklin Pierce*, 29.
8. Nichols, *Franklin Pierce*, 217.
9. Gara, *Presidency of Franklin Pierce*, 41.
10. Nichols, *Franklin Pierce*, 533.
11. Donald, *Charles Sumner and the Coming of the Civil War*, 208.
12. For the background on this section, see Potter, *The Impending Crisis*, and McPherson, *The Battle Cry of Freedom*.
13. For background on Pierce, see Nichols, *Franklin Pierce*.
14. Ibid., 235.
15. Ibid., 236.
16. Gara, *Presidency of Franklin Pierce*, 49.
17. See Nevins, *Ordeal of the Union*, vol. 2, pp. 43–44.
18. For Pierce's cabinet, see Gara, *Presidency of Franklin Pierce*, 44–47.
19. Nevins, *Ordeal of the Union*, 51.
20. Gara, *Presidency of Franklin Pierce*, 49.
21. Nevins, *Ordeal of the Union*, 72.
22. For the Ostend Manifesto, ibid., chapter 10.
23. For the Pacific railroad question, see Gara, *Presidency of Franklin Pierce*, 88–90.
24. For the politics behind the Kansas-Nebraska Act, see Rhodes, *History of the United States*, vol. 1, pp. 425–51.
25. Nichols, *The Stakes of Power*, 54.
26. Nichols, *Franklin Pierce*, 338.
27. Nevins, *Ordeal of the Union*, 145.
28. For the Know-Nothing party, ibid., 327–30.
29. Ibid., 455.
30. Boller, *Presidential Anecdotes*, 116.

CHAPTER VIII

1. Gienapp, "Buchanan, James," in Garraty and Foner, eds., *The Reader's Companion to American History*, 134.
2. Van Woodward, ed., *Responses of the Presidents to Charges of Misconduct*, 85.
3. Morison, *The Growth of the American Republic*, vol. 1, p. 651.
4. Nevins, *The Emergence of Lincoln*, vol. 1, p. 63.
5. Nevins, *Emergence of Lincoln*, has a good character study of Buchanan.

6. Ibid., 61.
7. Smith, *The Presidency of James Buchanan*, 13.
8. Klein, *President James Buchanan*, 275.
9. Boller, *Presidential Anecdotes*, 118.
10. Stampp, *America in 1857*, 48.
11. Ibid.
12. Boller, *Presidential Anecdotes*, 120.
13. The most complete account of Buchanan's life is in Klein, *President James Buchanan*.
14. Ibid., 34.
15. Ibid., 150.
16. Smith, *Presidency of James Buchanan*, 14.
17. Boller, *Presidential Anecdotes*, 117.
18. Klein, *President James Buchanan*, 229.
19. For Buchanan and the Dred Scott case, see Smith, *Presidency of James Buchanan*, 24–29, and Nevins, *Emergence of Lincoln*, 91–118.
20. Klein, *President James Buchanan*, 272.
21. For Buchanan and the Lecompton constitution, see Smith, *Presidency of James Buchanan*, 31–46.
22. Ibid., 41.
23. Van Woodward, *Responses of the Presidents*, 86–87.
24. Smith, *Presidency of James Buchanan*, 81.
25. For the Panic of 1857, see Stampp, *America in 1857*, 219–236.
26. For the Mormon War, ibid., 201–9.
27. A detailed account of the run-up to the Civil War is in Nevins, *Emergence of Lincoln*.
28. Rhodes, *History of the United States*, vol. 3, p. 150.
29. Boller, *Presidential Anecdotes*, 120.
30. Klein, *President James Buchanan*, 402.
31. Ibid., 427.

CHAPTER IX

1. Manchester, *Disturber of the Peace*, 116–117, and H. L. Mencken, *A Carnival of Buncombe*, 32.
2. Adams, *Incredible Era*, 115.
3. Parrish, *Anxious Decades*, 11.
4. Longworth, *Crowded Hours*, 324.
5. Russell, *The Shadow of Blooming Grove*, 230.
6. H. F. Alderfer, quoted in Adams, *Incredible Era*, 188–89.
7. Allen, *Only Yesterday*, 146.
8. Sinclair, *The Available Man*, 36–37.
9. Sullivan, *Our Times*, vol. 6, pp. 16–19.
10. Ibid., 22.
11. Sinclair, *Available Man*, 41–42, and Werner and Starr, *Teapot Dome*, 10.
12. Sullivan, *Our Times*, 29.

13. Russell, *Shadow of Blooming Grove,* 334.
14. Ibid., 341–42.
15. Werner and Starr, *Teapot Dome,* 23.
16. White, *Autobiography of William Allen White,* 584.
17. Ibid.
18. Sinclair, *Available Man,* 160.
19. Bode, *Mencken,* 178.
20. Adams, *Incredible Era,* 234–36.
21. Longworth, *Crowded Hours,* 324.
22. Werner and Starr, *Teapot Dome,* 38.
23. Russell, *Shadow of Blooming Grove,* 452.
24. Sinclair, *Available Man,* 231–35.
25. The transfer of the oil reserves can be followed in detail in Werner and Starr, *Teapot Dome.*
26. Adams, *Incredible Era,* chapter 22.
27. Russell, *Shadow of Blooming Grove,* 558.
28. Adams, *Incredible Era,* 323–24.
29. Sullivan, *Our Times,* 232–37; Werner and Starr, *Teapot Dome,* 95–100.
30. White, *Autobiography of William Allen White,* 619.
31. *Memoirs of Herbert Hoover,* vol. 2, p. 49.
32. Russell, *Shadow of Blooming Grove,* 597.
33. Quoted in Mee, *The Ohio Gang,* 115.
34. Adams, *Incredible Era,* 433–34.

CHAPTER X

1. Potter, "Nixon: Political Pitchman."
2. Blum, *Years of Discord,* 319.
3. *New York Times,* July 9, 1976.
4. Ambrose, *Nixon,* vol. 1, p. 39.
5. Patterson, *Grand Expectations,* 719.
6. For Nixon's domestic accomplishments, see Hoff, *Nixon Reconsidered.*
7. Wicker, "Richard M. Nixon," in *Character Above All,* 130.
8. *London Sunday Times* Team, *Watergate,* 79.
9. For Nixon's early life, see Ambrose, *Nixon,* vol. 1.
10. Wicker, "Richard M. Nixon," 142.
11. Ambrose, *Nixon,* 32.
12. Ibid., 27.
13. Wicker, "Richard M. Nixon," 135.
14. Ambrose, *Nixon,* 29.
15. Ibid., 72.
16. Ibid., 140.
17. Whitney, *The American Presidents,* 335.
18. Safire, *Before the Fall,* 690.
19. Ambrose, *Nixon,* vol. 2, p. 660.
20. Ibid., 560.

Notes

EPILOGUE

1. Ellis, *American Sphinx*, 8.
2. Berlin, *Russian Thinkers*, 187.
3. For a succinct evaluation of Jefferson's presidency, see McDonald, *The Presidency of Thomas Jefferson*.
4. Roosevelt, *The Naval War of 1812*, 5.
5. For a controversial study of Jefferson and civil liberties, see Levy, *Jefferson and Civil Liberties*.
6. Ellis, *American Sphinx*, 238.
7. Schlesinger, "The Ultimate Approval Rating."
8. Miller, *Spying for America*, 421.
9. Kennedy, *Public Papers of the President*, September 2, 1963.

BIBLIOGRAPHY

Ables, Jules. *In the Time of Silent Cal.* New York: Putnam's, 1969.

Ackerman, Kenneth D. *The Gold Ring.* New York: Dodd, Mead, 1988.

Adams, Henry. *The Education of Henry Adams.* New York: Modern Library, 1931.

Adams, Samuel Hopkins. *Incredible Era.* Boston: Houghton Mifflin, 1939.

Allen, Frederick Lewis. *Only Yesterday.* New York: Bantam, 1946.

Ambrose, Stephen E. *Nixon.* 3 vols. New York: Simon & Schuster, 1987–91.

Anderson, Donald F. *William Howard Taft.* Ithaca, N.Y.: Cornell University Press, 1968.

Bailey, Thomas A. *Presidential Greatness.* New York: Appleton-Century, 1966.

Barry, John M. *Rising Tide: The Great Mississippi Flood of 1927 and How It Changed America.* New York: Simon & Schuster, 1997.

Berlin, Isaiah. *Russian Thinkers.* New York: Viking Press, 1978.

Billings, Elden E. "Social and Economic Life in Washington in the 1890's." *Records of the Columbia Historical Society of Washington, D.C.,* 1966–68.

Blum, John Morton. *Years of Discord.* New York: Norton, 1991.

Bode, Carl. *Mencken.* Carbondale, Ill.: Southern Illinois University Press, 1969.

Boller, Paul F. *Presidential Anecdotes.* New York: Penguin, 1982.

Bourne, Peter. *Jimmy Carter.* New York: Scribner, 1997.

Britton, Nan. *The President's Daughter.* New York: Elizabeth Ann Guild, 1927.

Burner, David. *Herbert Hoover: A Public Life.* New York: Knopf, 1979.

Burns, James McGregor. *The Crosswinds of Freedom.* New York: Knopf, 1989.

Burton, David H. *William Howard Taft: In the Public Service.* Malabar, Fla.: Robert E. Krieger, 1986.

Butt, Archie. *Taft and Roosevelt.* 2 vols. Garden City, N.Y.: Doubleday, Doran, 1930.

Carpenter, John A. *Ulysses S. Grant.* New York: Twayne, 1970.

Carter, Jimmy. *Why Not the Best?* New York: Bantam, 1976.

Castel, Albert. *The Presidency of Andrew Johnson.* Lawrence, Kans.: Regents Press, 1979.

Catton, Bruce. *U. S. Grant and the American Military Tradition.* Boston: Little, Brown, 1954.

Class of 1947. U.S. Naval Academy. *The Lucky Bag.* Annapolis, Md.: 1946.

Coletta, Paolo E. *The Presidency of Wlliam Howard Taft.* Lawrence, Kans.: University Press of Kansas, 1973.

Coolidge, Calvin. *Autobiography.* New York: Cosmopolitan, 1929.

Cunliffe, Marcus. *The Presidency.* Boston: Houghton Mifflin, 1987.

Dallek, Robert. *Hail to the Chief.* New York: Hyperion, 1996.

DeGregorio, William A. *The Complete Book of Presidents.* New York: Dembner Books, 1984.

Donald, David. *Charles Sumner and the Coming of the Civil War.* New York: Knopf, 1967.

Donovan, Hedley. *Roosevelt to Reagan.* New York: Harper & Row, 1985.

Ellis, Joseph J. *American Sphinx: The Character of Thomas Jefferson.* New York: Knopf, 1997.

Fallows, James. "The Passionless Presidency." *Atlantic,* May 1979.

Ferrell, Robert H. *The Strange Deaths of President Harding.* Columbia, Mo.: University of Missouri Press, 1996.

———, ed. *Off the Record: The Private Papers of Harry Truman.* New York: Harper & Row, 1980.

Foner, Eric. *Reconstruction: America's Unfinished Revolution.* New York: Harper & Row, 1988.

Galbraith, John Kenneth. *The Great Crash.* Boston: Houghton Mifflin, 1955.

Gara, Larry. *The Presidency of Franklin Pierce.* Lawrence, Kans.: University Press of Kansas, 1991.

Garraty, John A. *The New Commonwealth, 1877–1890.* New York: Harper & Row, 1968.

Garraty, John, and Eric Foner, eds. *The Reader's Companion to American History.* Boston: Houghton Mifflin, 1991.

Giglio, James N. *The Presidency of John F. Kennedy.* Lawrence, Kans.: University Press of Kansas, 1991.

Glad, Betty. *Jimmy Carter.* New York: Norton, 1980.

Goldwater, Barry. *Goldwater.* Garden City, N.Y.: Doubleday, 1988.

Goodfellow, Guy. "Calvin Coolidge: A Study of Presidential Inaction." Ph.D. diss., University of Maryland, 1969.

Grant, U. S. *Personal Memoirs.* New York: Library of America, 1990.

Haas, Garland A. *Jimmy Carter and the Politics of Frustration.* Jefferson, N.C.: McFarland, 1992.

Hamilton, Holman. *Prologue to Conflict.* Lexington, Ky.: University of Kentucky Press, 1964.

Hertzberg, Henry. "Jimmy Carter." In *Character Above All,* edited by Robert A. Wilson. New York: Simon & Schuster, 1995.

Hesseltine, William B. *Ullyses S. Grant, Politician.* New York: Dodd, Mead, 1935.

Hicks, John D. *The Republican Ascendancy.* New York: Harper & Row, 1960.

Hoff, Joan. *Nixon Reconsidered.* New York: Basic Books, 1994.

Hofstadter, Richard. *The American Political Tradition and the Men Who Made It.* New York: Knopf, 1949.

Holt, Michael F. *The Political Crisis of the 1850s.* New York: John Wiley, 1978.

Hoover, Herbert C. *Memoirs of Herbert Hoover.* Vol. 2. New York: Macmillan, 1952.

Hoover, Irwin H. *Forty-two Years in the White House.* Boston: Houghton, 1936.

Josephson, Matthew. *The Politicos.* New York: Harcourt, Brace, 1938.

Kaufman, Burton I. *The Presidency of James Earl Carter, Jr.* Lawrence, Kans.: University Press of Kansas, 1993.

Kenin, Richard, and Justin Wintle, eds. *Dictionary of Biographical Quotations.* New York: Knopf, 1978.

Kennedy, John F. *Public Papers of the President, 1963.* Washington, D.C.: Government Printing Office, 1964.

Bibliography

Klein, Philip S. *President James Buchanan*. University Park, Pa.: Pennsylvania State University Press, 1962.

Lasky, Victor. *Jimmy Carter: The Man & the Myth*. New York: Marek, 1979.

Lathem, Edward C. *Meet Calvin Coolidge*. Brattleboro, Vt.: Greene Press, 1960.

Leuchtenberg, William E. *The Perils of Prosperity*. Chicago: University of Chicago Press, 1958.

Levy, Leonard W. *Jefferson and Civil Liberties: The Darker Side*. New York: Quadrangle, 1973.

London Sunday Times Team. *Watergate*. New York: Bantam, 1973.

Longworth, Alice Roosevelt. *Crowded Hours*. New York: Scribner's, 1933.

McCoy, Donald R. *Calvin Coolidge: The Quiet President*. Lawrence, Kans.: University Press of Kansas, 1988.

McDonald, Forrest. *The Presidency of Thomas Jefferson*. Lawrence, Kans.: University Press of Kansas, 1976.

McElvaine, Robert S. *The Great Depression*. New York: Times Books, 1984.

McFeely, William. *Grant*. New York: Norton, 1981.

McKitrick, Erich. *Andrew Johnson and Reconstruction*. Chicago: University of Chicago, 1964.

McPherson, James M. *Battle Cry of Freedom*. New York: Oxford University Press, 1988.

Manchester, William L. *Disturber of the Peace*. New York: Harper, 1951.

Manners, William. *TR and Will*. New York: Harcourt, Brace, 1969.

Matusow, Allen J. *The Unravelling of America*. New York: Harper & Row, 1984.

Mee, Charles L., Jr. *The Ohio Gang*. New York: M. Evans, 1981.

Mencken, H. L. *A Carnival of Buncombe*. Baltimore: Johns Hopkins University Press, 1956.

————. *A Mencken Chrestomathy*. New York: Knopf, 1949.

Miller, Nathan. *Spying for America: The Hidden History of U.S. Intelligence*. New York: Dell, 1989.

————. *Stealing From America: A History of Corruption from Jamestown to Whitewater*. New York: Marlowe, 1996.

————. *Theodore Roosevelt: A Life*. New York: William Morrow, 1992.

Morgan, H. Wayne. *From Hayes to McKinley*. Syracuse, N.Y.: Syracuse University Press, 1969.

————. *The Gilded Age: A Reappraisal*. Syracuse, N.Y.: Syracuse University Press, 1963.

Morison, Samuel Eliot. *The Growth of the American Republic*. Vol. 2. New York: Oxford University Press, 1966.

Morris, Edmund. *The Rise of Theodore Roosevelt*. New York: Coward, McCann & Geoghegan, 1979.

Mowry, George E. *The Era of Theodore Roosevelt*. New York: Harper, 1958.

Murray, Robert K., and Tim H. Blessing. *Greatness in the White House*. University Park, Pa.: Pennsylvania State University Press, 1988.

————. *The Harding Era*. Minneapolis: University of Minnesota Press, 1969.

————. *The 103rd Ballot*. New York: Harper & Row, 1976.

Nevins, Allan. *The Emergence of Lincoln.* 2 vols. New York: Scribner's, 1950.

———. *Hamilton Fish: The Inner History of the Grant Administration.* New York: Dodd, Mead, 1936.

———. *Ordeal of the Union.* 2 vols. New York: Scribner's, 1947.

Nevins, Allan, and Henry Steele Commager. *A Pocket History of the United States.* New York: Washington Square Press, 1986.

Nichols, Roy F. *The Disruption of American Democracy.* New York: Macmillan, 1948.

———. *Franklin Pierce: Young Hickory of the Granite Hills.* Philadelphia: University of Pennsylvania Press, 1931.

———. *The Stakes of Power.* New York: Hill and Wang, 1961.

Noggle, Burl. *Teapot Dome: Oil and Politics in the 1920's.* Baton Rouge, La.: Louisiana State University, 1962.

Parmet, Herbert S. *JFK: The Presidency.* New York: Penguin, 1984.

———. *Richard Nixon and His America.* Boston: Little, Brown, 1990.

Parrish, Michael E. *Anxious Decades.* New York: Norton, 1992.

Patterson, James. *Grand Expectations.* New York: Oxford University Press, 1996.

Peterson, Merrill D. *Jefferson in the American Mind.* New York: Oxford University Press, 1962.

———. *Thomas Jefferson and the New Nation: A Biography.* New York: Oxford University Press, 1970.

Potter, David M. *The Impending Crisis.* New York: Harper & Row, 1976.

Potter, Phillip. "Nixon." In *Candidates 1960,* ed. by Eric Sevareid. New York: Basic Books, 1959.

Potts, Louis W. "Who Was Warren G. Harding?" *The Historian,* August 1974.

Pringle, Henry. *The Life and Times of William Howard Taft.* 2 vols. New York: Farrar & Rinehart, 1939.

Reeves, Richard. "John F. Kennedy." In *Character Above All,* ed. by Robert A. Wilson. New York: Simon & Schuster, 1995.

———. *President Kennedy.* New York: Simon & Schuster, 1993.

Reeves, Thomas. *A Question of Character: A Life of John F. Kennedy.* New York: Free Press, 1991.

Rhodes, James Ford. *History of the United States from the Compromise of 1850.* Vol I. New York: Macmillan, 1910.

Ridings, William J., and Stuart B. McIver. *Rating the Presidents.* Secaucus, N.J.: Citadel Press, 1997.

Roosevelt, Theodore. *Autobiography.* New York: Da Capo, 1985.

———. *The Naval War of 1812.* Annapolis, Md.: Naval Institute Press, 1987.

Rossiter, Clinton. *The American Presidency.* New York: Mentor, 1956.

Rugoff, Milton. *America's Gilded Age.* New York: Holt, 1989.

Russell, Francis. *A City in Terror: The Boston Police Strike.* New York: Viking, 1975.

———. *The President Makers.* Boston: Little, Brown, 1976.

———. *The Shadow of Blooming Grove.* New York: McGraw-Hill, 1968.

Safire, William. *Before the Fall.* Garden City, N.Y.: Doubleday, 1975.

Schlesinger, Arthur M., Jr. "The Ultimate Approval Rating." *New York Times Magazine,* December 16, 1996.

Sick, Gary. *All Fall Down: America's Tragic Encounter with Iran.* New York: Random House, 1985.

Sievers, Harry J. *Benjamin Harrison.* Vols. 1–2, New York: University Publishers, 1952, 1959. Vol. 3, Indianapolis: Bobbs-Merrill, 1968.

Sinclair, Andrew. *The Available Man.* New York: Macmillan, 1965.

Smith, Elbert B. *The Presidency of James Buchanan.* Lawrence, Kans.: University Press of Kansas, 1975.

Smith, Hedrick. *The Power Game.* New York: Random House, 1988.

Socolofsky, Homer, and Allan B. Specter. *The Presidency of Benjamin Harrison.* Lawrence, Kans.: University Press of Kansas, 1987.

Stampp, Kenneth. *America in 1857.* New York: Oxford University Press, 1990.

Stoddard, Henry L. *As I Knew Them.* New York: Harper, 1927.

Stone, Irving. *They Also Ran.* New York: Signet, 1968.

Stroud, Kandy. *How Jimmy Won.* New York: Morrow, 1977.

Sullivan, Mark. *Our Times.* 6 vols. New York: Scribner's, 1926–1935.

Thomas, Lately. *The First President Johnson.* New York: Morrow, 1968.

Trefousse, Hans L. *Andrew Johnson.* New York: Norton, 1989.

———. *The Radical Republicans.* New York: Knopf, 1969.

Triani, Edward P., and David L. Wilson. *The Presidency of Warren G. Harding.* Lawrence, Kans.: Regents Press, 1977.

Tuchman, Barbara. *The Proud Tower.* New York: Macmillan, 1962.

Wecter, Dixon. *The Hero in America.* Ann Arbor, Mich.: University of Michigan, 1963.

Welles, Gideon. *Diary,* vol. 3. Boston: Houghton Mifflin, 1911.

Werner, M. R., and John Starr. *Teapot Dome.* New York: Viking, 1959.

White, Leonard. *The Republican Era.* New York: Macmillan, 1958.

White, William Allen. *The Autobiography of William Allen White.* New York: Macmillan, 1946.

———. *A Puritan in Babylon.* Macmillan: New York, 1938.

Whitney, David C. *The American Presidents.* Garden City, N.Y.: Doubleday, 1985.

Wicker, Tom. "Richard M. Nixon." In *Character Above All,* edited by Robert A. Wilson. New York: Simon & Schuster, 1995.

Wiebe, Robert H. *The Search for Order.* New York: Hill and Wang, 1967.

Williams, R. Hal. *Years of Decision: American Politics in the 1890s.* New York: Knopf, 1978.

Wilson, Edmund. *Patriotic Gore.* New York: Oxford University Press, 1962.

Wilson, Woodrow. *A History of the American People.* Vol. 5. New York: Harper, 1902.

Woodward, C. Vann. *Responses of the Presidents Charges of Misconduct.* New York: Dell, 1979.

INDEX